D0857190

AMERICAN LABOR

FROM CONSPIRACY
TO
COLLECTIVE BARGAINING

WAR-TIME STRIKES
AND THEIR ADJUSTMENT

Alexander M. Bing

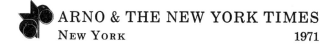

ARNO & THE NEW YORK TIMES
NEW YORK   1971

WAR-TIME STRIKES
AND THEIR ADJUSTMENT

WAR-TIME STRIKES
AND THEIR ADJUSTMENT

BY

ALEXANDER M. BING

WITH AN INTRODUCTION BY
FELIX ADLER

NEW YORK
E. P. DUTTON & COMPANY
681 FIFTH AVENUE

PREFACE

THE writer has endeavored in the following pages to give as complete an account as space and available material will allow of the labor difficulties which occurred during the war and of the machinery which was created to adjust them. It has, of course, been impossible to deal with every one of the thousands of strikes which took place—even controversies of considerable size and importance had to be omitted—nor has any attempt been made to thoroughly cover the events of the post-armistice period. But inasmuch as most of the labor difficulties after the signing of the armistice were directly connected with those which took place during the war itself, it was considered desirable to include some of these later occurrences as far as such a course was practicable.

This book is based upon the writer's personal experiences in Government work during the war, upon statements made to him by officials of Government Boards, employers, union leaders and others, and upon awards and reports of labor adjustment agencies, the testimony taken at many hearings, the Monthly Labor Review of the Bureau of Labor Statistics and other publications of the U. S. Department of Labor, economic journals and the publications of trade unions, corporations and employers' associations, the Congressional Record, and the newspaper files.

Many of the chapters have been submitted to the men who were connected with the labor boards during the war. Some of the errors which are almost unavoidable in a presentation of facts covering so wide a range have in this manner been eliminated. The writer wishes to acknowledge his indebtedness for this help and also for the cordial coöperation with which his requests for information and material have been received by members of labor adjustment boards, employers and labor unions. It would be impossible to give the names of all of the persons who have given their assistance; he wishes, however, to especially mention Mr. Payson Irwin, Mr. V. Everitt Macy and Mr. Stanley M. Isaacs, Prof. Henry R. Seager, Prof. Wm. Z. Ripley, Prof. Edwin

R. A. Seligman, Miss Julia O'Connor, President, Telephone Operators' Department of the International Brotherhood of Electrical Workers; Fred Hewitt, Editor, *Machinists' Journal;* B. M. Squires, chairman, New York Harbor Adjustment Board; John Fitch, and Harold Stearns for assistance on the manuscript.

CONTENTS

PART II. PRINCIPLES

PART III. THE PSYCHOLOGICAL BACKGROUND OF INDUSTRIAL UNREST

INTRODUCTION

THE author of this book was rarely equipped for the work he undertook. An employer of labor of large business experience, he was one of the dollar-a-year men who gave their services to the Government during the war, was assigned first to the Housing Department of the Shipping Board, then to the Ordnance Department, and took an active part in the settlement of labor controversies. He thus came into touch at first hand with the matter of such disputes, and the various methods by which it has been attempted to settle them. He supplemented the personal knowledge of the subject he thus gained by a comprehensive study of the material contained in official reports and other available documents.

In the book thus produced, two qualities seem to shine out: painstaking accuracy and deep sympathy with the human factor in industry.

Mr. Bing's bias as a so-called capitalist might be expected to incline towards the group to which he belongs. On the contrary, nothing is more apparent than his eager desire to be absolutely just in presenting the case of labor. It is exceedingly difficult to be just. The author has scrupulously endeavored to be so.

I have no doubt that this work will form a valuable addition to the library of social reform, and that it will be widely read, appreciated and pondered by those who are interested in the supreme practical question of our time.

FELIX ADLER.

PART I. THE MEDIATING AGENCIES

WAR-TIME STRIKES
AND THEIR ADJUSTMENT

CHAPTER I

The Industrial Background

THE war created an emergency in which it was necessary, besides recruiting and drilling an enormous army [1] and building up the navy to the required war strength, to embark on a shipbuilding program of hitherto unthought of size, hastily to construct cantonments each of which was as large as a city, and to produce quantities of munitions, food, clothing, aeroplanes, and other essentials on a scale that dwarfed into insignificance any former activities of the Government. The United States faced an unprecedented production program. To meet it successfully required an augmented supply of labor and continuous work, unhampered by strikes and other causes of inefficiency; it was absolutely essential to remove every factor that would interfere with production and to take advantage of every factor that would promote it.

Obviously it was not a time for social experimentation. Yet if to prevent strikes, to augment morale, and to increase efficiency, it was necessary to attack fundamental industrial wrongs of long standing, then such action can be justified as a *war* measure to the extent to which it was useful for this purpose.

To form an intelligent estimate of the problem, a knowledge of industrial conditions before the war is as essential as a knowledge of the effects upon industry of the war itself. The labor problem

---

[1] In one year and a half the army grew to twenty times its former size. In March, 1917, it consisted of 189,674 men and in November, 1918, of 3,554,000. Report of Secretary of War for 1918, page 9. Similar figures could be quoted for the Navy and other branches of the service.

which confronted the nation, upon our entry into the European conflict, resulted from adding to the existing causes of bad industrial relations those emergency elements which magnified and intensified the factors of unrest that had previously been present. The most important causes of strife in the pre-war period were inadequate wages, long hours, and opposition to collective bargaining and unionism. These, together with others of lesser importance, will be briefly examined before considering the effect of the war upon the industry of the country, and the labor disturbances which followed.

GENERAL CAUSES OF UNREST—WAGES

The United States Commission on Industrial Relations, reporting in 1915, found that "between one-fourth and one-third of the male workers 18 years of age and over, in factories and mines, earn less than $10 a week; from two-thirds to three-fourths earn less than $15, and only about one-tenth earn more than $20 a week . . . from two-thirds to three-fourths of the women workers . . . in industrial occupations generally, work at wages of less than $8 per week." [1]

The Railroad Wage Commission reporting in May, 1918, to the Director General of Railroads found that 51% of all railroad employees during December, 1917 (at a time when costs of living had already gone up materially), were receiving $75 per month, or less; 80% were receiving $100 per month, or less. Less than 3% received from $150 to $250 a month. [2] The average weekly earnings of laborers in Western sawmills for 1915 was $9.58; [3] in the steel mills and the packing plants and other trust-controlled industries up to 1915, prevailing wages for unskilled men varied from 15 cents to 20 cents per hour, averaging about 18 cents. [4] For ten hours a day and six days a week, this meant weekly earnings of $10.80 or $562.60 per year. Stockers in 1915 averaged 74.8 hours and earned $13.95 per week. And these

[1] Report of B. M. Manly, Director of Research and Investigation, Final Report of Commission on Industrial Relations, page 31.
[2] *Monthly Review*, Bureau of Labor Statistics, June, 1918.
[3] *Bulletin 225* of Bureau of Labor Statistics, page 11.
[4] N. C. Adams in a study of wages for the steel industry says that the rates for common labor in 1915 were 15 cents to 16 cents in the eastern district, and 19 cents in the Pittsburgh and Great Lakes districts. *Monthly Review*, Bureau of Labor Statistics, March, 1918.

figures are typical of the wages paid, prior to the war, to semi-skilled and unskilled labor in the United States. Nor were low wages in all cases confined to workers of little skill; in many cases skilled men and women fared little better.[1]

HOURS

The history of industry, since the inauguration of the era of factory production, is the story of constant struggle by the workers for the reduction of hours of work. In the years immediately preceding our entry into the war, considerable progress had been made in the introduction of the eight-hour day (that is to say, the forty-eight-hour week), yet there were still many industries in which the normal working week was over seventy-two hours. The rule was still twelve hours a day and seven days a week in a substantial number of places.[2]

OPPOSITION TO UNIONISM

A large part of our industrial workers, in addition, were prevented from joining labor unions by the bitter opposition of their employers and were refused the benefits of collective bargaining. Among the large trusts where, prior to 1915, wages had been lowest, this attitude particularly prevailed, but it was also to be found in the metal trades and in hundreds of other occupations. Although the employers themselves had increasingly united in industrial combinations—that is to say, in trade associations and in chambers of commerce—there existed on the part of a large proportion of the employers of the country the determination to treat with their employees as individuals only and to prevent them by every means in their power from associating themselves with their fellow workmen in organizations "of their choice." Perhaps the most striking, as certainly the most unfortunate, survival

[1] President Wharton of the Railway Employees Department, A. F. of L., in addressing the Fourth Biennial Convention of that Department, said that an examination of Railroad payrolls showed hourly wages in some cases as low as the following: machinists, 24 cents; machinist helpers, 18 cents; millwrights, 21 cents; pattern workers, 30 cents; pipe fitters, 26 cents. *Official Proceedings*, page 130.
[2] The President's Second Industrial Conference, reporting as late as March 6, 1920, says at page 33: "There are large basic industries which still employ substantial numbers of men in exhausting work for eighty-four hours per week and longer."

of this opposition was manifest in the first of the President's recent Industrial Conferences at Washington, which ended by the withdrawal of the labor delegates.[1]

OTHER CAUSES

Another source of unrest was the bad sanitary conditions under which many men and women worked, and the absence of adequate protection against accidents. Much progress had been made in both of these respects yet much remained to be done. Some of the large corporations, which offended most with respect to inadequate wages, long hours, and anti-union discrimination, had nevertheless done splendid work toward the prevention of accidents and, to a lesser degree, toward the betterment of sanitary conditions. In some of the hazardous occupations, however, such as mining and in many less dangerous callings, there was a failure to observe State and Federal law and an indifference to obvious dangers, which were followed by an unnecessarily large number of fatal accidents. Inevitably unrest increased because of the workers' feeling that the laws had been violated and that many injuries and deaths could have been prevented. So also with respect to conditions of health and sanitation: Dissatisfaction and resentment were augmented by bad physical conditions, especially in labor camps and isolated communities, although by no means there alone. In fact, because sanitation was immeasurably better, in some places, than it had been in previous years, was precisely the reason why those industries and localities that had failed to keep up with the progress which elsewhere had been accomplished were made all the more irritatingly conspicuous.

There can also be no doubt that the employer had not given adequate thought to the problem of labor management. His attention had been absorbed by other difficulties of production, as well as by questions of distribution and finance. His relations with labor questions—whether or not his workers were able to live on the wages which they received; how they were affected by seasonal idleness or the monotony of their daily task, whether or not general working conditions were as they should have been—

[1] See New York *Times,* Sunday, October 26, 1919, for statement by the late Mr. Endicott, a "public" delegate although himself a large employer.

these, and dozens of similar questions, were quite outside the horizon of most business men. It is only in the last few years when all employers have experienced great difficulty in getting and keeping men that these questions have received any appreciable amount of study. It is only recently, for example, that labor turnover has been recognized by the employer as an industrial evil, costly alike to the worker, the employer, and the community. The employment manager, in whom responsibility is now vested for better relations between management and men, is a late development in industry. Prior to the war, very few firms realized the need for this expert service, and in addition very few men or women were available to supply it.

Moreover, the large number of foreign born workers, millions of whom were unable to speak our language, the overcrowding in large industrial centers, and the bad housing and sanitary conditions which resulted (from which small communities were also sufferers) contributed to the awakening of that antagonism and that dissatisfaction which were part of our general industrial unpreparedness.

Not only were relations between employers and employees bad for the reasons recited above, but two things were lacking which would have been of inestimable value in the crisis that was about to confront the nation.

First: A public opinion at least moderately informed as to actual industrial conditions, and reasonably in agreement as to general policies to be adopted and measures immediately to be taken.

Second: Government machinery ready to aid in making the necessary adjustments from a state of peace to one of war, including (1) means for handling the problems incident to a shifting of the working population to new industries; (2) means for the training of workers to supply emergency needs; (3) means for giving aid to private employers in increasing the efficiency of their labor force by better management, especially with respect to those matters making for better industrial relations; and (4) the necessary machinery for the avoidance or prompt adjustment of industrial disputes so that production might proceed uninterruptedly.

We needed not only the knowledge of industrial conditions and the physical equipment necessary to cope with the emergencies that confronted the nation, but also an expert personnel reënforced by an enlightened public opinion.   Every one of these elements was almost completely lacking.

THE WAR AND OUR INDUSTRIAL UNPREPAREDNESS

With the outbreak of the European War in 1914 there was at first a cessation of all industry in the warring countries.   Widespread unemployment occurred in spite of the fact that millions of men were being inducted into the armies, a fact which under normal conditions would have created an acute labor shortage. Much of the normal production of peace time came to a standstill simultaneously with the universal consternation that followed the beginning of the war.   A considerable period was needed before the idle men could be absorbed into the newly organized warmaking industries.   But the growth of the munition plants and the manufacture of other articles needed to carry on the war on the gigantic scale on which it was being waged, together with the increasingly heavy drafts upon the male population of the Allied countries for military service, soon did absorb the men whom a general stoppage of industry had made idle.   Gradually, too, peace industries were resumed, creating additional demands for workers.[1]

In a short time, in fact, a labor shortage was created, which as the months wore on became more and more acute.   This shortage was partly met by the introduction of women workers into industry in ever increasing numbers,[2] partly by the abrogation of trade union customs which tended to curtail production, and partly by the absorption into industry of old men and others who, in normal times, for one reason or another, were unemployed and in some cases unemployable.   In these ways, principally of course by the first, means were found to provide enough men for the

[1] See Mary Conyngton, *Monthly Review*, U. S. Bureau of Labor Statistics, April, 1918, p. 204, for an account of the effect of the war upon the employment of women in England.   At first they were thrown out of work in large numbers, relief work having been needed in thousands of resulting cases of destitution.   Gradually the unemployed women were reabsorbed into industry and hundreds of thousands of others drafted into it.

[2] Thus, *The Labour Gazette,* London, November, 1917, quoted in *Monthly Review,* U. S. Bureau of Labor Statistics, Jan., 1918, p. 65, states that there were 1,421,000 more females employed in Great Britain in July, 1917, than at the outbreak of the war (an increase of almost 50%).

armies and enough workers to meet the enormous demands made by modern warfare for manufactured articles of every description.

In the United States there occurred a similar industrial crisis in August, 1914, not so severe, however, as that originally experienced in European countries. Our ordinary peace industries were slowed down, whereas in Europe many of them were almost wiped out. It was several months before the full resumption of normal peace industries in this country, together with the demand for war materials from abroad, absorbed our unemployed man power. Gradually, as factory after factory was built to supply the needs of the Entente Nations, as our shipbuilding plans began to develop, and as the demand for food products at home and abroad constantly increased, an oversupply of labor was changed to a labor shortage.

Upon our own entry into the European war in 1917, industrial conditions were once more disturbed and large numbers of men were thrown out of employment. These, however, were soon absorbed by the recruitments for the army and navy and by our rapidly expanding war production program, which during 1918 assumed gigantic proportions. As a result, our labor shortage soon became acute.

SPECIFIC CAUSES OF UNREST

Our difficulties, like those of England (and other European countries), were much complicated by the concentration of war industries into certain sections of the country where housing and transportation, all too poor before the war, became, by reason of the influx of additional workers, almost unbearable. In addition, from August, 1915, on, there occurred a constant and increasingly rapid rise in the cost of living. By June, 1917, the increase amounted to 29%; by June, 1918, 58%; by December, 1918, 74%; by December, 1919, the cost had almost doubled.[1] Up to the fall of 1917, in spite of the great increase in the cost of practically every article that entered into the workingmen's budget, there were many industries and localities in which no substantial wage increases had occurred.

[1] *Monthly Labor Review,* U. S. Bureau Labor Statistics, June, 1920, p. 79. The estimates of the National Industrial Conference Board, Research Reports Nos. 9, 14 and 25, are somewhat more conservative: June, 1918, 52.3%; November, 1918, 65.9%; November, 1919, 82.2%.

We have seen that the general wage level prior to the war was in a majority of cases too low to permit of proper living standards. If our workers were to avoid acute suffering, adequate wage increases became imperative. Moreover, the injustice resulting from the lessened purchasing power of the worker's wages was felt with added keenness because of the general belief (which was substantially correct) that the employers were making large profits and that the mounting costs of the necessities of life were due in part at least to profiteering.

Furthermore great irregularity in wages and conditions of employment attended the changing of the nation from a peace to a war footing. There were numerous causes responsible for this result. Most important of these was the stealing of labor which accompanied the efforts of Government contractors and departments to speed up their work. After our entrance into the war the Government awarded contracts on cost plus basis.[1] War psychology, as well as the demands of Government departments, laid emphasis on speed rather than economy. Contractors and Government officials, in their eagerness to get their particular pieces of work done, disregarded the effect of their actions on other Government work, and the stealing of men from one plant to another was freely indulged in, Government departments and employers bidding against each other for men and supplies. Many firms, when they wanted men, showed themselves absolutely unscrupulous in the manner in which they disregarded the wishes and even the express orders of Government officials regarding wages and overtime.

As a result, some workers remained at the old wages, whereas others doing the same work in the same community were paid much more by aggressive employers—or perhaps by some agency of the Government itself—having profitable contracts to fill and eager to get men. Wages in one branch of an industry might remain stationary, while another part of the same industry received large increases. These inequalities affected men in different parts of the Government service as well as in private plants.[2] Thus a mechanic in the shipyards might be receiving 50% more

[1] H. B. Endicott in the New York *Times,* March, 1918, says that "the cost plus method was apparently the cause of more unrest among workingmen than any other single factor."

[2] Specific instances of these inequalities will be cited in subsequent chapters.

than an equally skilled worker in the same community and trade, working, for instance, in a munition plant.

The unrest which was bound to follow inequalities of this kind was greatly augmented, not only by the high living costs and the bad conditions produced by overcrowding and inadequate transportation, but also by the continued refusal of many employers to grant collective bargaining, and by their persistence in practices of discrimination against labor unions. To make matters worse, the urgent need for production and the publicity which this need received, in an effort to make the best use of every particle of the nation's resources, gave the workers a realization of a strength which before they had neither realized nor possessed.

But now, both realizing and possessing this new power, they desired, naturally enough, not merely to have their wages keep pace with the rising cost of living but also to effect an improvement in pre-war conditions. Even in 1916 there occurred the largest number of strikes in any one year of the country's previous history,[1] and in addition a tie-up of the entire railway system was averted only by Congressional action which forced the railroads to grant the men's demands. Furthermore, the workers realized that the time to enforce demands was when men were scarce, not when they were plentiful.[2]

As against these factors making for conflicts of great magnitude can be set the war psychology, making powerfully for the maintenance of industrial peace. Patriotic fervor demanded universal sacrifices for the nation, and it was realized that increased production was essential for the winning of the war. Interruption of the manufacture of munitions or ships or of the production or transportation of food, might result in national defeat. Yet the patriotic motive, although genuine and potent, was not of itself sufficiently strong to overcome the many adverse conditions making for severe industrial conflicts. It was a real element in the situation, but never a determining one, and in the first

[1] See Appendix No. 1 for statistics relative to strikes.
[2] The correctness of this point of view has been demonstrated by the events of 1920. Curtailment of credits together with excessive prices of commodities made it necessary to decrease production in many industries. Taking advantage of this condition there were employers who not only refused legitimate wage demands but deliberately closed their factories to weaken the strategic position of the workers.

year of our participation in the war there occurred an even larger number of strikes than in the record year of 1916.

PRE-WAR MEDIATING AGENCIES

What the war disclosed was the fundamental need of a method by which the workers could obtain redress of grievances without resorting to the strike. Machinery for mediating these grievances was utterly lacking as was also any compulsion—other than fragmentary and ill-informed public opinion—to procure the acceptance of arbitral decisions by either side.

Prior to our entry into the war, the only governmental machinery for the adjustment of labor disputes was as follows:

(a) **The Department of Labor.** The Conciliation Bureau of the department did excellent work in some cases, but it was for several reasons inadequate to meet the emergency. In the first place, the Labor Department was insufficiently supplied with funds[1] and Congress was unwilling to make additional appropriations. It was furthermore thought by many of the largest employers that the department was under the control of organized labor. The law under which the department was organized states its purpose to be "to foster, promote and develop the welfare of the wage-earners of the United States."

In fact, the purpose of the department is regarded by most people as that of protecting the interests of labor rather than of administrating measures for the improvement of relations between employer and employee—which would include projects to secure increased productive power as well as improved working conditions. The fact, too, that the Secretary of Labor is the ex-cfficial of a powerful national labor union has helped to secure for the department the confidence of organized labor, but has had the opposite effect on employers who are unsympathetic with labor organizations. The members of the Secretary's staff had also been more successful in gaining the confidence of the men than of the employers, although these members had been recruited from different walks of life, some having been lawyers and employers, others, labor leaders and college professors. Another reason why the department could not take care of the war emergency was that it has always been opposed to the undertaking

[1] Report, Secretary of Labor, 1917, page 10.

of arbitral functions by its commissioners, believing that the usefulness of the department, in the long run, would be greater if it confined its efforts to mediation and conciliation. But the war called for the exercise of larger powers than the Labor Department possessed and made the exercise by other agencies of arbitral determinations of wages and other questions absolutely necessary.

(b) **The Board of Mediation** appointed under the Newlands Act of 1913 for the settlement of industrial disputes on the railways. The jurisdiction of this board was limited to men engaged in the movement of the trains, and in the absence of agreement between the parties it had no powers of arbitration but only of conciliation. It had an excellent record, and continued its work for those railroads—only the smaller and less important ones—which were not taken over by the Government.

(c) **Boards of Conciliation** existed in many of the States. They were, however, never—except in a few cases—important factors in the settlement of industrial disputes. The shortcomings of the Mediation Bureau of the Department of Labor applied to most of the State Boards of Conciliation; in addition these boards were unable to do the work of which a national board was capable, because their jurisdiction was too narrow.

(d) **Joint Boards of Adjustment,** in some industries, resulted from agreements—usually concluded annually—between employers' associations and labor unions. These agreements fix wages and hours for the period covered by the agreement, and provide a method of adjusting other questions that may arise. In the anthracite coal mines of Pennsylvania the board of conciliation was the outgrowth of the Roosevelt Commission of 1903, and has been maintained by the renewal, from time to time, of the agreement under which the board was created. In other industries, such as in many of the building trades, the glass blowers, and a portion of the needle trades, similar agreements had been made. But difficulties frequently arose when the time arrived, upon their expiration, for the renewal of these agreements. No machinery existed to facilitate this process other than that above set forth, which in many cases proved ineffectual. Moreover, these agreements were made under circumstances so different from those which confronted the nation during the war that even in the trades in which they existed they were frequently insufficient to meet the war emergency. In some cases there had been so rapid an advance in the cost of living that the workers were unable to get along on the wages set for the industry by the trade agreement made one or two years previously. Thus joint trade agreements, which had been of the greatest service in normal times in preserving industrial peace, were in the war emergency inadequate.

Because of the conditions above set forth the United States after the declaration of war drifted into a condition of affairs that rendered serious labor troubles almost inevitable. Millions of workers whose pre-war wages were insufficient to support a proper standard of life found their earnings every day more inadequate because of the increase in the cost of food, clothing, and shelter. In some cases increases in wages took place; in comparatively few, however, in the first year of the war, were they as great as the added living cost, and in many cases no increases whatever was made. The feeling was strong that this was the time to insist upon remuneration more in keeping with the worker's ideas of his deserts.

The eight-hour day, required by law for Government work, was the goal of labor everywhere. Although largely extended in 1916, it was nevertheless denied in a substantial number of localities and industries. Most serious of all, however, in the difficulty presented of reconciling capital and labor were the differences in regard to unionism. The men's insistence upon their right to join trade unions and in some instances their demand for union recognition and the closed shop clashed with the very strong desire of many employers to deal with their workers as individuals and their dislike of labor organizations in themselves. And although both sides were patriotic, neither was unmindful of its own interest, and each side was afraid that the other would take advantage of the unusual conditions to secure changes which would have been impossible in normal times. Employers desired profits and held tenaciously to pre-war industrial prejudices, even in cases where to do so meant to jeopardize production. Workers, on the other hand, were not deterred by the war from efforts to improve conditions. The difference between the two was that because of constant increases in the cost of living the worker had in almost all cases to take the initiative, if he was to secure an amelioration of his grievances—even to the extent of the maintenance of the status quo ante—and this often meant that he had to resort to the strike. And we must also remember that the temptation to do so was all the stronger because, due to the scarcity of labor, a strike was almost certain to be successful.

CHAPTER II

The Emergency Construction Wage Commission

IMMEDIATELY after the declaration of war the construction of cantonments was commenced. It was planned to construct 16 National Army Cantonments to accommodate 40,000 men each, and to rush them to completion in 90 days.[1] The task seemed utterly impossible of achievement as each cantonment practically amounted to a city in itself. So great was the desire for speed that the contractors did not wait to receive signed contracts from the Government but proceeded immediately with work amounting to many millions of dollars on verbal orders.

The building industry in large cities had been conducted almost exclusively under the closed shop, the men having been very strongly organized. There were, however, hundreds of thousands of mechanics in rural districts—and also not a few employed by smaller contractors in the cities, who were not members of unions.

It was essential that a contractor be in a position to avail himself of the labor nearest at hand, irrespective of whether or not it was union or non-union. It was also necessary that disputes for any cause be not permitted to develop into stoppages of work. There were a number of contractors engaged on heavy construction, especially in the country districts, such as the building of dams, power plants, and railroads, who conducted open shops and who were alleged by the unions to discriminate against union men. Owing to the nature of the cantonments, combining road-building, sewage systems, and power plants, some of these contractors seemed by their past experience best fitted for the work and one of them was awarded the contract for the construction of a cantonment at Indianapolis. This contractor advertised all over the country for men, although it was claimed that members of unions, residing at Indianapolis, were unemployed and that the

---

[1] "To this requirement was almost immediately added the task of constructing 16 National Guard Camps of nearly the same size." Report of the Secretary of War, 1918, page 62.

14

contractor was discriminating against them. A strike occurred on this and other grounds and stoppages of work were also threatened elsewhere.

Growing out of the negotiations undertaken both to secure a return to work of the men at Indianapolis and to prevent any more occurrences of a similar nature, an agreement was made June 10, 1917, between the Secretary of War and the President of the American Federation of Labor, for the organization of the first War Labor Adjusting Board—the Cantonment Adjustment Commission.[1]

This was the first time in our history that the United States Government entered into an agreement with labor unions. The event is considered by many to mark the beginning of a new era in the history of American industry. The agreement provided for the adoption of union wages and hours in the vicinities in which the work was located, but it was understood that union men were not to object to the employment of men who did not belong to the union.[2] Three members of the commission were provided for, one to represent the public, one the army (as employer), and a third to be nominated by the President of the American Federation of Labor.

As so frequently happened during the war, the work to be performed by the commission was very much underestimated at the time it was organized. It was thought that cantonment construction would last only a few months, and it was not expected that the work of the commission would extend over a long period, or be of an arduous nature; with the development of our war activities, however, it became necessary for the Government to undertake a construction program of vastly greater size than was at first contemplated.[3] A large part of this work was placed

[1] In the original agreement the Secretary of War and the President of the American Federation of Labor signed as individuals; in subsequent amplifications thereof they signed in their respective official capacities. See Appendix II for personnel of the board and agreements under which it was constituted.

[2] The agreement was short and indefinite and in the early period of its history the commission was loosely organized. See Louis B. Wehle, *The Quarterly Journal of Economics,* November, 1917, p. 122.

[3] By November 1, 1918, the original 32 projects had grown to 448, including only major undertakings. At one time no fewer than 400,000 workmen were employed on work coming under the jurisdiction of the board, the buildings having been erected at the total expenditure of $1,250,000,000. See Report of the Secretary of War for 1918.

under the jurisdiction of the Board—first, army aviation fields and storage facilities; later Navy shore construction. With this expansion of the activities of the Board its name was changed to the "Emergency Construction Commission."

The country was divided into districts and an examiner appointed for each district, who at first was not a regular employee of the commission but was employed on a per diem basis. With the increase in the scope of the Board's duties two examiners, usually army officers, were placed in charge of labor adjustments for each district. A competent statistical bureau was also developed which studied the earnings and efficiency of the workers, their regularity of attendance, and the relation of absenteeism to overtime work. (Use will be made in subsequent chapters of some of the material collected by the commission.)

The work of labor adjustment was much facilitated by the fact that all of the contracts let by the Government were on a basis of cost plus a fee and that there was incorporated in each contract the so-called labor clauses by which the contractor agreed that in the event of any labor dispute he would notify the Government and accept the instructions of its representative in relation thereto.

With the exception of small local flareups the commission maintained almost uninterrupted peace in places where it had jurisdiction, all national unions abiding by the policy under which it was organized, except the carpenters, who claimed not to be bound by the signature of the President of the American Federation of Labor [1] (of which they were members) and who objected to the waiver of the demand for the closed shop—which was involved

At the time of the signing of the armistice the Emergency Construction Wage Commission estimated its own shortage of labor at 200,000 men and for all trades in the country at one million. It planned to bring 50,000 to 75,000 men from Porto Rico and the Bahama Islands and before the war ended they had brought in about thirteen thousand Porto Ricans and three thousand from the Bahamas. These men were all sent back shortly after the signing of the armistice. See "A Report of the Activities of the War Department in the Field of Industrial Relations During the War."

[1] Technically this contention was undoubtedly correct; but the carpenters accepted the benefit of the Baker-Gompers Agreement and in any event were not justified in refusing to join all the other building trades in recognizing its validity.

in the agreement under which the commission was created. There was, however, very little serious trouble until after the signing of the armistice.

In the spring of 1918, the commission undertook to standardize wages in the building industry all over the country. It was a stupendous undertaking, requiring conferences with representatives of labor and of employers for all building trades in every locality. In the midst of the work, after the organization of the War Labor Policies Board and its determination to standardize wages for every war industry in the United States, the Emergency Construction Commission was requested to discontinue its work and turn over its material to the Labor Policies Board, which it did. The latter board, however, never completed its task and unfortunately nothing was done towards the standardization for which the Emergency Construction Wage Commission had expended so much effort.

The rule under which wages were adjusted by the Emergency Construction Wage Commission was a peculiar one and unlike that used by any other war labor board. It ascertained the wages for any given locality which had been adopted by bona fide agreements between employers' associations and labor unions, and accepted these wage scales, irrespective of its judgment as to their fairness. The work of wage adjustment was thus simplified and reduced to the mechanical process of determining the standards which had already been fixed by previous agreements, and the application of these standards. The weakness of this procedure, however, was that it led to the exertion of great pressure by local unions upon local employers to change wage rates in order to induce the commission to adopt these new scales which had been locally agreed to. Such changes, naturally enough, might thus be arbitrarily made. On the other hand there arose towards the end of the war cases in which this rule, of adopting local standards, prevented the Board from making increases which the equities of the situation demanded and which otherwise it would have made. At the beginning of the war employers generally were more willing to concede local wage increases than towards the end of the war when there was a common belief that a period of declining prices confronted them. In such cases the maintenance by the Commission of the existing wage scale did not end the difficulties and the Commission seemed helpless to effect an adjustment.[1]

This rule of wage adjustment was adopted more or less hastily at a time when it was believed that the Commission's work would not last very long; nevertheless when the scope of the Commission's activities was enlarged and its life indefinitely prolonged by the extension of its jurisdiction over many kinds of building work which were undertaken by the War and Navy Departments, the rule was never changed.

The greatest evils connected with war labor administration, the abuse of overtime and the stealing of men from one plant to another, first became prominent with the commencement of cantonment construction.[2] Looking back over the war period, the important facts which stand out in this connection are that the cantonments were finished and occupied in an incredibly short period and that our army was sent to France with corresponding expedition, arriving there in time to be one of the deciding factors of the war. As compared with this achievement, very little else is of much significance. Yet the same results, tremendous though they were, could doubtless have been accomplished without the

---

[1] The carpenters' strike in New York City in the fall of 1918 was a case in point.

[2] To meet this condition there was organized in the Hampton Roads District (Virginia) a Board of Control charged with the duty of reconciling the conflicting claims for materials and men created by the pressure of Government work in this locality. In close proximity were Newport News with its shipbuilding plant, embarkation depots and army cantonments and Norfolk and its Navy Yards, aviation fields and other war plants. These activities were all carrying on building and war production programs of great magnitude. Each was short of labor and competed with every other enterprise—Government as well as private—for its share of the inadequate supply. Hence the organization of the Board of Control with Rear Admiral F. R. Harris, as Chairman representing the Navy, the U. S. Shipping Board, the Emergency Fleet Corporation, the U. S. Housing Corporation and the War Industries Board and other representatives of the War Department, the U. S. Employment Service and the Railroad and Fuel Administrations. The Board did not attempt to make independent wage adjustments but working closely with the Emergency Construction Wage Commission and containing representatives of every Government agency employing building mechanics in the district, it was able to prevent the adoption by any one department of a wage scale which was not in accordance with the rate fixed for the district. That is to say, it coördinated the work for this district of the different wage boards so that uniform scales and conditions would prevail.

riotous competition for men which accompanied the actual work, or the reckless employment of overtime with its consequent abnormal daily earnings—in some cases as high as twenty dollars a day. These excessive war time earnings had the unfortunate effect of leading the workers to expect in normal times earnings which industry on a peace basis was incapable of affording.[1] The disillusion of the workers which inevitably followed the armistice is no doubt in part responsible for much of the recent labor unrest.

[1] This will be discussed in greater detail in a subsequent chapter, as will the confusion in wage fixing which resulted from the fact that in addition to the Emergency Construction Commission, three other agencies were fixing wages in the building trades for men engaged on construction work over which they had jurisdiction.

CHAPTER III

Shipbuilding

SHIPBUILDING LABOR ADJUSTMENT BOARD

THE need for ships and for Government assistance, if that need was to be promptly met, was realized some time before our participation in the war; and resulted in the bill which created the Shipping Board. This bill was passed in September, 1916; and the organization of the board was immediately begun, although not completed until considerably later. The early months of 1917 saw the launching of Germany's unrestricted submarine campaign, followed by our entry into the war. These events were accompanied by very large sinkings of the merchant ships of the Allies, and by great fear as to their ability to maintain the necessary ocean shipping. The delays in our own shipbuilding program gave rise in the public mind to a feverish anxiety for ship production, and the attention of this country as well as of almost the entire world was fixed upon the activities of the United States Shipping Board in its efforts to meet the situation.

The task which confronted the board was one of unusual difficulty—unusual even at a time when difficult and seemingly impossible tasks confronted every branch of the Government. Of the many problems with which the board was faced the labor problem was probably the most perplexing. The shipping industry had, until some time after the outbreak of the European war, been an unprofitable one, and most of the shipbuilders were or had been in receivers' hands. The result was that the yards were in poor physical condition—the best of them without even proper toilet facilities; lockers, baths, and hospitals were usually lacking, and, in this extra-hazardous calling, even provision for first aid was utterly inadequate. Modern ideas in regard to the treatment of labor had not reached the shipyards, and men were still hired and fired in the same haphazard way that was the custom twenty-five or fifty years ago. There was probably not a single yard at the time of our entry into the war using the services of an efficient employment manager.[1] Wages also had lagged behind the point which had been reached in most prosperous industries,[2] and it was further claimed that cutting piece rates was practiced in many of the shipyards.

During this period transportation facilities from the workers' homes to the yards became so overtaxed that it was stated at many of the hearings that large numbers of the men were traveling two hours in the morning to reach the yards and an equal length of time in the evening to reach their homes. Conditions, which were well described as approaching a riot, prevailed during the rush hours on many of the trolley lines—men rode on fenders, they clung to the outside of the cars, with the natural result of frequent cases of serious injury and, so it was reported, of several fatalities. It was in the face of such conditions and of the universal shortage of labor that the vital need for ships made it necessary to augment the force of shipyard workers from about ninety thousand at the time of our entry into the war to close to four hundred thousand at the time of the armistice,[3] an increase of over four times, in less than two years.

These general conditions were at first not fully appreciated by the members of the Shipping Board, but as time went on the Government groped its way to a more thorough understanding of what they implied. The reader must keep in mind these peculiar difficulties with which the Shipping Board was confronted in order to comprehend the steps that were taken to get men, to prevent strikes, and to increase production.[4]

[1] P. H. Douglas and F. E. Wolfe in the *Journal of Political Economy* for May, 1919, Volume XXVII, page 376, state that at as late a date as January 1, 1918, only 13 shipyards had employment departments in any organized form. (At that time the yards were employing about 146,000 men.)

[2] A representative of the unions stated at the Philadelphia hearings of the Board, December, 1917, that when he arrived in the Delaware River section (a few years before) boilermakers were getting 29 cents an hour—a rate which he stated to have been the lowest paid anywhere in the United States. Another witness said that the rate for blacksmiths had remained stationary for thirty years.

[3] P. H. Douglas and F. E. Wolfe in the *Journal of Political Economy* for May, 1919, Volume XXVII, page 372.

[4] One of the first steps was the granting of industrial exemption for all shipyards workers. (Work in the shipyards and in the actual operation of vessels wer the only occupations for which a specific exemption, irrespective of the importance of the individual to the in-

Indeed the forces making for unrest in the yards were stronger, especially for the first year of the war, than the efforts of the Shipping Board to counteract them. For in spite of the dangerous crisis which the world faced during the months succeeding our entry into the war, threats of strikes and actual cessations of work were taking place in our Atlantic Coast shipyards, delaying the construction of new ships and the repairs to the requisitioned German merchant vessels. Still more serious troubles were threatening on the Pacific Coast.

To meet this situation, the Shipbuilding Labor Adjustment Board was created on August 25, 1917, by agreement made between the Government, the President of the American Federation of Labor, and all the International Unions doing the work of shipbuilding (except the carpenters). This agreement as amended in December, 1917, provided for the adjustment of disputes by a board of three, one a representative of the public, one of the Shipping Board Emergency Fleet Corporation, and the Navy jointly, and one representing organized labor, nominated by the President of the American Federation of Labor.

The first task of the board was to prevent threatened stoppages of work on the Pacific Coast. Both sides came to Washington and hearings were held, in the midst of which, however, the authority of the member of the Commission representing the Shipping Board was suddenly withdrawn by that body.[1] The hearings had to be suspended in spite of the fact that trouble had arisen in all the shipbuilding cities of the Pacific Coast, and in Seattle had gone so far that an actual strike order for September 5th had been issued. The labor representatives from the coast returned home with their grievances unsettled, and called out their men on what was to be one of the most serious labor disturb-

dustry, was given under the draft regulations.) A preferential was also determined upon, in the wages of mechanics engaged in the building of ships, over those in every other occupation. The construction of houses was undertaken by the Government in many shipbuilding centers, and, in addition, the patriotic side of work in the shipyards was emphasized. Efforts were also made to improve the physical conditions of the yards, as well as the method of labor management.

[1] A fact which never became known to the public.

ances of the war. The board was thereupon reconstituted, traveled to the Pacific Coast, and held hearings in all the large shipbuilding centers, many of the men in the meantime continuing on strike.[1]

The testimony taken at these hearings shows the extreme bitterness which existed between most of the employers, especially in the steel shipyards, and their men. The demands included wage increases, no discrimination against union members, the elimination of "10-hour lumber." In Portland the closed shop was also asked for, but the demand was withdrawn when its inconsistency with the understanding under which the board was created was pointed out. The employers attributed their difficulties to a comparatively few "agitators," failing to realize that their troubles were due to a general condition of unrest and dissatisfaction among all the workers—a state of mind which, with all the other elements affecting the situation, was destined to make the war period a time of the largest number of strikes in the country's history.

After the board had held its hearings in Seattle, decision was postponed until San Francisco and Portland had been heard, and although other unions favored a return to work pending the announcement of an award, the Brotherhood of Boilermakers and Iron-shipbuilders held out, and they at first refused to go back until their grievances were settled. Only after great pressure from their national officers were they finally induced to return to work. At the conclusion of the San Francisco hearing the board set uniform wage scales for all Pacific Coast shipyards, awarding an increase of 31% over the wages established by joint agreements on June 1, 1916, in San Francisco and Seattle. This

---

[1] In San Francisco the men had been induced to return to work through the efforts of Mr. Gavin McNab, who acted as President Wilson's personal representative. Elsewhere on the coast, however, the strike was still on when the board held its hearings. Although labor adjustment boards have usually insisted that men return to work before they will take jurisdiction, the Shipbuilding Labor Adjustment Board felt that, under all the circumstances, it would be unwise to adhere strictly to this rule.

percentage was the estimated increase in the cost of living from that date.[1]

Dissatisfaction with the wage award and with certain features of the agreement under which the board was constituted led to danger of another strike and hence to the execution of a supplementary agreement of December 8, 1917, making changes in the Pacific award, equivalent to a further increase in wages.[2]

In the meantime while the Shipbuilding Labor Adjustment Board was on the Pacific Coast trying to induce the men of Portland, Seattle, and San Francisco to return to work, the troubles which had been threatening in the East came to a head in strikes at Fore River, Newark Bay, and Baltimore. None of these were, however, of long duration,[3] and shipbuilding now proceeded peacefully under labor adjustments made by the board, until interrupted on the Atlantic Coast by disputes with the carpenters in February, 1918, resulting in a dramatic exchange of telegrams between Chairman Hurley of the Shipping Board and Mr. Hutcheson, President of the Brotherhood of Carpenters, and ending finally in the famous "Will you coöperate or will you obstruct?" telegrams of the President of the United States to the carpenters, urging them to return to work and submit their

[1] In accordance with the agreement the award should have been based on wages of July 15, 1917, but wages up to that time not having kept pace with increases in living costs, an award based on wages in effect at the later date would have been insufficient to meet the entire increased cost of living and would have failed to keep the men at work. As it was, one of the Seattle shipyards had advanced rates very much faster than its competitors and in some instances had been paying its men considerably higher rates than those awarded by the Board.

[2] The new agreement provided for a war bonus of 10%, contingent until February 1, 1917, upon regularity of attendance; after that date it became a permanent addition to wages. It also provided for appeals from the decision of the board and eliminated representation from the wooden shipbuilders' unions, which had been provided for in the original agreement, because of the refusal of the carpenters to become a party to the agreement.

[3] Henry Endicott, Chairman of the Commission on Public Safety for Massachusetts, was accepted as arbitrator for the Fore River dispute, and Vice-Chairman Stevens of the Shipping Board secured a return of the men at Baltimore. The latter testified before the Senate Committee in December, 1917, that strikes in the shipyards had, up to that time, caused a loss of 536,992 working days—an equivalent of 20,000 men working for one month.

grievances to the orderly determination of the Shipbuilding Labor Adjustment Board, which resulted in a return of the men.[1]

Another period of comparative peace in the shipyards now ensued, to be broken only after the signing of the armistice by the dissatisfaction of the metal trades of Seattle because of the denial by the board of their request for a wage increase to $1.00 an hour. The decision of the board was appealed, and the Board of Appeals, whose membership was evenly divided between capital and labor, was deadlocked. This was construed by the Shipping Board as an affirmation of the decision of the board. The men refused to accept this interpretation. Protracted negotiations with the Shipping Board followed, during which the workers endeavored to obtain permission to negotiate directly with their employers for a wage increase, which permission the board at first gave but later withdrew.[2] The early decisions of the Shipbuilding Labor Adjustment Board had fixed minimum rates, but in a great many cases these became maximum rates as well, by reason of the fact that the shipyard owners had agreed in their contracts with the Shipping Board not to increase rates without the permission of the board, which the board was unwilling to grant.[3] During the progress of the war, it more and more became the general practice for the adjustment boards to establish rates of wages as maxima as well as minima, the object of this being to prevent one employer from bidding against an-

[1] The Carpenters' Union was never reconciled to the abandonment during the war of union labor's demand for the extension of the closed shop. It also desired separate representation in the Adjustment Board, when matters were being heard concerning its membership. Upon the failure of President Hutcheson in his negotiations on these and other points with the Shipping Board, the carpenters in Staten Island and Baltimore shipyards quit work (Mr. Hutcheson claimed against his wishes), and refused to submit their grievance to the Shipbuilding Adjustment Board. Public opinion strongly condemned the carpenters' stand, and Mr. Hutcheson appealed to President Wilson for an opportunity to present to him the grievances of the men, whereupon the telegrams of the President above referred to were sent.
[2] See The Strike in Seattle by Theresa S. McMahon, *The Survey*, March 8, 1919, p. 822.
[3] Some of the yards were prevented from increasing wages by reason of the fact that their work was on the basis of cost plus fixed fee for every ship built and the Shipping Board would not reimburse them for wage payments in excess of the awards of the S. L. A. B.

other for men, and the consequent shifting from one plant to another. The unions had acquiesced in this restriction during the war, although a good deal of resentment was caused by the Government's having prevented employers from paying more than the fixed rates, even when they wanted to. Now that the war was over, it was felt very strongly that the Government should not prevent an employer from paying as high wages as he chose.

These Seattle negotiations seem to have been taken out of the hands of the S. L. A. B. and to have been conducted in person by Mr. Piez, the General Manager of the Emergency Fleet Corporation.[1] His final decision was not to permit individual shipyards to increase their rates of compensation, and after much negotiation, upon refusal of the yards to grant their wage demands, on January 21, 1919, the men walked out in Seattle, Aberdeen and Tacoma.[2]

There now followed one of the most dramatic labor struggles of the war. After the strike had been in progress only a few days, the metal trades of Seattle requested the Central Labor Council, with which all the labor unions of that section are affiliated, to call a general sympathetic strike in support of the metal trades. The Council, upholding the metal trades in their demands, and feeling that the Shipping Board should either have granted their wage increase or have permitted the men to negotiate directly with the shipyards, decided upon a general strike, subject to ratification by the individual unions. With very few exceptions the unions agreed to aid the metal workers, and the date of February 6 was set for the commencement of the strike. By that time no fewer than 110 unions had fallen in line, in-

---

[1] Mr. Piez in a telegram to the shipyard owners said: "The Fleet Corporation feels that the men in your district have had every opportunity for a proper and fair hearing. That the men in striking violated the spirit and letter of their agreement with the Government . . . that if they were successful in securing their demands . . . the future of the entire shipbuilding industry would be jeopardized. The Fleet Corporation stands by the Macy Board decision and will do nothing more." *Seattle Post-Intelligencer*, January 26, 1919.

[2] V. E. Macy in the *National Civic Federationist*, February 5, 1919, said that the Seattle situation was 60% the fault of selfish employers, who violated all orders of the S. L. A. B. by paying wages far in excess of the scale authorized, and 40% the fault of the radical leaders, who thought themselves strong enough to defy their national officers.

cluding street-car workers, teamsters, restaurant workers, and electricians and other building trades men.[1]

This general strike was a most remarkable phenomenon. Not only were the grievances of the metal workers, in calling the original strike, less acute than those of the workers in most other controversies during the war period, but in addition the strike was called against the decision of the S. L. A. B., a wage adjusting agency which contained in its membership a representative of the metal trades and which had earned a general reputation for fairness. It is true that the men in Seattle had never been satisfied with any of the awards of the board—unlike the workers in other sections of the country the men of the Pacific Coast shipyards had not profited by the awards of the S. L. A. B. because wage scales in the West had been higher than in other parts of the country. In the general wage leveling process that inevitably accompanied the war the tendency of the board toward standardization resulted in very much smaller wage increases in the West than in the East. Seattle, which had enjoyed a particularly high scale, was most adversely affected by this policy. The high level there was due partly to the degree of labor organization and partly to the action of some thoughtless and unscrupulous employers who offered rates far in excess of either the local rates or those set by the board.

From the standpoint of the Shipping Board and of the general public the men of the shipyards had been very liberally treated during the entire war period. The rates which they received were high, and when supplemented by overtime, resulted in very large earnings. But for the men of Seattle the rates were not high and the cutting off of overtime immediately upon the signing of the armistice accentuated their dissatisfaction with the awarded scale. It was therefore especially hard for them to realize that, for the general good, it was necessary to maintain standardized rates even if this worked to the disadvantage of a particular community.

On its side, the community felt, in the early months succeeding the signing of the armistice, that the cost of living was going to come down and that therefore wages ought not to be any

[1] An effort was also made to call a general strike at Tacoma at the same time as the strike at Seattle. This was not successful.

further increased. The business interests of the country were extremely positive on this point as were a substantial number of labor men and liberal thinkers.[1]

The insistence of the Seattle metal trades, therefore, upon their demand for an increase of wages to $1.00 an hour was frowned upon throughout the country, and when this demand was denied by the S. L. A. B., its decision met with popular approval. The strike appeared to involve both a violation of the agreement under which the S. L. A. B. was organized (although to be sure, the Seattle metal trades claimed that the agreement was a violation of the constitution of their international union and that they were, therefore, not bound by it), as well as an unreasonable demand for which no justification could be found in the equities of the situation.

In spite of all the weaknesses in the workers' position, and in spite of the fact that this was one of the least justified strikes of the war period—although, of course, a different psychology had followed the signing of the armistice—the remarkable thing was that a general sympathetic strike should have been called at all, and that it should have met with an almost unanimous response from the labor unions of Seattle.[2] As a demonstration of solidarity in the ranks of labor this showing was impressive.[3]

The effect of the strike[4] upon the residents of Seattle and

[1] This expectation, as succeeding events have shown, was too sanguine. Up to the summer of 1920 the cost of living continued to increase.

[2] In all cases except one the strike call received a majority vote; in most cases, however, a two-thirds or three-fourths vote was necessary, and in a few instances these large majorities were not polled.

[3] It is interesting to note that there has resulted a corresponding solidarity on the part of the employers who have since the general strike formed a powerful association of their own.

[4] The general strike lasted until February 11th, and was conducted with great ability and moderation; there seems to have been no violence, and the general strike committee, which was formed to take charge of the situation, not only organized a special labor guard composed of 300 ex-service men but by means of subcommittees arranged for the exemption from strike of certain necessary functions. Thus the electric light workers were allowed to maintain power for the city water supply, the teamsters were authorized to collect such garbage as was a menace to the health of the community, and other essential operations were permitted to go on undisturbed; otherwise, the life of the city came to a complete stop. Sixty thousand workers laid down their tools; trolley cars, taxicabs, and trucks were stopped for several

upon the country generally was electrical; a great many people seemed to feel that a general revolution was at hand. In Seattle there was a rush for firearms, coupled with a fear of violence and catastrophe out of all proportion to the events which called it forth.[1] To-day there is a great deal of difference of opinion as to the extent to which an industrial revolution was contemplated; there can be no doubt, however, that there were some of the workers who hoped that the upheavals of Europe would be duplicated in the United States and that the Seattle strike was only the beginning. As a matter of fact the strike committee did adopt as one of its maxims that of revolutionary socialism (from the old international manifesto)—"you have nothing to lose but your chains and the world to gain." Yet radical as many of the leaders of the strike undoubtedly were, it does not appear that revolutionary opinions and motives animated either their calling or their conduct of the strike. Certainly the actions of the strike committee were not those of a body of men who seriously contemplated revolution.

Tremendous pressure from the international officers of a number of important unions concerned in the strike resulted in an early return to work of the street-car men, teamsters, and others;[2] and on February 11th the general strike was declared off (although the strike in the shipyards continued). Its concrete result was practically nil; but its psychological effect was not confined to the city of Seattle but spread all over the country and was most unfortunate. It sharpened the antagonism of the employer toward, and increased his fear of the labor union, which antagonism, in turn, has served to increase the bitterness of the workers. Other general strikes had occurred during the war and

days, and almost all the industrial activities of the city were brought to a standstill. The strike committee organized restaurants at which as many as 30,000 meals a day were served; milk stations were opened for the supply of milk to babies, and coöperative enterprises of various kinds were started. No matter what we may think of the occasion for this particular strike, or of the legitimacy of ever calling a *general* strike, we cannot but admire the efficiency and organizing skill with which it was carried out.

[1] See The Seattle General Strike. Issued by the History Committee of the General Strike Committee, published by the Seattle Union Record.

[2] See The Seattle General Strike, p. 37.

indeed a general lockout,[1] yet these events aroused no particular excitement. The mere fact that the Seattle strike was larger would not of itself explain this difference; the temper of public opinion at the time the strike was called, as well as the sensational publicity which each side gave to the occurrences at Seattle, must be taken into account, if the focussing of public opinion upon this strike is to be understood and the intense intolerance it aroused explained.

[1] In September, 1917, a general strike occurred in Springfield, Ill. The street car workers were out and a parade had been organized as a demonstration in their favor. This parade was stopped by the police and as a protest a general strike of union workers of Springfield took place. The miners were particularly active and the A. F. of L. weekly newsletter for September 29, 1917, states that in all 10,000 workers joined the strike. Later the deputy sheriffs were dismissed and assurances given that the right of free assemblage would be maintained. . . . But the most important general strike which occurred during the war itself (the Seattle Strike took place after the armistice) was that of March, 1918, at Kansas City. Here also the strike was sympathetic; this time with the laundry workers and drivers who had sought recognition of their union (a demand not sanctioned by the Government's war labor policy). There seems to have been little disorder during the seven days that the strike lasted, until an attempt was made to run the street cars. Rioting then occurred and the National Guard had to be called in. The feelings stirred up by this general strike may have been in part responsible for the creation of the Kansas Industrial Court, which will be dealt with in subsequent chapters. . . . At about the same time a general strike occurred at Waco, Texas, which was likewise sympathetic but this time with street car men who had been locked out. . . . A general lockout occurred at Billings, Montana, in April, 1918. It seems that in the previous year all the workers under the jurisdiction of the Federated Labor Union had quit work in sympathy with mechanics in the building trades who had been locked out by the Billings Employers' Association. The men who struck included icemen, city employees, gasmen, creamery workers, truck drivers and others. The strike lasted two weeks and was finally settled by the men receiving an increase in wages and a return to their former positions. But when, in April, 1918, the laundry workers struck for a further increase, the members of the Billings branch of the Montana Employers' Association locked out all of the employees affiliated with the Building Trades Council "as well as the clerks, cooks and waiters, laundry workers, common laborers and teamsters in the jurisdiction of the Trades and Labor Assembly." The purpose of the lockout as stated in the Third Biennial Report of the Montana Department of Labor and Industry, page 39, seems to have been to force the acceptance of the open shop. The trouble spread to other trades and a number of the employers were declared unfair and, as such, boycotted by the workers. Although wages were increased when the men resumed work, the lockout seems, on the whole, to have been successful.

The difficulties of the Shipping Board were not confined to cases of actual or threatened stoppages of work; other troublesome issues arose which seriously threatened production.[1] Thus early in the war, as the number of wooden shipyards and their activity increased, the demand for caulkers rapidly outstripped the limited supply. To add to the difficulty, the caulkers themselves, for many months, refused to permit any increase in the percentage of apprentices. Indeed the situation became so acute that a number of otherwise finished ships could not be used because of a shortage of men to caulk them. Finally in December, 1917, Government pressure (and the acquiescence by the local representative of the board to a rate of $8.50 a day, which the shipyards had been paying caulkers in their efforts to get an adequate labor supply) induced them to meet the plans of the board for the training of new men, and the shortage was gradually relieved. Still another typical difficulty was the effort of the metal trades of the Pacific Coast to extend trade unionism and the closed shop, the men refusing to work on "unfair" material and to install boilers made in non-union plants. This issue, similar to the one which had led to the strike in the wooden shipwards (of September, 1917), was finally overcome by a waiver of the men's demands that only "union" materials be used.

INDUSTRIAL RELATIONS DIVISION EMERGENCY FLEET CORPORATION

In September, 1917, the Emergency Fleet Corporation of the Shipping Board established an Industrial Service Section, which at first was mainly concerned with the procurement and training of labor for the shipyards and with questions relating to draft exemption. To these functions others were gradually added and in May, 1918, in order to better organize the work, the Industrial Relations Division was created.[2] We are concerned, in this book,

[1] In order to prevent the shifting of men from one yard to another, decisions, which at first were for single yards, were made to cover larger and larger territory until in the last decisions of the board one award was made for the Pacific Coast and one for all other districts of the country. Uniform wage scales were established in both awards for the higher paid occupations.

[2] Second Annual Report, United States Shipping Board, p. 152.

with only one of the activities of the new Division, to wit, the Labor Section, charged with the settlement of labor controversies arising in plants having contracts for materials for ship construction. As we have seen in the first part of this chapter, the Shipbuilding Labor Adjustment Board had jurisdiction over all labor questions arising in the shipyards. In many cases, however, a shipbuilding company would sublet a contract for the manufacture of mechanical parts of the ship or for machinery needed in its construction. Labor disputes occurring in shops engaged on filling such orders were referred to the Labor Section.[1]

In order to insure the necessary harmony between the two boards, the director of the Industrial Relations Division was also a member of the Shipbuilding Labor Adjustment Board. The nature of the work of the Labor Section and its methods of procedure were similar to those of the Industrial Service Section of the Ordnance Department, which are set forth in some detail in a subsequent chapter and need not, therefore, be examined at this place.

[1] John J. Casey was in charge.

CHAPTER IV

Shipping

MARINE AND DOCK INDUSTRIAL RELATIONS DIVISION

THE adjustment of wages and working conditions of men operating coastwise and deep sea vessels was undertaken by the Shipping Board itself. In the organization of its own work the Board had delegated to Vice-Chairman Stevens supervision of all labor matters directly affecting it. When Mr. Stevens went to Europe in December, 1917, the supervision of labor matters was placed in the hands of Robert P. Bass. Finally, a few months before the armistice, the Shipping Board decided to create the Marine and Dock Industrial Relations Division in order to give more definite structure and standing to the work which hitherto had been accomplished in a less formal way, and Mr. Bass became Director of this new division.[1]

The jurisdiction of this division covered generally three different groups of workers—the dock workers, that is to say, the longshoreman, the harbor men, who operate tugs, barges, lighters, and other harbor craft, and the licensed officers and crews of coastwise and deep sea vessels. As we will see in the next section the Shipping Board coöperated with other Government agencies in establishing the National Adjustment Commission charged with the duty of fixing wages and general labor condition for the dock workers. In theory the Shipping Board—and later its Marine and Dock Industrial Relations Division—was

---

[1] The purposes of the division are stated as follows, in the Second Annual Report of the United States Shipping Board, page 84: "It is the duty of the new division to act as a coördinating agency in all labor matters affecting the Board; to supervise labor questions which pertain to the operation of vessels and marine equipment including the work of loading and unloading; to secure peaceful adjustment of disputes," etc. John G. Palfrey was Assistant Director. On January 1, 1919, Herbert B. Ehrman became Director.

supposed to exercise general supervision over these activities, so far as they concerned the Shipping Board itself. As a matter of fact this supervision was exercised through the election of the Shipping Board's representative as Chairman of the National Adjustment Commission. The Marine and Dock Industrial Relations Division dealt primarily with the officers and crews of ocean-going vessels, leaving to the local commissions which were affiliated with the National Adjustment Commission (except in the Port of New York, where a special commission was created) [1] the framing of wages for harbor craft.

In considering the labor problems of the workers on ocean-going and coastwise vessels, a further division will be found convenient, and in this case again the division will fall naturally into three sections. Each section will represent roughly one of the three geographical divisions into which the marine shipping industry of the country is naturally divided—the Atlantic and Gulf Ports, the Great Lakes, and the Pacific Coast. The conditions of the industry and the methods of handling labor differed vitally in all three localities. These differences, as far as they concerned the workers, arose chiefly from questions relating to the unions. And as was so often the case during the war the attitude of the employers toward unions largely determined the degree of industrial peace which was maintained in any port, that of the employers on the Atlantic and Pacific Ports presenting a sharp contrast to that of the employers on the Great Lakes.

In the Atlantic and Gulf Ports, where a majority of the men (65%) were members of the International Seamen's Union and where the employers were willing to coöperate with the Government by dealing with these organizations, little trouble was experienced during the period of active hostilities (in fact none until 1919). In May, 1917, a conference was held between the Shipping Board, the Shipping Committee of the Council of National Defense (of which shipowners were members), and the International Seamen's Union, at which what became known as the "Atlantic Agreement" was worked out. This agreement fixed wages and bonuses, provided for the training of apprentices, the dilution of the trade, and for the recruiting of men by a joint appeal of representatives, of owners and workers, known as the "Call

[1] *I. e.*, the New York Harbor Wage Adjustment Commission, discussed in the concluding section of this chapter.

to the Sea," the object of which was to induce men who had been seamen to return to their former occupation.[1] Later ratified by the employers and the union, this constituted the first written agreement ever made between American shipowners and the Seamen's Union.

A second conference was held a year later, when the Atlantic seamen agreed to leave the adjustment of wages to the Shipping Board, and the owners agreed to accept such adjustments for privately owned vessels. Shortly thereafter the board issued new wage scales awarding the men substantial increases.[2]

After the armistice, demands of the men for wage increases, for shorter hours, and for changes in union status threatened a stoppage of shipping. To prevent a strike, and if possible to provide permanent machinery for the adjustment of future disputes, the Shipping Board in June, 1919, once more called the parties in interest to an industrial conference in Washington. The marine section of this conference[3] was unable to come to any agreement, having been deadlocked on the question of preferential treatment of union men.[4]

Conferences continued but the men were unwilling to accept the wage increases which the Shipping Board offered, and the attitude of the private owners on the question of preferential treatment for union men was one of unalterable opposition. A strike ensued and for more than two weeks the entire ocean-going and coastwise shipping at Atlantic and Gulf ports was completely tied up. The settlement was a compromise, giving the men substantially the wages they had demanded, but not the preferential union treatment.[5] The eight-hour day was allowed while vessels

[1] See Report of Director of Marine and Dock Industrial Relations Division, submitted as of December 31, 1918.
[2] A standing committee of five was arranged for, charged with the improvement of sanitary conditions and other employment problems.
[3] There were also two other sections—a Dock Section and a Harbor Section. See B. M. Squires in *Monthly Labor Review,* U. S. Bureau of Labor Statistics, July, 1919, page 14.
[4] It is interesting to note that here again is an illustration of the difficulty which, after the armistice, employer and employee found in coming together, who, during the war, had been able to adjust their differences without serious trouble.
[5] The steamship companies did not expressly agree to give preferential treatment to union men but there seems to have been a tacit understanding that such preference would in practice be given.

were in port, but the three watches which the men had demanded at sea were refused.

On the Pacific Coast, where before the war 95% of the seamen had been organized, wages were fixed by joint agreement between the private owners and the men, and the Shipping Board agreed to accept, for the vessels under its control, the wage scales thus reached. Arrangements for recruiting former seamen and for the dilution of the trade, similar to those on the Atlantic Coast, were made. On both coasts the war record was excellent. The Shipping Board succeeded in keeping the rapidly increasing merchant marine fully manned.

In contrast to the record of both Atlantic and Pacific Coasts is the record of the Great Lakes. Here the opposition of the employers to the union—strengthened as the union was by the national crisis—produced a situation in which disastrous strikes were on two occasions averted by only the narrowest margin. On the Great Lakes 80% of the tonnage was handled by the Lake Carriers' Association, alleged to have been controlled by the United States Steel Corporation. Whether this claim was true or not, its labor policies were extremely hostile to the Seamen's Union.

It had been the practice of the Association to recruit its men from the assembly halls of its so-called Welfare Association, and to require them to carry "Continuous Discharge Books," in which officers of the vessels made reports on the men leaving their employ. The men claimed that these discharge books, which had to be deposited with the ship operator on entering the employment and without which no new job could be obtained, were used to discriminate against the union. The great resentment which this aroused resulted—as in many other places during the war—in demands that the cards and the assembly halls be abolished. The Lake Carriers' Association being unwilling to recede from its position, a strike for this and other grievances was ordered to commence October 1, 1917.

Through the intervention of Mr. Stevens of the Shipping Board the wage differences—one of the matters in controversy—were adjusted. The Board also promised to investigate "the discharge books," and thereupon the strike was indefinitely postponed. After an examination of the facts, the Shipping Board directed the Lake Carriers' Association to discontinue the use of these books, allowing them to substitute certificates of discharge, from which, however, certain objectionable features, such as the personal opinion of the discharging officer and notations that might indicate union activity, were eliminated.

Nevertheless the Lake Carriers' Association devised a method of making use of these discharge certificates which was as objectionable to the men as the old discharge books had been. The association "substituted for the discharge book a 'certificate of membership,' with a pocket in it, as a container for the individual discharge certificates, and that all the papers had as before to be produced and deposited at the time of employment."[1] The men claimed that this would also be used for discriminatory purposes and demanded its abolition, as well as the practice of hiring men at the assembly halls, which the association had maintained.

Another source of irritation was the attitude persistently taken by the association toward the union. Its representatives had refused to attend the Marine Conference because of the presence of representatives of the Union. Furthermore, when a Government Committee on recruiting had unanimously recommended that the coöperative arrangement, contained in the "Atlantic Agreement," be extended to the Great Lakes and the Pacific Coast, the association refused to do so. It also refused to sign the "Call to the Sea," which had been signed by Atlantic and Pacific shipowners. Nor would it adopt the method of training provided for in the "Atlantic Agreement." The reason given by the Lake Carriers for these refusals was that to accede to any of these requests would have been equivalent to recognizing the union. Irritated by these extreme manifestations of hostility, the men now insisted not only on the elimination of the discharge certificates, and the hiring of men at the assembly halls, but that the owners sign the "Call to the Sea," and that they adopt a training plan similar to that contained in the "Atlantic Agreement" for recruiting men to the service.

Wage demands could easily have been adjusted, but the association held out firmly on the other matters, and a strike was declared for July 28. A week or two before the date set, the Shipping Board ordered a change in the discharge certificate, eliminating its objectionable features and directing that it should

[1] Report of the Director, Marine and Dock Industrial Relations Division, p. 24.

state on its face that it was the property of the man, and that it need not be produced or deposited at the time of hiring. The Shipping Board also decided questions of overtime, and announced that it would immediately adjust wages. The men, however, persisted in their full demands. The situation became tense, and feeling ran very high indeed. To have tied up shipping on the Great Lakes in July, 1918, would have meant irreparable damage to the nation's fighting ability, as these vessels transported grain for the Allies' Armies and iron ore for the principal steel mills of the country.

Four days before the date set for the strike, Chairman Hurley, of the Shipping Board, issued a statement in which he reviewed the circumstances and the men's demands, and he concluded that "The Shipping Board does not feel that there are any grievances of such a nature as to justify a strike at this time." The statement was published in large advertisements by the association and was bitterly resented by the union, which objected not only to the conclusion, but also to a portion of the statement in which it said that, "The Board has not decided to use the Great Lakes for training and recruiting marines." The men felt that this was either a misstatement or that the Shipping Board had "suddenly decided to change its policy . . . to recall the letters sent to the unions and the shipowners last month, and to lay aside its program with reference to the national use to be made of the Great Lakes, because the Lake Carriers' Association has refused coöperation."[1] The men held their grounds, and it looked as if the strike could not be averted. As a result, however, of last minute conferences with each side the Shipping Board issued orders compelling substantial compliance with the union's demands, and the strike was called off.

The action of the Lake Carriers' Association furnishes the only example that has come to the writer's attention in which an employer refused to attend a national conference called by the Government, because of the presence of the members of a union. Most of the associations composing the Industrial Conference Board cannot be accused of fondness for unions, and probably a large majority of the firms comprising the membership of these associations are just as unwilling to "recognize" unions as was

[1] Letter from Victor Olander, Secretary International Seamen's Union to H. B. Ehrman of the Shipping Board.

the Lake Carriers' Association. Yet to meet the national emergency five representatives of the Industrial Conference Board joined with five representatives of unions in the organization of the National War Labor Board. In the shipbuilding industry, every shipbuilder submitted to labor adjustments by a board of which a representative of organized labor was a member. This did not constitute recognition of the union, nor did the actions which the Lake Carriers' Association refused to take. And yet if a strike had occurred, the public would doubtless have blamed the union whose affirmative action would have actually brought it on. But would not the strike, as a matter of fact, have been to a much greater degree the result of the association's stubbornness and lack of coöperation?

NATIONAL ADJUSTMENT COMMISSION

To adjust disputes between longshoremen and their employers, strikes having already occurred in several ports, the Shipping Board and the War and Labor Departments coöperated in August, 1917, in the organization of the National Adjustment Commission, by agreement with shipping operators, the American Federation of Labor, and the International Longshoremen's Association.[1] It was also provided that local Commissions be appointed in important ports with memberships of three—one to represent the Shipping Board and War Department jointly, one, the Longshoremen's Union, and one, the employers.[2]

The jurisdiction of the board extended over the entire Atlantic Coast and the Gulf of Mexico. But because of the opposition of the employers of the Great Lakes[3] and the Pacific Coast[4] to the presence of union representatives on both the board

[1] The Board was to consist of one member nominated by the Shipping Board, one by the War Department, one by the Longshoremen's Association, and two representatives of the shipping interests, one of whom was to act in cases involving deep sea and the other coastwise shipping. See Chairman's Report National Adjustment Commission.

[2] Local Commissions were established at 26 ports.

[3] One group of employers, the Lumber Carriers' Association of the Great Lakes, adopted the agreement of the National Adjustment Commission on August 22, 1918, and a local Commission was established at Chicago for the lumber industry. Local commissions were also established at ports on the Great Lakes to adjust disputes in the coal-handling industry.

[4] In Seattle and Tacoma, Washington, the principal shipping companies adopted the agreement with the proviso that any disputes not

and the local commissions, the authority of the National Adjustment Commission in these localities was confined to special cases.

In the original agreement by which the Commission was created, its jurisdiction was limited to longshoremen's work. This was, however, extended by special agreements of the parties in interest, including the Shipping Board, to the adjustment of wages and working conditions on harbor craft, and many of the local commissions organized by the Natioaal Adjustment Commission exercised a likewise broadened jurisdiction.

In the fixing of wages it was found that the employees, while striving to establish uniform scales for the same kind of work at different ports, felt that differences in compensation should be made for handling different cargoes in cases where a special hazard to life or health was involved. Thus the men desired uniform scales of wages set for all Atlantic and Gulf ports, but they asked for double wages when handling wheat in the bottom cf the hold, or uncrated barbed wire, or when loading explosives "down stream." The employers, on the other hand, took exactly the opposite view on both questions. They insisted that differences in compensation which had for a long time existed in the different Atlantic ports were founded on differences in the cost of living and should be maintained. And they claimed that little if any differential should be established for handling different kinds of merchandise.[1]

In its earlier decisions the commission set different scales for the different Atlantic ports and for deep sea in contrast to coastwise longshore work. As the war continued, however, it became increasingly necessary to be able to shift men from one point to another and from one kind of work to another as the emergencies demanded, and this made a uniform scale imperative. A second reason for a uniform scale was that it was a method for obtaining higher wage levels which were especially needed in those ports where the wages were lowest. The tendency had been for skilled

settled locally should be referred to the Commission. A local commission was established in Portland, Oregon, with representatives in its membership of the Longshoremen's Union; but this was the only Pacific port at which such a local commission was created. For the Puget Sound District a special local commission was organized, consisting of only one member—a local agent of the National Adjustment Commission.

[1] For a discussion of standardization of wages during the war see Chapter XV.

longshoremen to drift into better paid occupations, particularly the shipyards. Inasmuch as shipyard wages were being standardized on the entire coast—that is to say, inasmuch as all of the shipyard workers were receiving the rates of the highest paid yards—the competition of the shipyards in places where longshore wages were low was particularly severe. For this reason uniformity, meaning as it did the adoption of the highest scales, would better enable all ports to keep their longshoremen in spite of competition of other occupations.

For these reasons the awards of the Commission, of October and November, 1918, established uniform rates for deep sea and coastwise longshore work for all the ports included within the North Atlantic Division (New York, Baltimore, Boston, and Hampton Roads District); and in November, 1918, a similar award was made for deep sea work for the Gulf ports. The policy of standardization was also applied in the deep sea award of December, 1918, fixing rates for the South Atlantic ports, lower than those established for the North Atlantic and Gulf ports but uniform within the South Atlantic District.

The Commission was able to prevent the occurrence of any serious strike during the active war period, although many controversies arose in which peace was maintained with a great deal of difficulty. Thus on the Pacific, where the employers' opposition to the unions prevented the creation of local commissions, disputes occurred in the Puget Sound district very similar to those which, as we have seen in the previous section of this chapter, took place on the Great Lakes. Here, as there, the men demanded the abolition by the use of employers of "rustling cards" (identical in principle with the "discharge certificates") and of "hiring halls." In an effort to avoid a strike the board summoned respresentatives of both sides to Washington. The greatest difficulty was experienced in reaching an award which would be accepted by both sides; the decision as finally. announced abolished rustling cards—which the board's representatives for the Puget Sound District, Professor Carleton Parker, had found to have been used for discriminatory purposes. The award permitted the continued use of the hiring halls but only under the supervision of an appointee of the Shipping Board and provided that in any event the use of the halls be discontinued by July 1, 1918. The board's decision, especially this last part of it, was virtually forced by the men; it aroused bitter resentment on the part of the employers, who felt—with some degree of justice—that on this point they had not been given an opportunity to be heard. Feeling ran high and it was only by the exertion of severe pressure on both sides by the Government that peace was maintained. A rehearing was held on June 25, 1918, which the employers failed to attend. By this time, however, the extension of the work of the U. S. Employment Service, sanctioned by Presidential order, opened the way for an easy solution of this troublesome point. The employers were directed either to close the halls or to put them under the supervision of the U. S. Employment Services (of which the President of the Longshoremen's Association was Director of dock labor).

Another case, which has a certain human interest, developed out of the men's demand in New York that a foreman by the name of Frank Laguiro be discharged. Over an issue apparently so insignificant, the entire shipping of the Port of New York was almost tied up at a critical period during the war. The commission found that the evidence did not warrant ordering his discharge, but that, in view of the fact the men at his pier were so hostile to him, it recommended that he be transferred to another pier.

The longshore industry at the Port of New York is another of the many industries in which, although no serious strike occurred during the war, the difficulty of preserving industrial peace in the period immediately following is clearly exemplified, and this in spite of the fact that longshore work was one of the few industries in which an attempt was made to continue as a piece-time agency, war machinery for the adjustment of disputes.[1]

In June, 1919, the dock section of a conference called by the

---

[1] The creation of permanent arbitral machinery is all the more noteworthy in view of the fact that strong union organization in the longshore industry was a matter of very recent growth. B. M. Squire, in the *Monthly Labor Review*, U. S. Bureau of Labor Statistics, December, 1919, points out the casual nature of longshore work and the checkered history of longshoremen's unions. He states that in 1911 the International Longshoremen's Union had a membership in the port of New York of 3,200. In 1914, after consolidating with a rival union, its members were over 6,000. In 1918 the membership included practically every member of the trade, variously estimated at from 40,000 to 60,000.

Shipping Board (referred to in the second part of this chapter) reached an agreement for the continuance during peace times of the National Adjustment Commission, with certain changes in its structure and personnel. These changes recognized the desire which many of the employers had expressed during the war for the maintenance—especially after the war was over—of separate wage scales at the different ports and the country was divided into nine districts with separate commissions for each, but with one chairman (named by the Shipping Board to represent the public) serving on all the commissions. The agreement which constituted the National Adjustment Commission provided that pending its awards there should be no strikes, and that its awards be accepted by both sides. A convention of the Longshoremen's Union unanimously authorized a committee to enter into an agreement embodying these general terms, and later both the executive council of the union and the employers' association ratified the agreement, with some few changes.[1]

At the Port of New York demands had been made of wage increases for longshore work to $1.00 an hour for straight time and $2.00 an hour for overtime, and late in September, 1919, the reconstituted commission for the North Atlantic deep sea district commenced its hearings. Upon its announcement on October 6, 1919, of an award of 70 cents for straight time and $1.10 for overtime (increases of 5 and 10 cents respectively), the men refused to accept it and quit work. The President of the Longshoremen's Association had been a member of the Commission and he, together with the other representative of the men, had voted against the award. He did all in his power, however, to induce the men to accept it and remain at work. The strike was led by men who had quarreled with officials of the International Longshoremen's Union. It lasted about four weeks, paralyzed the shipping of New York during that time, and through its interference with the export of food and other vitally needed materials intensified, in other parts of the world, the suffering which the war had already caused. All branches of the Government were firm in their insistence that the award of the National Adjustment

[1] In August, 1920, the Shipping Board announced its unwillingness to continue its membership in the reconstituted Commission. On October 1st, the Commission formally dissolved and there was thus abolished the only one of the war adjustment agencies which had survived as a permanent peace-time organization.

Commission be respected. The Secretary of Labor, however, after appealing to the strikers to return to work, made the tactical blunder of appointing a conciliation committee, including in its membership F. P. A. Vacerelli, the insurgent leader of the strikers. Mayor Hylan and one of the Labor Department's conciliators were the other members. The appointment of this committee led to the prolongation of the strike, inasmuch as it revived the hopes of the men that they would receive further concessions. But the employers, as well as the officers of the International Longshoremen's Association, insisted upon the validity of the award of the National Adjustment Commission. Gradually the men returned to work, yet not, unfortunately, until after the efforts of the strikers to prevent members of the International Longshoremen's Union from going back had resulted in a number of riots, in one of which two fatalities occurred.

The award of the commission had provided that if the Government's efforts to reduce the cost of living should prove unsuccessful the case would be reopened on December 1 (or if it appeared at that time that there had been an improvement in the efficiency of the workers—the award calling attention to the lack of efficiency then prevailing). The cost of living did not decline and late in November the commission reopened its hearings and awarded the men a further increase of 10 cents an hour. In the meantime the commission had heard the Gulf case and announced an increase coincident in time and practically identical in provision with the revised New York award.

But the wages of coastwise longshoremen had all this time remained unchanged at 65 cents an hour, in spite of the increase granted to deep sea men of 15 cents an hour.[1] The coastwise shipping industry had become unprofitable. The Government guarantee of income, which, together with the railroads, these shipping interests had received upon the Government's assumption of war-time control, had not been continued under the Act of Congress under which the railroads and the coastwise shipping lines were restored to their private owners. It therefore seemed impossible to increase wages until higher railroad and shipping

[1] There had, before the war, been a differential between the two of about 5 cents which was justified by the fact that there was somewhat steadier work for the coastwise longshoremen, but during the war, as we have seen, this differential had been abolished.

rates could be established.   The coastwise longshoremen, resenting the continuance of the 15 cent differential between the deep
sea men and themselves, went on a strike, which continued for
many months and brought about innumerable complications.

THE NEW YORK HARBOR WAGE ADJUSTMENT BOARD

In the fall of 1917 a strike was threatened at the Port of New
York by the men on all the harbor craft.   Such a strike—in the
midst of the war—would have been a calamity.   Not only would
it have tied up all the ferries connecting Manhattan Island with
New Jersey, Brooklyn, and Staten Island, and the lighters upon
which New York City is absolutely dependent for food and fuel
and for the movement of much of the freight in and out of the
city needed in war manufacture, but it would also have brought
all ocean shipping to a standstill.   And inasmuch as more than
half of our shipments to the Allies were sent through the Port of
New York, the seriousness of the situation will readily be understood.

Among the unions whose members were employed in harbor
work a movement had begun in 1913 for closer association.   This
movement culminated in 1917 when practically all of the unions
became united in the Marine Workers' Affiliation of the Port of
New York.   The opposition of the employers to this organization
and their unwillingness to deal with some of the unions which
composed it, had led in the spring of the year to the breaking
off of negotiations for the settlement of demands of some of the
harbor crafts.   Persistent efforts to adjust the difficulties, participated in by Federal and State mediators, had failed, and a
strike seemed imminent.

The situation was so threatening that in October, 1917, Mr.
Stevens, Vice-Chairman of the Shipping Board, came to New
York and in separate conference with both sides endeavored to
get them to agree to the organization of a local board of adjustment, of the type provided for in the agreement creating the
National Adjustment Commission—that is to say, consisting of
one representative of the public, one of the employers, and one
of the employees.   The men were willing to accept a board of
this kind, but the employers claimed that the Marine Workers'
Affiliation did not represent their employees, as to whom they

made the statement, so often made under these circumstances, that "a majority of their employees are satisfied and loyal . . . and have no knowledge of any threatened strike." [1]

They refused to meet representatives of the Affiliation, and "challenged the patriotism of any set of men who when their country is at war will attempt to form a union in this great Port of New York where unionism was never before known for the purpose of taking advantage of the times and compelling towboat interests to join with them in the extortion of unheard of and exorbitant prices at the expense of the commerce of the port." [2]

As a compromise, an agreement was reached on October 20, 1917, whereby a board was created known as the Board of Arbitration, New York Harbor Wage Adjustment, of which all three members were to be Government representatives—one from the Shipping Board, one from the Department of Commerce, and one from the Department of Labor. It was also provided that the board was to have no authority over the question of the open and closed shop, but on the other hand the employers agreed not to discriminate against the men for union membership. Its first award, on November 16, fixed a new scale of wages; and the succeeding months were taken up by efforts of the union to have the scale put into effect by all the employers, many of whom denied the jurisdiction of the board and were unwilling to comply with its award. The situation was further complicated by the fact that boats were owned not only by private companies but also by the railroads—soon to be taken over by the Federal Government—and by the City and the State of New York, as well as by different departments of the Federal Government. In December, 1917, one hundred employers—including marine departments of the railways and City and State agencies—were complained against for not putting the award into effect. By the end of January 200 complaints had been received. Many private employers openly defied the authority of the board and as the unrest

[1] Statement of the New York Towboat Exchange, quoted by B. M. Squires in *Monthly Labor Review* for September, 1918. The reader is referred to this and other articles by Mr. Squires in other issues of the *Monthly Labor Review*, and also in the *Journal of Political Economy*, Volume XXVII, Number 10, December, 1919, for an excellent account of labor adjustments and industrial conditions in the port of New York.

[2] Statement of employers to Shipping Board.

among the workers increased new demands by the union were made and a strike once more threatened. As a result of a conference called in March, 1918, by the Shipping Board a committee of the employers was formed to enforce compliance. Many employers claimed to be paying the wages fixed in the award but an inspection of the payrolls of 80 of them showed that 60 were not doing so. Thereupon those who still refused to comply were summoned before the Shipping Board, and in some cases it was necessary to threaten to commandeer their boats before they could be induced to fall in line.

During all this time the membership of the union was growing by leaps and bounds. The extent of this growth was largely attributable to the non-compliance of the boat owners with the award. If his employer was unwilling to grant an increase in wages, the individual, unorganized worker did not know how to secure it. Nor was the union organizer slow to take advantage of the opportunity which the employer thus created, since in practice, by reason of his knowledge, experience, and spare time the union representative was best fitted to bring the complaints of the men to the attention of the board and thus secure, for any group of workers, the benefits of the award. A great deal of time was thus necessarily consumed before the new wage scale was adopted by all of the boat owners, and in the meantime the unrest caused by their resistance was intensified by the conflicts of jurisdiction between the Harbor Board, the Railroad Administration, and the Municipal and State authorities.[1]

Even before the general acceptance of the award new demands were accumulating, and when on March 20, 1918, the board refused to consider these new demands until September 30, the men became indignant and appealed to the newly organized National War Labor Board. Without attempting at that time to decide the controversies, the War Labor Board, by means of conferences with all of the parties in interest, brought about a

[1] It should be noted that the adjustment of wages for State and Municipal employees was complicated by legal difficulties—wages in some cases being prescribed by law. The Railroad Administration, faced the obstacle of having to fix wages for the entire country. It was, therefore, difficult for it to make an exception in the case of employees at the Port of New York. Yet granting this, there can be little doubt that the Railroad Administration failed to give to the other departments of the Government that degree of coöperation which the emergency demanded.

modification of the arbitral agreement so as to enlarge the membership of the Harbor Board by including a representative of employers and employees. The board as thus constituted held hearings and granted a new wage scale; before this became effective, however, the first general award of the Railroad Administration was announced, which gave the railroad harbor employees a higher rate of wages than had been granted to them by the Harbor Board. The Railroad Administration was induced to hold its award in abeyance so far as it affected New York harbor men, and in an effort to overcome the difficulties resulting from this conflict of jurisdictions the agreement was again amended so as to add to the Harbor Board a representative of the Railroad Administration and a second representative of the employees, thus bring the membership of the new board up to seven. A rehearing was now held before this new board and another award promulgated, to be effective until May 31, 1919, "unless in the judgment of the board conditions warranted a change prior to the date thus fixed for expiration."

Even now the troubles of the harbor were not at an end. It was the employers' turn to be dissatisfied, partly with the award itself and partly with the indefiniteness of its duration, and they appealed to the National War Labor Board for a hearing.[1] In the meantime, because of protests of the railroad men, the Railroad Administration had put General Order Number 27 into effect wherever the wages under the order were greater than those fixed by the Harbor Board. General Order Number 27 had also the effect of disturbing the processes of standardization in the rates of men employed by different railroads at New York harbor, and lead to demands from the railroad men for uniform rates—that is to say, for a standardization upward. This resulted in a new and more vigorous protest from the owners.[2]

The next few months witnessed a struggle by the railroad employees to receive the maximum benefits accruing to them under General Order Number 27, including the basic eight-hour day, which was referred to although not expressly granted in this order, but which, as a matter of fact, the Railroad Administration

[1] No action was taken on this appeal.
[2] The situation was further complicated by the reluctance of the City, State and Federal authorities to put the award into effect, which very much increased unrest, and came very near resulting in strikes.

had been extending in other branches of the service.[1] It is unnecessary to go into all the difficulties that arose as a consequence
of these conflicts of jurisdiction except to say that they were extremely irritating, needlessly adding to the complications of a
situation which for months had been almost at the breaking point.[2]

The demand of the railroad men for the eight-hour day finally
led to the adoption of this demand by the entire Marine Workers' Affiliation. So serious became the danger of a strike that
shortly after the armistice, the Harbor Board (which had a
few weeks before recommended its own dissolution on account of
the conflicts of jurisdiction, but which had, in spite of this, remained in existence) called a hearing for December 6, 1918. The
employers now refused to submit to the board's jurisdiction on
the ground that the termination of the war (by the armistice)
had ended the authority of the board. A new board was proposed which the employees were willing to accept, but the employers, although willing to submit to a new board the question
of wages, were unwilling to arbitrate the question of the eight-
hour day, and the employer member resigned from the Harbor
Board.

Efforts to induce the National War Labor Board to assume
jurisdiction failed on the ground that the Harbor Board was still
in existence, and that it should immediately hear the controversy.[3]
But because both the Railroad Administration and the private

[1] See Chapter VIII for a more detailed discussion of railroad adjustments and of the effect of General Order Number 27.

[2] Robert P. Bass, in the Report of the Director of the Marine and
Dock Industrial Relations Division, U. S. Shipping Board, says at
p. 29: "The New York harbor situation stands out as a striking
example of the futility of agreements to arbitrate, which include only
a portion of the employers and employees in a given locality and
industry. Because of the lack of a complete or unified system of
arbitration, and because of the attempt to enforce conflicting standards of wages and working hours in a single labor market, the
situation at New York was always precarious, and throughout the
latter part of 1917 and all of 1918 steadily drifted toward open
rupture."

[3] While the dispute was at its height, the Shipping Board issued the
following statement: "There are still in the American armies in
Europe over a million and a half men, and it is inconceivable that
the American people or its Government would permit of any action
which would imperil the movement of food and supplies to these
Americans, now that their actual task of fighting is over. In addition
to the maintaining of our own armies, there is the obligation to feed
and clothe the peoples of our allies in Europe in a large measure

boat owners refused to agree to accept the decision of the board, its remaining members declined to act and recommended that the case be again presented to the National War Labor Board.

Once more the War Labor Board held a hearing and once more the Railroad Administration and the private boat owners refused to accept its jurisdiction. Proposals by the employers for a new board, coupled with a thirty-day investigation of conditions, were rejected by the men, and the War Labor Board felt unable to act.[1]

A few days later the boat owners issued advertisements in the press setting forth their side of the controversy. In these statements the employers, as was so often the case (see Chapter XVI), attempted to exploit the patriotic motive by capitalizing the fact that any action taken by the men to enforce their demands would result in suffering to the boys "over there," forgetting their own share of the responsibility for such an outcome. On the other hand, they pointed out—with some degree of justice —the peculiar conditions of their industry, which differentiated it,

impoverished and destitute because of their long resistance to the German power . . . There is also the nation's obligation to its citizens to bring back to America as rapidly as circumstances will allow hundreds of thousands of American troops awaiting transportation on the other side. In the performance of all of these tasks the Government will find itself seriously crippled by reason of any stoppage of work on the part of the harbor craft operators and employees of New York Harbor." (New York *Times,* December 17, 1918.)

[1] The Board issued the following statement:

"The National War Labor Board finds itself unable to secure a settlement of the controversy with reference to the New York Harbor situation for the following reasons:

1. The private boat owners and the Railroad Administration failed to comply with the order of the board of December 21, 1918, to fill the vacancies existing on the New York Harbor Wage Adjustment Commission.

2. The private boat owners and the Railroad Administration refused to submit the case to the National War Labor Board and to agree to abide by its decision.

Under the principles and policies of the National War Labor Board we cannot proceed further and give assurance of rendering a definite and binding decision, except in case of joint submission.

3. The private boat owners refused to submit the question of an eight-hour day to any other proposed form of arbitration except after an investigation for a period of not less than thirty days by a specially created conference committee, supplementary to the Arbitration Board."

as far as the eight-hour day was concerned, from normal factory work.

A strike which lasted three days immediately followed, and completely tied up every activity in the harbor. Appeals to the President for relief resulted in his cabling from Paris an urgent request to both sides to submit to the War Labor Board. In this emergency all of the Government bodies, including the troublesome Railroad Administration, signified their willingness to accept the finding of the War Labor Board. The employers, however, remained obdurate, except that one of them submitted to the jurisdiction of the Board, thus giving their counsel a standing in the subsequent hearings.

The strike ended upon the assumption of jurisdiction by the War Labor Board. Extended hearings were held which were marked by the most intense bitterness on both sides. The War Labor Board was deadlocked in regard to the issues in controversy, and the case was referred to an umpire, Mr. V. Everett Macy (Chairman of the Shipbuilding Labor Adjustment Board).

His decision came as a great disappointment to the men. At this particular time (March, 1919) the labor market was oversupplied with workers, due to the returning soldiers, the shutting down of war production and the fact that peace production had not yet been resumed. It was thought that commodity prices were going to be substantially reduced and wage increases were deprecated because they interfered with the hoped-for reductions in the cost of living. The umpire concluded that no case had been made out for an increase of wages over the Harbor Board's decision of July, 1918. The eight-hour day was awarded for a few of the harbor occuptions but denied to the most important ones. The Marine Workers' Affiliation considered the award absolutely unsatisfactory and refused to accept it. On March 4th, they declared another strike which was directed not alone against the private owners (only one of whom had joined in the submission to the War Labor Board) but also against the Railroad Administration which had been a party to it, and a great deal of indignation was caused by the failure of the workers to abide by the decision of the umpire.

The Railroad Administration, after insisting for a time that the men abide by the decision, finally granted the strikers the eight-hour day and wage increases, which were also conceded by other Government agencies. The strike continued, however, for many weeks against the private owners until settled by the acceptance by the workers of a ten-hour day with an agreement by both sides to arbitrate the question of wages.[1]

[1] The anomalous condition was thus produced of an eight-hour day for harbor men working for the railroads and a ten-hour day for those employed on privately owned boats. This resulted in another strike, caused by the transfer to a private company of a number of the boats owned by one of the railroads. The men claimed that the transfer was not bona fide but was merely part of a plot on the part of the railroads to get rid of the eight-hour day.

CHAPTER V

The President's Mediation Commission

In order to understand the circumstances surrounding the creation of the President's Mediation Commission we must go back to the early months of the war. At that time very little war mediating machinery had yet been provided—none whose jurisdiction extended beyond a particular industry. And yet, the necessity for adequate methods for adjusting labor disputes, which were occurring in almost every trade, was then every day becoming apparent.

Production of spruce lumber in the Pacific Northwest (vitally needed for aeroplanes and shipbuilding) was practically at a standstill because of the bitter antagonisms between the lumber jacks and their employers. Copper mining in the most important producing areas had almost entirely ceased; industrial warfare, resulting in most serious stoppages of public service operations and war industries, was threatening from the Atlantic to the Pacific.

Long-standing grievances of the workers, employers' opposition to collective bargaining, the use to which an unlimited supply of immigrant labor had been put to keep wages of the unskilled at an abnormally low level, the belief that the rise in the cost of living was largely due to profiteering—all of these factors were contributing to stoppages of work which seriously threatened the Government's war program. These labor disturbances, especially in the Far West, were met by ruthless and illegal reprisals on the part of both employers and Government officials. These reprisals were ostensibly directed against the I. W. W., but in fact were indiscriminate and branches of the A. F. of L. as well as more radical organizations suffered from them. The national leaders of the A. F. of L. were consequently driven to appeal to the President, in an effort to protect their members, and to aid in restoring production.

General conditions, brought to a focus by these protests, resulted in September, 1917, in the appointment of a Mediation Commission, the purpose of which was to bring about the adjustment of disputes which at that time were of paramount importance, and to investigate the general causes of industrial unrest and recommend methods for abating it.

This body, like the National War Labor Board, which was created seven months later, was quite different from all of the other war Labor Adjustment Boards. It was the product of Presidential proclamation—not of agreement with labor unions— and its jurisdiction was not limited to one place or one trade but extended over the entire country. The Secrétary of Labor was Chairman of the Commission, the other members of which were representatives of labor and capital.[1] Felix Frankfurter, afterwards to become the Chairman of the National War Labor Policies Board, was secretary.

The industrial troubles of the packing plants in Chicago, of the mines and lumber fields of the West, of street railways, of telephone operators and oil workers of California were investigated and the Commission secured the return of the strikers in all but one of these industries. It was one of the first Government agencies to establish collective bargaining by the appointment of shop committees and to insist that they be dealt with by the employers and the excellent work accomplished by these committees and the publicity which attended their installation was a powerful factor in the extension during the war of the shop committee movement. The Commission appointed administrators who settled the details of controversies and, acting as arbitrators in some cases and as mediators in others, maintained peace for the balance of the war period.

The President's Mediation Commission induced the meat packers to submit to arbitration their differences with the men, although two separate agreements for this purpose were necessary, one with the employees through their unions,[2] and one with the

[1] Ernest P. Marsh, Verner Z. Reed, Jackson L. Spangler and John H. Walker.
[2] It is interesting to note that in its efforts to organize the packing house workers, the Chicago Federation of Labor under the leadership of John Fitzpatrick and William Z. Foster devised a form of industrial unionism by which all of the workers in the packing industry were united. A Stockyard Labor Council was formed which included local

employers. Judge Alschuler was appointed arbitrator, and his award provided for materially increased wages, the basic eight-hour day, collective bargaining, and the right to trade union membership.[1] Conditions were established which made for peace throughout the war period—that is, until a number of months after the armistice.

In the copper mines where the production of millions of pounds of copper had been stopped by strikes tying up the richest fields

unions of many trades such as butchers, blacksmiths, colored laborers, electrical workers, leather workers, machinists, office employees, railroad carmen, firemen, engineers, switchmen, teamsters, etc. The local unions were affiliated with the A. F. of L. and received permission from their Internationals to join the Stockyard Council, although at the time of its formation some of the locals had no members in the stockyards. A vigorous organizing campaign then followed, in which among others, two negro organizers were employed. The spread of the movement was facilitated by discontent with conditions in the industry and strikes occurred in Omaha, Kansas City and Denver. At a national conference in Omaha in November, the Amalgamated Meat Cutters and Butcher Workmen decided upon demands for an eight-hour day, wage increases, etc. The presentation of these demands was, it is claimed, followed by the discharge of a number of members of the union. The packers refused to discuss the matters in dispute with representatives of the union and a strike followed. This resulted in the intervention of the President's Mediation Commission and the agreement above referred to. Before the submission of the points at issue to the arbitrator, 18 separate demands of the men were referred to a committee of four—Carl Mayer and J. G. Condon, representing the employers and Frank P. Walsh and John Fitzpatrick, the men. This committee agreed upon 12 of the demands. The other six which included wages and the eight-hour day were submitted to arbitration. John E. Williams was originally appointed arbitrator but ill health compelled his retirement and he was succeeded by Judge Samuel Alschuler. Recent disputes between the Stockyard Council and the International Officers of Amalgamated Meat Cutters and Butcher Workers of North America lead to the demand that the Council be abolished. Upon the refusal of a large number of locals to sever their connections with the Council, their charters were revoked.

[1] Judge Alschuler's decision, reprinted in the *Monthly Labor Review*, U. S. Bureau of Labor Statistics, May, 1918, gives an excellent picture of the packing industry, showing that from the date of the last strike in 1904 (in which the men were badly beaten and their union crushed), wages had remained at 18 cents per hour for many stockyard occupations, in spite of increased cost of living and the utter inadequacy of that remuneration to afford a minimum of subsistance. After the European War and the consequent cessation of immigration, the packers, in order to keep their men, were forced to make substantial wage increases. But owing to the increased cost of living and the originally low wage levels, the men's compensation was before Judge Alschuler's award quite inadequate and very much less than that paid in other industries.

of the country [1] the Commission was successful in procuring a return to work of all of the men. It set up or reëstablished local machinery for collective bargaining and appointed an administrator to adjust any differences which the copper companies and the men could not settle by themselves.

With the administrator's aid strikes were avoided during the remainder of the war period. And the readjustments to a peace basis, which in the copper industry were particularly difficult, were made with a minimum of friction.[2]

The Mediation Commission also attempted to settle the differences in the lumber districts of the Northwest, but here its efforts were not so successful. The I. W. W. was in control of the labor in this field,[3] and the Commission, although holding hearings in the lumber belt at which both employer and employee were called

[1] See Chapter XIX for more detailed account of copper strikes and Bisbee deportations.

[2] In a letter to the Conciliation Division of the Department of Labor, dated October 20, 1919 (Report of the Secretary of Labor, 1919, page 20), Mr. Hywel Davies, Labor Administrator for the Arizona copper industry, states that by the latter part of January, 1919, the copper industry "was confronted with an accumulated surplus of over 1,000,-000,000 pounds of copper produced at a maximum cost under war conditions and with an expected market price of 26 cents but which had now slumped to about 15 cents per pound." The wage agreements made during the war had provided for a sliding scale depending upon the selling price of copper. In view of the seriousness of the situation which confronted the industry a conference was called at Washington, and reductions in wages of $1.00 a day during February and March, 1919, in Montana, Arizona, Utah, and Nevada were decided upon and approved by representatives of the men. The administrator comments upon the fact that no such wage reductions were made in any other war industry and gives the men great credit for having accepted them without any serious stoppage of work. The only disturbance of any consequence was at Jerome, Arizona, where the mines were shut down for four months. The employers also are praised for not having insisted upon the full wage reduction called for in the sliding scale . . . in Montana the Anaconda companies accepted the men's demand that after July, 1919, the sliding scale be abolished and a flat rate be established, restoring the $1.00 per day by which the wages had been reduced. (There was, however, a strike of the metal workers who demanded a larger increase.) The report gives details of other adjustments and shows that the spirit between the operators and the miners has improved to a marked degree during the war and post-armistice period.

[3] Robert Bruere in "Following the Trail of the I. W. W." page 17 (reprinted from the New York Evening Post), states that the I. W. W. membership in the Washington lumber districts was variously estimated at from 7 to 30 thousand, and that the organization was rapidly growing.

upon to testify, failed to hear any of the members of the I. W. W., either individually or as members of that organization.[1] The efforts of the Commission to restore lumber production were unsuccessful, and it was not until a number of months later when the Loyal Legion was organized by a representative of the War Department that industrial peace was secured in the lumber belt.[2]

In the California oil fields a threatened strike was averted by the willingness of the independent companies to follow the lead of the Standard Oil Company and adopt the eight-hour day. It is interesting to note that the agreement made by the companies not to discriminate against their men for union membership was limited to unions affiliated with the American Federation of Labor.[3]

The report of the Commission, covering the work that it accomplished and analyzing the underlying causes of the labor difficulties which it had investigated, is probably the ablest laboi document which the war produced—a document which has permanent value for peace times as well as for the special emergencies of the war. The recommendations of the Commission were so excellent intrinsically, that it is a pity some of their practical value was lost because they were couched in general terms, whereas what was needed at this particular time was suggestions of such definiteness that they would naturally result in speedy administrative action.

[1] This position was in strange contrast to the attitude toward the I. W. W. taken by the Commission in its report to the President. This report gives an eminently fair and illuminating account of the origin and status of the I. W. W.—in fact, so fair to that body that it was introduced by members of the I. W. W. as evidence in their favor at a number of Federal prosecutions.

[2] See Chapter XIX for a more detailed account of the I. W. W. and of the Loyal Legion of Loggers and Lumberman.

[3] The Federal Oil Inspection Board, set up by agreement between employers and their men through the efforts of Verner Z. Reed of the President's Mediation Commission functioned as labor adjuster in the California oil fields until May 12, 1919, and during that time prevented any cessations of work. See Seventh Annual Report Secretary of Labor, p. 23.

CHAPTER VI

Special Agencies of the War and Navy Departments

ADMINISTRATOR OF LABOR STANDARDS IN ARMY CLOTHING

One of the first needs of our new army to receive the attention of the War Department was the need for uniforms. The clothing manufacturers were in part prepared to meet this demand because in the earlier days of the war the Allies—especially England—had placed large orders in this country for the manufacture of uniforms and army coats. Our Government had the British experience to draw on. At first England had given out contracts for complete garments. That is to say, the manufacturer furnished the cloth as well as the labor and delivered a completed article for a definite price. But England soon found it more satisfactory to purchase the materials, receiving bids from manufacturers for the labor only. And this practice, adopted by our Government, very much simplified the bidding and resulted in keener competition. It also lessened the contractor's risk and at the same time limited his profits to what he could make solely out of the labor involved. Thus the pressure to cheapen labor costs by subletting the work to the tenement house "sweat shop" sub-contractors was very much increased.

Soon the War Department was flooded with complaints that some of the work was being done under insanitary conditions, that army uniforms were being manufactured in the tenements and in unsafe and unhealthy factories. The situation was further complicated by the existence of two rival unions, whose contests for domination resulted in frequent quarreling and often in strikes. (The Amalgamated Clothing Workers of America, whose members manufactured most of the army uniforms, was the more radical organization. It was organized in 1914 by men who had seceded from the United Garment Workers of America, which is affiliated with the A. F. of L.) Another element of difficulty was the fact that many of the employers were men who themselves had recently risen from the ranks of the workers, and, as was usual in these cases, they were very reactionary and strongly anti-union.

In view of the general situation the War Department appointed a committee of three to investigate and this committee developed into the Board of Control for Labor Standards in Army Clothing. To this board there were appointed an army officer, a former clothing manufacturer, and the executive secretary of the Consumers' League. Because the dominant union in this industry was not affiliated with the A. F. of L., no labor representative was appointed.

The board found much need for improvement in the conditions under which the uniforms were being manufactured. Some of the employers had induced the army to station soldiers in uniform in front of the factories presumably to give to their plants the atmosphere of an official Government agency. And in certain cases the pressure of patriotic appeals induced the employees, including many women, to work long periods of overtime. Sanitary conditions were, in some places, exceedingly bad, and an energetic campaign was inaugurated to get the manufacturing of uniforms out of the tenements. In these respects the Commission was successful, and under its direction, the sweat-shops were abolished, the making of army uniforms was carefully supervised, and the sanitary and safety conditions of factories improved. It did not, however, function as a mediating agency.

In December, 1917,[1] there was substituted for the board of three a single individual, who was known as the Administrator of Labor Standards in Army Clothing, and whose office was made a subsidiary branch of the Industrial Service Section of the Quartermaster's Department. The position of Administrator was at first filled by Mr. Kirstein, one of the members of the original board, and in April, 1918, Professor William Z. Ripley, who had served as one of the experts of the Railroad Wage Commission, succeeded Mr. Kirstein.

Under the direction of the Administrator, the work of sanitary inspection was continued, with the function of labor adjustment added. The Administrator sought to prevent union discrimina-

[1] Report of the Activities of the War Department in the Field of Industrial Relations During the War.

tion and to maintain a position of neutrality between the two rival unions. He insisted upon collective bargaining, but followed the National War Labor Board rules in connection therewith.

In the eagerness of the men to obtain concessions to which they considered themselves entitled, strikes were called for various reasons, frequently against the wishes of the national officers of the unions. These strikes were contrary to the labor policy of the Government, and met with the rebuke of the Administrator.[1] On the other hand, he also experienced a great deal of difficulty with some of the employers who also violated the labor policies of the Government and who sometimes attempted by indirection to accomplish their purpose of weakening the union. In some cases the Administrator had to threaten manufacturers with the removal of their names from the list of approved contractors in order to secure their compliance with his decisions.

Because much of the labor involved in clothing manufacture was in some localities done under the piece work system, many disputes arose as to piece work rates, and a staff, expert in calculating costs of manufacturing, was developed to adjust these disputes (and also to advise the contract branch of the Quartermaster's Department). On that part of the work which was done on a basis of a weekly wage, considerable difficulty was experienced in keeping up the efficiency of the men. At one time the cutters, dissatisfied with their pay, were shown to have deliberately limited output in order to force a wage advance.[2]

At the time of the armistice a very serious strike occurred in New York because of the insistence of the Amalgamated Clothing Workers of America upon receiving the forty-four-hour week, which, at their May convention, they had decided to demand. Although work was continued on Government orders, the stoppage applying only to private work, Mr. Ripley offered his services as labor adjuster. The employers seemed willing to accept the arbitration of the Labor Administrator and of the War Labor Board. The union, however, for some time, insisted upon its demands be-

[1] See decision of Administrator in Pahl-Hoyt Co. Brooklyn.
[2] An abuse which the Administrator tried very hard to correct. In the case of Zeeman and Grossman, N. Y., decided in November, 1918, the Administrator found that production had decreased 50 per cent since May, 1918.

ing granted and refused to arbitrate.[1] The strike that followed lasted three months and was finally adjusted through the efforts of an advisory board, consisting of Mr. Ripley, Chairman; Felix Frankfurter, of the War Labor Policies Board and Louis Marshall, a promiment attorney. After the submission to this board, but before it had time to reach a decision, the manufacturers conceded the forty-four hour week [2] and the other questions were submitted to the board.[3]

A campaign now followed for the adoption of the forty-four-hour week all over the country, and soon thereafter the shorter week was adopted in all of the important clothing centers. In some places, notably Cincinnati, this result was only achieved after a very bitter struggle.

[1] Its reason for taking this attitude was probably the feeling that there was very little likelihood of receiving a favorable verdict from any Government board, the War Labor Board favoring the eight-hour day for factory work, but not the 44-hour week. See Chapter XIV.

[2] Shortly before the concession of the 44-hour week by the New York manufacturers—indeed one of the facts which induced this action —the largest clothing factory in the country, Hart, Schaffner and Marx, of Chicago, had entered into an agreement with the Amalgamated, providing for the 44-hour week.

[3] The advisory board made three separate reports—the first was preliminary and recommended the adoption of the 44-hour week, the return to work of the men and that studies be made in reference to wages and the creation of machinery to improve "efficiency, discipline and production." In the second this machinery was provided for as follows: Disputes which the representative of the union and the "Contractors Appeal Agent" were unable to settle were to be referred to an Impartial Chairman. The discharge of employees, which had been a source of controversy in this industry, was to be regulated by an Employment Agent, designated by the manufacturers, with the consent of the Advisory Board and subject to the approval of the Impartial Chairman. No discharges except "in aggravated instances" were to be made without written notice to employee and Employment Agent, who was directed to hold hearings—with appeal to the Impartial Chairman in whom was vested the power of review. In the Board's final report a wage increase was granted and provision made for adjustments in the event of a "substantial reduction in the cost of living." The necessity of coöperation by the workers with the manufacturers "to the end that there shall be assured efficiency in production and adequacy of output" is emphasized. And the report states that: "The voluntary or deliberate interference with efficiency or reduction of output is a matter of such seriousness as to be regarded as justifying the immediate suspension by the Employment Agent with the sanction of the Impartial Chairman of any worker committing such an act."

ARSENAL AND NAVY YARD WAGE COMMISSION

The Government had always maintained a number of its own plants for naval construction and ordnance manufacture.[1] But even in peace times they did not have sufficient capacity to supply the comparatively small needs of our regular army and navy. With our participation in the war, vast quantities of ordnance were ordered from private corporations and in addition the facilities of the Government arsenals and navy yards were enlarged and the work very much speeded up.

It was especially important to avoid strikes in these Government plants, both because of the vital need for their products and because of the effect which an inability of the Government to maintain continuous production in its own factories would have upon private industry. In certain respects the task was easier here than elsewhere. The eight-hour day had been established as in other government work, and it was also required by law that wages paid to Government employees be equal to those received by workers in private industry in the immediate neighborhood. Most of the Government workers were members of unions and questions of discrimination, which were so prominent elsewhere, did not arise.

The chief task was therefore to increase wages in accordance with the advance in living costs and in accordance with the changes which were taking place in wages in the vicinities. For this purpose the Secretaries of War, Navy and Labor coöperated and on August 15, 1917 the Arsenals and Navy Yard Commission was organized.[2] A number of hearings were held on the basis of which the Navy was prepared to fix new scales for Navy Yards. The War Department, however, was not at that time ready to join, and the Navy Department made an independent award for Navy Yards.

[1] The principal arsenals are located at Watertown and Springfield, Mass.; Watervliet, N. Y.; Picatinny, N. J.; Frankford Arsenal, Philadelphia, Pa., and Rock Island, Ill. See A Report of the Activities of the War Department in the Fields of Industrial Relations During the War.

[2] The members were Franklin D. Roosevelt, Assistant Secretary of the Navy; Walter Lippmann, representing the War Department, and William Blackman, representing the Department of Labor; Stanley King succeeded Mr. Lippmann and Rowland B. Mahaney, Mr. Blackman.

The Ordnance Department assigned Major B. H. Gitchell, afterward head of the Industrial Service Section, to consider the question at each arsenal separately and the scales arranged by him, in consultation with arsenal commanders and representatives of the men, were formally approved by the Commission and made effective November 1, 1917.[1] From time to time thereafter new scales were established by both the Army and the Navy. The two Departments consulted informally before making awards, but the Commission as such ceased to function.

NATIONAL HARNESS AND SADDLERY ADJUSTMENT COMMISSION

The manufacture of harness and saddlery had, in recent years, very much fallen off due to the increasing use of automobiles and auto trucks. The war, however, made very large demands upon this industry as it did upon so many others. As a result of the unusual activity of the trade and of the increased living costs the men demanded wage increases, which the employers were unwilling to meet. Disputes also arose as to the application of the Federal eight-hour law and as to whether or not it applied to sub-contract as well as to direct Government work. During the summer of 1917 the situation became acute and a general strike in the industry threatened. Fortunately this was averted by the organization in September, 1917, of the National Harness and Saddlery Adjustment Commission. The agreement under which it was formed was signed by almost all of the manufacturers in the country and by the United Leatherworkers International Union. It was one of the few agreements to provide expressly that no interruption of work should take place during the war. All disputes were to be left to the adjustment of the Commission, which was to consist of two representatives appointed by the Secretary of War (one of whom was to act as chairman) one by the employers and one by the union.[2]

In order to prevent the heavy turnover due to competition among employers for men, the rates fixed by the commission (at

[1] A Report of the Activities of the War Department in the Field of Industrial Relations During the War, p. 25.
[2] Stanley King, of the Secretary of War's office, was the first chairman of the Commission; he was succeeded by Major S. J. Rosensohn. The other representatives of the War Department were Lt. Col. John

first fifty cents an hour for skilled men and then sixty cents) were made maxima as well as minima. Somewhat later the competition for men having taken the form of giving them excessive amounts of overtime instead of increases of pay, the commission limited the number of hours which any employee was permitted to work to 55 hours in summer and 58 hours in winter.[1]

The commission accomplished its purposes so successfully that there were no strikes of any consequence in this industry. It was formally dissolved by the Secretary of War on January 15, 1919.

S. Fair, and Major John R. Simpson, who acted in matters concerning the Quartermaster and Ordnance Departments respectively. The employers were represented by Henry Diegel and the union by W. E. Brown.

[1] It was also provided that men might be permitted to work 60 hours on certificate of necessity from the employer member of the commission and "that in case of extraordinary emergency, upon a certificate from a duly authorized representative of the War Department stating that the needs of the Government demand that a particular manufacturer shall operate his factory more than 60 hours and that the needs of the Government cannot otherwise be supplied, the Commission may authorize a manufacturer to permit his employees to work more than 60 hours."

CHAPTER VII

Special Agencies of the War and Navy Departments (continued)

INDUSTRIAL SERVICE SECTIONS OF ORDNANCE, QUARTERMASTER AND AIRCRAFT

ALTHOUGH the War Department had, as early as June, 1917, appointed a Commission to adjust labor conditions in connection with the construction of cantonments and although it had created all of the other boards which we have just described, yet it had not organized the task of supervising industrial conditions and preventing strikes in the hundreds of private plants, in all parts of the country, in which munitions were being manufactured. Nor can this omission be explained on the theory that no labor difficulties had been encountered in connection with the manufacture of guns and powder and all of the many articles which the Ordnance branch of the War Department was striving with feverish haste to have manufactured. As a matter of fact, strikes had occurred in the munition factories of Bridgeport, Bethlehem, Newark and elsewhere. Unrest prevailed throughout the entire industry, due not only to the abnormal conditions prevailing generally, but also to the opposition of most of the large munition companies to the existence and growth of the machinists' union.

Under these circumstances it seems very strange that the War Department did not follow the practice it had adopted in all of these other cases, and create machinery, which we can now see was so urgently needed, to adjust labor conditions in ordnance plants. The Department itself has stated that its reason for this omission was its belief, in the early months of the war, that Congress had placed in the Labor Department the functions of labor adjustments and that its best course was to refer these difficulties to the Labor Department.[1] (The action of the department in

[1] See A Report of the Activities of the War Department in the Field of Industrial Relations During the War, p. 26.

creating the boards mentioned above is considered merely as an exception to this general policy.) There can be very little doubt, however, that the War Department was further influenced by the fact that the large munition firms were opposed to the intervention of Government boards. This opposition had been shown in the objections of these firms to the inclusion of the "labor clause" [1] in munition contracts. They feared that the growth of the unions would be accelerated if the Government became active in the adjustment of labor problems and they wanted more than anything else to retain the freedom of action, in these matters, which they had possessed in times of peace.

Whatever the reasons may have been, it was not until the fall of 1917 that the organization of an Industrial Service Section was undertaken by the Chief of Ordnance, and not until January, 1918, that it was formally constituted.[2] The Section was organized by dividing its work into different branches, each of which had jurisdiction over one activity such as employment management, housing, community organization and mediation. The Mediation Branch (later known as the Wages and Working Conditions Branch) with which we are mainly interested, was organized in February, 1918, for the adjustment of labor disputes.[3]

In the summer of 1918, the Industrial Service Section adopted a decentralized form of organization, maintaining a main office in Washington but opening branch offices in each of the districts into which the Ordnance work of the country was divided.[4] It was in close touch with both manufacturers and union, and endeavored to anticipate strikes by composing difficulties. In many cases, however, this was absolutely impossible. In the spring of 1918, as a consequence of the rapidly increasing cost of living

[1] See Appendix No. IX.
[2] In the first months of the war the Secretary appointed Felix Frankfurter as special assistant, for labor matters. Shortly thereafter Walter Lippmann was appointed in a similar capacity. Later still Stanley King and E. M. Hopkins succeeded Messrs. Frankfurther and Lippmann.
[3] Major William H. Rogers was in charge; he was succeeded by Major James Tole.
[4] It should be pointed out that the representatives of the Industrial Service Section acted, as a rule, as mediators rather than arbitrators. There was no general agreement that both sides should submit controversies to the adjustment of the Industrial Service Section. Some of the contracts for ordnance work contained the "labor clause" but very many did not and a great deal of munition work was in the hands

and of the wage increases in other industries, especially the shipyards, the machinists union formulated a series of wage demands,
which were presented to manufacturers all over the country.
These demands were resisted by the employers, practically everywhere, and the important strikes at Bridgeport, New York,
Newark and elsewhere were due to the resulting conflicts.

If a commission had been established for this industry, similar
to the Shipbuilding Labor Adjustment Board or the National Adjustment Commission, these demands could have been handled
in an orderly manner, a fair wage could have been established
for different localities commensurate with the increased cost of
living and with the pay of the men doing similar work in the
shipyards and other war industries. The fact was, however, that
the War Department was slow in the creation of the necessary
machinery, and when created, this machinery proved inadequate
in that it lacked authority and was not expanded rapidly enough
to meet the growing difficulties.

The disastrous situation at Bridgeport resulting largely from
the causes outlined above will be treated in greater detail in the
next section of this chapter. In New York, where the conflict between the two sides was not as acute, the strikes which did occur
were not of so serious a nature. Two things characterized the
New York situation—the manufacturers were not united in a
strong association and the men, although highly organized, were
more conservatively led. Upon the occurrence of strikes in a
number of the larger shops, because of the failure of the employers

---

of sub-contractors who had no contractual relationship whatever with
the Government. The situation was further complicated by the fact
that some contracts were for fixed sums, others were cost plus; many
factories were engaged in private as well as Government work. Some
contracts were profitable and the employers in their eagerness for men
with which to execute them, were willing to pay the high wage rates
of the shipyards. In other cases employers had not realized the disadvantageous conditions under which work would have to be done and
had taken contracts at a price which made it very difficult for them
to keep pace, in wages, with the increased cost of living. To be sure,
if their agreements contained the labor clause, they would receive from
the Government the added costs due to wage increases. If however
their contracts did not contain this clause, they would have to bear the
loss, and it was not until the war was almost at an end that the legal
difficulties which seemed to prevent the amendment of ordnance contracts, by the addition of the labor clause, were overcome.

to meet the demands of the machinists union,[1] an award was made by the representative of the Industrial Service Section (acting in this case in coöperation with the Navy, whose work was also affected) for all of the plants in the vicinity of New York. Although this award was a general one intended to apply to all of the plants in the vicinity, only the employers whose men had been on strike, comprising only a small proportion of the New York shops, had agreed to accept it. Every day, for months thereafter, complaints were received that individual factories were not paying the wages called for in the award. And the men were frequently forced to strike to compel the payment of the Government scale. If the shop were not working on contracts containing the labor clause, the Government had no authority whatever to compel the payment of the scale. Even in such cases the employer usually acceded to the demands of the men soon after it was pointed out that these demands had the Government's approval and that they were being met by most of the other employers in the community. These strikes were therefore seldom of long duration.[2]

The situation in Newark was a most interesting, although unsatisfactory one. Most of the employers were members of a powerful association and were bitterly anti-union. The men, before the war, had not been strongly organized. But the union, whose leader was extremely aggressive and radical, took advantage of the general unrest and the reactionary attitude of the employers to conduct a vigorous campaign for members.[3] As the union grew in strength the opposition of the employers was redoubled. And when the demands for wage increases were presented early in the summer of 1918, the employers not only disregarded them, but urged the War Department to keep its hands off and allow them to fight matters out themselves. In spite of the fact that the men were willing to submit to arbitration by the National War Labor Board or by the Ordnance Department, the employers persisted in this attitude. Faced by the very general dissatisfaction of many of the manufacturers with its labor policy, the War Department determined not to intervene

[1] A hearing had been held in Washington but no award had been made.
[2] The many strikes which occurred in New York to enforce the closed shop in particular plants are referred to in Chapter XIII.
[3] See Chapter XVII.

but to allow the men to go out if the employers could not themselves adjust the controversy. When, however, the strike occurred and the Government found that work had been stopped on some of the things it needed most for the army in France, it quickly intervened—against the most violent protests of the employers—and the men returned to work on the promise of Government adjustment.[1] Major B. H. Gitchell, who came to Newark with authority from both War and Navy Departments to settle the strike, conferred with both sides and issued an award similar to that made by him in other localities. Although only one of the Newark employers had agreed in advance to abide by Major Gitchell's decision, many of them were willing to accept it after it was made. The men, however, were dissatisfied because the award failed to provide for a basic eight-hour day and appealed to the National War Labor Board. Hearings were held but the employers maintained their previous unwillingness to submit to the Board's jurisdiction and urged that inasmuch as the men had agreed to abide by the War Department's decision, their appearance before the War Labor Board was a violation of their agreement. On this and other grounds they maintained their refusal to come under the jurisdiction of the War Labor Board.

Wages aside, the most important cause of strikes in munition plants was the question of discrimination for union membership. This was especially so after the enunciation by the President of the principles of the War Labor Board. These principles were adopted by the War Department and reinstatement was always ordered when it appeared that the dismissal was solely for union activity. The case of the Smith & Wesson Company, of Springfield, Mass., was a flagrant example of the violation of these principles. The company had maintained a closed non-union shop requiring each employee to sign an agreement not to join a labor union without giving the company one week's notice. During the summer of 1918 when wages of machinists all over the country were being readjusted, a new wage scale was put into

[1] In their brief before the National War Labor Board, the manufacturers, speaking of the Government's promise to intervene if the men would immediately return to work say, "no such promise should have been made. By striking the men were holding back guns and munitions from our troops. They should have been dealt with sternly, not tenderly." See Chapter XVI for more detailed discussion of this attitude on the part of employers.

effect at the Springfield Armory. The Smith & Wesson Company was unwilling to meet this scale and went so far as to discharge a committee of its own employees, who asked for a wage increase.[1] Under these circumstances a number of men joined the union and were discharged. A strike followed and the Secretary of War asked the War Labor Board to hear the controversy. The case was squarely within the principles of the War Labor Board and its award ordered the reinstatement of the men and the abolition of the individual contracts by which each man had agreed with the Company not to join a union. In spite of the fact that its agreements with the War Department contained the labor clause and that the firm had therefore agreed to submit any labor controversy to the determination of the nominee of the Secretary of War, the Smith & Wesson Company refused to recognize the jurisdiction of the National War Labor Board or to accept its decision. Thereupon the War Department exercised its most drastic remedy by taking over the plant. The fact that this occurred during the same week in which the Bridgeport workers refused to abide by the War Labor Board's decision, gave the Government an excellent opportunity to show both sides that it would insist impartially upon both employer and employee living up to decisions which they had agreed to accept. The fact that the action of this company was so patent a violation not only of the Government's war labor policy but of its own agreement makes it all the more remarkable that the press in so many places should have attacked the Government for this action,[2] and that a group of New England manufacturers should have written a letter of protest to the Secretary of War.

In certain other cases the Secretary referred disputes to the National War Labor Board, which in this way settled strikes in the most important munition factories in the country. Among these were some of the largest plants of the General Electric Company and of the Bethlehem Steel Company.[3] The mechanics involved in settlements made by the Industrial Service Section were predominently machinists, but molders, blacksmiths and other machine shop employees were also not infrequently the subjects

---

[1] See A Report of the Activities of the War Department in the Field of Industrial Relations During the War, p. 34.
[2] One of these attacks is reprinted at page 252.
[3] See Chapter X.

of wage adjustments. The department was likewise active in adjusting disputes in the building trades of men engaged in constructing plants and additions for munition factories.[1]

Immediately after the signing of the armistice, notwithstanding the confusion which was bound to follow the readjustments of munition plants to a peace basis and notwithstanding the fact that many months would have to elapse before all of the claims arising out of war-time awards could be settled, the War Department decided to abolish the Industrial Service Section. The International Association of Machinists wrote to the Secretary and protested against this action, but Mr. Baker insisted that it would be "unwise for the War Department to continue their functions in labor matters when, as now, the problems of production of war supplies had given place to the problems of reconstruction."[2]

The Industrial Service Section was speedily demobilized, and a great deal of confusion resulted, together with a material increase in the feeling of labor unrest. Many of the men believed that war promises were not kept and that with the end of the extreme emergency the Government had suddenly lost its interest in their welfare. That the men had a good deal of justification for this feeling there can be very little doubt, and the action of the War Department is one of the many illustrations of the Government's haste to rid itself of practically all war emergency boards.

It is interesting to note that some months later the Department changed its policy and decided to retain during peace times an Industrial Service Branch to supervise the handling of the labor problem at the arsenals and elsewhere.[3]

INDUSTRIAL SERVICE SECTION—QUARTERMASTER CORPS

Most of the labor problems affecting the work of the Quartermaster Corps were settled by special boards which have already

[1] In these cases the Industrial Service Section coöperated with the Emergency Construction Commission investigating the facts and reporting them to that body with recommendations for its action.

[2] Letter Secretary of War to International Association of Machinists, November 20, 1918.

[3] Payson Irwin, who was Special Assistant to Chief of Industrial Service Section from the time of its organization, succeeded Major Gitchel and was in charge of the Section during the period of plant demobilization. He became the first head of the new peace-time organization.

been considered. Thus the Emergency Wage Adjustment Commission adjusted the difficulties which arose in connection with the construction of cantonments. The harness and saddlery industry was taken care of by the National Harness and Saddlery Board. The Administrator of Labor Standards in Army Clothing adjusted difficulties in connection with the manufacture of uniforms and raincoats. This latter function was placed under the jurisdiction of the Industrial Service Section but in practice its activities were largely independent.

Dr. E. M. Hopkins, in December, 1917, became chief of the Industrial Service Section of the Quartermaster Corps. Later he was transferred to the office of the Secretary of War and placed in general charge of the labor problems of that entire department, and Mr. John R. McLane took charge of the Industrial Service Section. Mr. McLane also acted as one of the Board of Referees for the Clothing Industry of Cleveland.[1] But, partly because of the facts above set forth and partly because of special circumstances surrounding some of the industries in which Quartermaster's supplies were manufactured,[2] the activities of the section itself remained comparatively unimportant.

INDUSTRIAL SERVICE SECTION—AIRCRAFT

The problems faced by the Bureau of Aircraft Production were very similar to those of the Ordnance Department, the trades employed by each of them being largely the same. Much of the machine work of the Bureau was done in sub-contract shops, and many factories were engaged at the same time on work for both departments. In January, 1918, an Industrial Service Section was organized.[3] It did not, however, become very active until the following spring, when Major Gitchell, in charge of the Industrial Service Section of Ordnance, was placed in a similar

[1] The other members were Dr. Hopkins and Major Rosensohn. Stanley M. Isaacs acted as Secretary.

[2] Thus in the shoe trade the Massachusetts State Board of Conciliation and Arbitration had for a number of years acted as arbitrator for that portion of the industry—the largest and most important—which was located in that State.

[3] Charles P. Neill was appointed chief and W. Jett Lauck Assistant Chief. The services of both were soon thereafter requisitioned by other important boards, Mr. Neill serving with the Railroads and Mr. Lauck becoming Secretary of the National War Labor Board.

position for Aircraft. The policy of decentralization adopted in the Ordnance Department was carried out for the Bureau of Aircraft and branch offices were opened in each district into which the work of the Bureau was divided. Although the personnel in each of the departments was distinct, coöperation between them was facilitated by reason of the fact that Major Gitchell was in charge of both sections and similar wage scales and policies were maintained.

THE BRIDGEPORT STRIKES

The series of strikes at Bridgeport, Connecticut, are singled out for extended description because they illustrate so vividly the important factors of industrial strife during the war. A further reason for giving closer attention to this controversy is the prominence which it received by reason of the refusal of the men to obey the award of the National War Labor Board, resulting in the dramatic order of President Wilson in which he demanded that the men return to work. The Bridgeport situation is also illustrative of the fact, to which reference has often been made, that war labor difficulties were the direct outgrowth of bad pre-war industrial relations.

Labor unrest at Bridgeport had long antedated the war, and this city as well as practically all of New England, had seen a struggle in the machine shop industry between the unions and the type of employer who refuses to have any dealings whatever with them, and who does his best to prevent the spread of unionism among his employees.

Frequently this attitude of the employers is responsible for breeding radicalism in the unions, and many examples can be cited where coöperation on the part of the owner of the industry with organizations representing his employees has been accompanied by a conservative and coöperative spirit on the part of the men and their leaders—whereas an attitude of bitter antagonism to any organization of the men has been met with radicalism and added bitterness by the employees.

In this particular case, for example, the Bridgeport local union—although a branch of the International Association of Machinists, affiliated with the A. F. of L.—was led by radical socialists (just as was the machinists union at Newark, where similar opposition on the part of the employers prevailed). In spite of its hard struggle against the hostility of the manufacturers, it maintained a flourishing existence, and published the *Labor Leader,* whose radical utterances hardly made it easier to keep the peace.

Bridgeport was one of the first American cities to receive large war orders from the Allies and as the war continued from year to year their ever growing demands for greater and greater quantities of ammunition kept the manufacturers of Bridgeport working night and day—expanding their plants, taking on added forces of men, straining the housing facilities of the town, crowding more and more men into increasingly congested quarters. Rents were soaring and the cost of living was rising even more markedly than in most other parts of the country.[1]

Bridgeport was seething with life, booming with war orders. Most of the workers believed that the employers were, as a result, rolling in wealth. And when the United States entered the war this belief was intensified by their knowledge that contracts were doubled and trebled. Although the profitableness of the contracts undoubtedly varied very much—they were let in a great rush on a rising labor market; in some cases they were very profitable, in others not profitable at all [2]—the men nevertheless believed that there was a fortune in every one. Furthermore the leaders in Bridgeport were radical socialists to whom any profits were irritating and these supposedly large *war* profits especially so.

There is a good deal of conflict of evidence as to whether or not the pay of the Bridgeport workers kept pace with increased costs of living, and whether, considering the prosperous condition of the industry (a condition which the men undoubtedly exaggerated) wages had increased as much as might reasonably have been expected. But of this there can be no doubt. At the beginning of Bridgeport's war labor troubles the workers in the ammunition plants did not enjoy nearly such good wages nor such

[1] If any one were to ask which of the communities of the country suffered most from intolerable overcrowding of industrial workers during the war, the towns of Bridgeport, Chester, Wilmington, Erie and Newport News would at once come to mind. In all of them much work was being done for the Army and Navy, and a greater or lesser amount for the Shipping Board.

[2] One of the largest firms was in great financial difficulties during a large part of the war period, and its notes were selling in the open market at about 60% of their par value.

favorable overtime rates as did their fellow workers in the Navy and shipbuilding plants, located in this very same community and throughout New England—and the men were aware of this difference.[1] Furthermore, their dissatisfaction with their pay was intensified by the fact that not only was their union not recognized, but that a systematic effort to crush unionism, by means of a blacklist and otherwise, was practised in Bridgeport. And it was made difficult, if not impossible, for some of the active union workers to secure employment in the machine shops, even at a time when men were extremely scarce, and when the national need for the products of Bridgeport factories was greatest.

Demands were made in the summer of 1917, which looked at now, appear to have been quite reasonable. These were, among others, the eight-hour day; the right to join unions without discrimination; reference of differences between employers and their workers to shop committees, with arbitration in case of disagreement; a 10% increase in wages with a minimum rate of 60 cents for toolmakers and 50 cents for machinists, and overtime at time and one-half for the first three hours, thereafter and on Sunday and holidays double. A demand for the closed shop was also made, but not pressed.

These demands were followed up by a letter on August 14, 1917, asking for a conference. The employers thereupon went to Washington and in accordance with uncontradicted evidence before the War Labor Board laid the matter before the Attorney General, asking for criminal action. The matter was referred by the Department of Justice to the War Department, and Mr. Walter Lippmann, special assistant to the Secretary of War, was sent to Bridgeport. Conferences were held with both sides, but no definite adjustments were made at that time.

In February, 1918, the Machinists' Union wrote to the Remington Arms Company [2] demanding a rate of 80 cents for tool-

[1] Union scale of wages of machinists in manufacturing shops in Bridgeport in May, 1918, are stated in Bulletin Number 259 of the U. S. Bureau of Labor Statistics (page 167) to have been 55 cents an hour with time and a half for overtime on weekdays; at the hearings of the National War Labor Board, the employers testified that the average hourly earnings of machinists June 22, 1918, were 57.5 cents; Shipping Board rates at this time throughout New England were 62½ cents for second class and 72½ for first class machinists.

[2] The Remington Arms Company was by far the largest producer of rifles and small arms in this country and formed the center of the ma-

makers and 70 cents for machinists. The Company (whose contract contained a clause by which all wage disputes were to be submitted to the War Department) referred the union to the office of the Secretary of War. Thereupon the business agent of the union saw representatives of both the War and Labor Departments.

The War Department referred the matter to its recently organized Industrial Service Section of the Ordnance Department, and the Labor Department sent one of its mediators, Mr. Mahaney, to Bridgeport to investigate. On Mr. Mahaney's arrival he found that some of the Remington men were out in protest against the refusal of the Company to pay time and one-half for overtime on Good Friday. The men were induced to return to work but demands were presented for wage increases to 70 cents for machinists (which was approximately shipyard rates) and 80 cents for toolmakers.

After more negotiations the Industrial Service Section of the War Department once more took the matter in charge, this time dispatching Payson Irwin and a number of assistants to study wage and labor conditions in Bridgeport. In the meantime the men had taken a strike vote, which showed that they were overwhelmingly in favor of going out. Mr. Irwin, on reaching Bridgeport, induced them to stay at work, promising that the Ordnance Department would make a definite wage adjustment. In addition, Major William C. Rogers, who had now been placed in charge of the mediation branch of the Industrial Service Section, wrote to the machinists' union, promising them that the award would be made retroactive from May 1, 1918. Major Rogers, however, instead of at once taking up the Bridgeport matter was compelled to go to the Middle West because of a situation there that seemed even more pressing.

Still more weeks elapsed, and no action was taken by the Government. And when on April 29 the men, already impatient with the delays, received from the contract shops a flat refusal of their demands, they took a strike vote, and on May 3 went out in

chine industry in Bridgeport. At the time of the entry of the United States into the war this one firm employed many thousands of men and women. It also supplied many of the smaller shops of Bridgeport, and indeed those throughout New England, with a considerable portion of their work.

twenty-two of these shops, and on May 8, at the Remington Arms Company.

Major Rogers now hurried to Bridgeport; held conferences with both sides, and got the men to return to work by repeating his promise of an award by the Ordnance Department, retroactive from May 1. Because of the bitterly anti-union feeling of the employers, these conferences were held separately with employers and men. They showed how completely the manufacturers misconstrued the temper of their workers by blaming their troubles upon a few agitators. As a matter of fact the resentment of the men, because of union discrimination and because of the discrepancy between their wages and that of the shipyards, was almost universal.

On May 23 a hearing was held in Washington before a special board consisting of Major Rogers, Major Tole, and Mr. Irwin. Both sides appeared before this board and presented their case. On June 8, having received the approval of the Secretary of War, the award was made public. But as is often the case, it satisfied neither side. Nevertheless the men finally accepted it. The employers, on the other hand, flatly refused to do so, and exerted the strongest possible pressure upon the Secretary of War to have the award withdrawn. Weeks passed, and the employers still continuing to ignore the award, a strike resulted in one of the large plants, and a strike vote was taken in all the others. Secretary Baker now telegraphed the men that he had referred the entire matter to the Taft-Walsh Board, and urged them to stay at work.

The men, however, regarded the Secretary's action in not compelling the manufacturers to accept the award of the special board created by his own department as a surrender to the manufacturers' association and a breach of faith with them. On June 26 all machinists stopped work.

With production at a standstill in the most important munition center in the United States, the War Labor Board took jurisdiction, promised speedy action, and persuaded the men to return to work after they had been out about two days. All of the manufacturers now agreed to abide by the War Labor Board's decision, and the union did likewise. Hearings were held in Bridgeport which lasted many days. The testimony, like that of so many other hearings of the War Labor Board, is full of bitter accusations by the men against the employers. They charged systematic discrimination against those who were active in the union,[1] and the use of the draft as a means of intimidating the workers and keeping them from striking.[2] The demand for classification, with minimum wage rates for toolmakers, machinists, and helpers,[3] which had previously been granted by the special board of the Ordnance Department, was strongly urged by the men and even more bitterly opposed by the employers. In support of this the men claimed that their fellow machinists in the ship and navy yards, and in arsenals, and hundreds of private plants in other localities, were working under a minimum wage scale. And this demand for classification and a minimum rate was the point at issue about which each side felt most strongly.

The War Labor Board was unable to agree, and after a great deal of difficulty Otto M. Eidlitz, a prominent New York builder and Director of Housing in the Labor Department, was chosen as umpire. His decision gave the men an eight-hour day (which had already been introduced in most shops), and established an elaborate system of collective bargaining. But he did not give them what they most wanted—classification with a minimum wage scale,[4] for which the machinists' union, all over the country, had been contending. Instead, he awarded a flat wage increase of 15% to the lower paid workers, with smaller increases to the better paid and no increase whatever to the men who already received 78 cents an hour.

---

[1] The testimony amply sustains the men's contention on this point.
[2] See Chapter XVI.
[3] See Chapter XV.
[4] In a letter to the War Labor Board, written by Mr. Eidlitz on September 14, 1918, interpretating the award, he says, "I felt that it was not fair for me to establish classification of trade and minimum wage at this time, under all the conditions existing at Bridgeport, but in view of the fact that the representatives of the employers and employees on the National War Labor Board had agreed that collective bargaining should be instituted at Bridgeport, and in addition that a Local Board with equal representation of employers and employees was to be inaugurated, that this Board, with the help of employers and employees of Bridgeport, would take up all questions on which the parties to the controversy were not in agreement . . . It would be fully within the province of this Local Board to create other subsidiary boards, and it was not the intent to bar the establishment of classification of trade and minimum wage." The failure of the Government to organize the Local Board made it impossible to carry out the suggestions contained in the umpire's letter.

The men were bitterly disappointed. They felt that the Government should have insisted upon the employers accepting the previous award of the War Department. Now after more months had elapsed, an umpire had, they claimed, adopted the viewpoint of the employers and denied them that to which they felt themselves richly entitled. In spite of the efforts of the national leaders to keep them at work,[1] the men refused to accept the award and once more went out on strike.

As will have been observed from this account, the situation was most unfortunately handled by the Government agencies, in that unpardonable delays took place and confusing conflicts of jurisdiction. We can, therefore, understand the indignation of the men, even though we cannot excuse their action in deliberately refusing to abide by the decision which they had previously agreed to accept. A strong letter followed from the President of the United States addressed, "on the joint recommendation of the Secretary of Labor, the Acting Secretary of War, and the joint chairmen of the National War Labor Board,[2] to the striking employees at Bridgeport. After pointing out the supreme importance of orderly procedure and the acceptance of "solemn adjudications of a tribunal to which both parties submitted their claims," the President concluded by requesting the men to return to work and threatening them that unless they did so, they would not be employed for the period of one year in any war industry in the community in which the strike occurred, that they could not claim draft exemption on occupational grounds, and that during that time the United States Employment Service would decline to obtain employment for them in any war industry elsewhere.[3]

The men thereupon, on September 17, 1918, voted to resume work. As they sought to return to their jobs, however, they found that the companies were discriminating against some of the men, refusing to reinstate them. The War Labor Board was notified

---

[1] There is a conflict of evidence as to the position taken by some of the national officers immediately after the award was announced. Later, they undoubtedly did their best to secure the acceptance by the men of the umpire's award.

[2] See Report of the Activities of the War Department in the Field of Industrial Relations During the War, page 33.

[3] *Monthly Labor Review,* U. S. Bureau of Labor Statistics, October, 1918, page 24.

that unless immediate action was taken the machinists would once more be on strike. The President now. telegraphed to the employers demanding that all of the men be reinstated. Even now the difficulty was not entirely settled, as the employers persisted in their refusal to reinstate a number of grinders, whose places they had filled with women. For three days these grinders stood alongside the women who were doing the work that the grinders had done before the strike, and finally got their places back (with pay for the three days).

Following its usual practice, the War Labor Board appointed an examiner to supervise the application of the award, which involved not only the payment of back wages in many plants and the setting up of machinery for collective bargaining in the various factories, but also the establishment of a local board of mediation and conciliation consisting of three members selected by the employers and three selected by the employees, presided over by a Chairman selected by the Secretary of War, "for the purpose of bringing about agreements on disputed issues not covered by" the umpire's award.

This local board might have developed into a most useful piece of machinery but its organization was never completed and it never got a chance to function. As a first step in the selection of their three representatives the men, under the supervision of the War Labor Board, elected delegates from each shop to a city convention. Of these 136 delegates it is remarkable that only 18 were members of labor unions and still more remarkable that the three men selected by the convention to represent all of the men were all members of the union—one of them was Sam Lavit, the union leader to whom the employers so strongly objected. Whether the composition of the committee was responsible for the failure to organize the mediation board is difficult to say. The first appointee of the Secretary of War as chairman of the board refused to serve and no other appointment was made so that the board was never properly organized. Mr. Winter, the Examiner appointed by the War Labor Board, acted informally as presiding officer, but in matters of importance the board was usually deadlocked and Mr. Winter not being officially appointed as its chairman could not settle the dispute. The employers had strenuously objected to that portion of Mr. Eidlitz's award which provided for collective bargaining of any kind.[1]   Nor were they satisfied with many of the rulings of the Examiner and especially with his very firm insistence that the election of shop committees take place (as was the War Labor Board's invariable rule) under his personal supervision.   They were particularly unfriendly to the idea of a general local board and this hostility was very much increased by the choice of active unionists as employee representatives.   It would therefore seem as though the failure of the Secretary of War to complete the board was somewhat more than an accident.

Finally the existence of the local board came to an end by the resignation of the employee members.[2]

---

[1] They claimed that they had not submitted to the War Labor Board the question of either hours or collective bargaining and that the umpire had exceeded his authority in making findings on either of these two points.

[2] During the summer of 1919 many strikes occurred in Bridgeport, for wage increase and the 44-hour week.   On the ground that Samuel Lavit, the business agent of the local Machinists' Union, had disobeyed the rules of the International Association of Machinists, by calling strikes without proper authority, he was removed from office.   The local voted to keep him in office and its charter was revoked.

CHAPTER VIII

Railroad, Fuel and Food Administrations

RAILROAD ADMINISTRATION

EVEN before the war the absolute necessity of maintaining un-interrupted operation of the railroads was sufficiently apparent to cause machinery to be created for the adjustment of labor disputes. This responsibility was vested under the Newlands and Erdman Acts[1] in a Board of Mediation and Conciliation, which, however, did not possess the power to serve as arbitrator unless both parties agreed to abide by its decision. Yet this board—together with special arbitration boards for particular controversies—had for many years succeeded in avoiding any interruption in railway service. And this in spite of the fact that the fixing of rates and the establishment of rules on the railroads had become an unbelievably complicated task.

In the early days of railroad operation the men engaged in the actual movement of the trains (i.e., conductors, engineers, firemen, trainmen) received wages based entirely upon the element of time. Gradually, however, there came to be added, as a further standard for the determination of wages, the distance actually traveled, and in this way there developed the dual standard of hours and miles by which to determine remuneration.[2]

---

[1] The Newlands Act was approved July, 1913, U. S. Statutes at Large, Volume XXXVIII, Part 1, pp. 103, 108. It superseded the Erdman Act of June, 1898, U. S. Statutes at Large, Volume XXX, pp. 424-428, which, in turn, had superseded the Act of October 1, 1888. Under all of these statutes provision had been made for the adjustment of disputes on the railroads. See Railroad Labor Arbitrations, Report of the U. S. Board of Mediation and Conciliation, 1916. Senate Document, number 493, 64th Congress, 1st session, pp. 8 and following.

[2] Before the enactment of the Adamson Law, the normal day's work consisted of 10 hours or 100 miles for freight and usually 200 miles for passenger service. See Julius H. Parmelee in *The Annals* of the Academy of Political and Social Science, January, 1917, page 2. The Adamson Law left the number of miles unchanged, but substituted 8 for 10 hours.

When collective bargaining was first instituted on the railroads, the groups involved in any wage adjustment were small in number. The early agreements covered only divisions of a road; gradually the area over which wage adjustments applied was extended to include the entire road, and then the entire system. Irrespective of the attitude of the railroads toward this extension of the area covered by collective bargaining, there was one point as to which the wishes of the railroads and those of the men were in sharp conflict. The railroads had sought to maintain variations in wage rates to fit differences which they claimed existed in the individual skill of the men, in the character of the service, and in the relative advantage of the locality in which the service was performed (such as differences in cost of living). On the other hand the employees sought greater simplicity in wage fixing, classification on broader lines ignoring minor differences, and standardization affecting ever wider areas of the country.[1]

This tendency toward greater uniformity was hastened by concerted movements affecting an entire section of the country. Finally, in 1916, for the first time in their history, the four brotherhoods joined together and presented identical demands to every one of the railroads. At this time the desire for the eight-hour day with time and one-half for overtime united the brotherhoods in a common demand. A "National Conference Committee" was formed, representing all of the important railroads of the country, and meetings were held with representatives of the men. Lengthy conferences followed, but no adjustment was reached. The railroads were willing to arbitrate; the men, on the other side, dissatisfied with the personnel and decisions of the recent arbitration boards, insisted upon their demands being granted and voted to strike.

This was in August, 1916, at a time when our entry into the war was becoming more and more probable and when the Entente powers, whose cause was favored by a large majority of our people, were in the greatest need of our supplies. The stoppage of railroad service would have been an international calamity, and the President, after fruitless efforts to effect a settlement, a strike then appearing to be imminent,[2] recommended that Con-

[1] See J. Noble Stockett, Jr., The Arbitral Determination of Railway Wages. Houghton, Mifflin; 1918.
[2] In a letter from Harry A. Wheeler, Chairman Committee on Rail-

gress establish by law the eight-hour day for men employed in operating the trains, and that a commission be appointed to study the workings of the new law. Although these demands had been made more than six months before, and although Congress had been repeatedly urged to take some definite action, by which, through an immediate investigation or otherwise, a solution could have been found based upon the facts, yet Congress followed its usual practice of doing nothing until matters had reached a crisis and then acted more or less in a panic. In the passage of the Adamson Law Congress accepted both of the suggestions of the President and the threatened strike was thus narrowly averted.[1] But the enactment of the law did not immediately settle the controversy; for the railroads fought its constitutionality, and, in the meantime, refused to put its provisions into operation. Once more, this time on the very eve of our entry into the war, the country was threatened with a strike. The President thereupon appointed a committee of four from the newly organized Council of National Defense to effect a settlement of the dispute.[2] Through the efforts of this committee the strike was postponed and a settlement reached by which both sides accepted the Committee's award on the very day on which the Supreme Court handed down a decision sustaining the constitutionality of the law. The provisions of the award were substantially an acceptance of the Adamson Law. There was also established a Commission of Eight to adjust any differences which might arise in

road Situation of the U. S. Chamber of Commerce, to the President, dated July 29, 1916, he says—"As a result of the meeting yesterday my conviction is deepened that an amicable settlement is remote and that while other orderly steps are yet to be taken before a final break is reached, yet such a break is inevitable unless some strong measures of intervention are speedily introduced."

[1] Perhaps no other legislative enactment has so aroused the opposition of employers, who are still denouncing the Administration for having yielded to the threats of the brotherhoods. Nor do the leaders of the men seem to have approved of the course taken by the Government. They would have preferred a test of strength, claiming that the strike would have lasted only a few hours, and that they would thus have obtained the adoption of the eight-hour demand in their own way. See W. N. Doak, Vice President, Brotherhood of Railroad Trainmen, in *Proceedings of Academy of Political Science,* January, 1920, page 180.

[2] This committee consisted of Secretaries Lane and Wilson, Samuel Gompers, President of the American Federation of Labor and Daniel Willard, President of the Baltimore and Ohio Railroad. Report of the Eight-Hour Commission, page 10.

the application of the eight-hour settlement. This commission was composed of equal representation of the railroads and the men—with no arbitrator or umpire. And its importance lay not only in the fact that it was able—always by unanimous vote—to adjust practically all the differences which arose,[1] but also because it became the model for all of the permanent wage boards which were created by the Railroad Administration during the war.[2]

Nevertheless the labor difficulties of the railroads were not solved by the enforcement of the Adamson Law. It must be borne in mind that the new law did not bring about any increase in wage rates. To be sure, the shortening of the hours from ten to eight did, in many cases, result in somewhat larger earnings, but this result was not sufficient for any length of time to keep the men satisfied in the face of the increased costs of living. Furthermore, the men had not received time and one-half for overtime, as this feature of their demands was eliminated by the President, when as a compromise he urged the passage of the Adamson Law.[3] Even if the Adamson Law had been sufficient to allay the unrest —which, as we have seen, it was not—it applied, after all, only to the men engaged in the actual movement of the trains, who as a matter of fact included only about 20% of the men employed by the railroads. It did not affect the shopmen, the station masters, the railway clerks, or innumerable others, and these men, as distinguished from the members of the brotherhoods, had been far less organized and not nearly so well paid.

The popular error that men in the railway service were re-

[1] W. N. Doak, in *Proceedings of the Academy of Political Science* for January, 1920, page 180. states that 30,000 disputes were adjusted with only three deadlocks, and these deadlocks were settled by the Board of Adjustment, Number 1, which likewise consisted of an equal number of representatives of the Railroads and the men.
[2] The jurisdiction of the Commission of Eight was confined to the men who operated the trains. It must not be confused with the Eight-Hour Commission, appointed by the President in accordance with the terms of the Adamson Law, "to observe the operation and effects of the institution of the eight-hour standard workday."
[3] The Adamson Law contained no reference whatever to overtime rates. The award of the Committee of the Council of National Defense provided that overtime should be paid for "at not less than" regular rates. No allowance of extra compensation was made in any trades which hitherto had not received it.

ceiving high wages has been referred to in a previous chapter.[1]
The fact of the matter is that although wage increases had been
made during 1915, 1916, and 1917, they were not relatively as
large as the increases which many workers were receiving in other
industries, and they were 'in most cases not sufficient to keep
pace with the increased cost of living.[2] The feeling of the men
at this time was described by the president of one of the brotherhoods as one of "unrest, if not desperation." [3] Especially were
the railroad shopmen and clerks dissatisfied with the pay they
were receiving, and in the summer and fall of 1917 a number of
strikes took place.[4]

At this time the railroads were facing demands of their men
for wage increases aggregating one billion dollars a year. Conferences had been held between the representatives of the four
brotherhoods and the President, as a result of which pledges had
been given to accept Federal mediation, but the men seemed un-

[1] See Chapter I, quoting the Railroad Wage Commission of 1918.
President A. O. Wharton of the Railroad Employees Department,
A. F. of L., speaking at their Fourth Biennial Convention in April,
1918, and explaining the work of the Wage Commission, which he
was assisting, said, referring to their current wages (page 129,
Official Proceedings), "I don't even know how they live under those
conditions. You take it for blacksmiths on the Bangor and Aroostook
Railroad, on the hourly basis, 23 cents an hour . . . On the Lehigh
Valley ten blacksmiths at 23. . . . I am only giving the lowest rate.
They go up above that, of course. Some blacksmiths' helpers get 13
cents an hour. One man on the Erie Railroad. I don't know how he
lives but he is there, according to this book . . . car repairers getting
18 cents an hour," etc.
[2] G. H. Sines, Chairman, Board of Railroad Wages and Working
Conditions, in *Proceedings of the Academy of Political Science*, February, 1919, page 96.
[3] W. S. Carter, President, Brotherhood of Locomotive Firemen and
Enginemen, and later Director of Labor, U. S. Railroad Administration, in *Proceedings of the Academy of Political Science*, February,
1919, page 64.
[4] Among the strikes affecting the railroads which occurred before
the Government took control, the following may be mentioned: July,
1917, Georgia, Alabama, and Florida Railroad (completely tied up).
A strike of the Boston and Maine machinists of September, 1917, was
referred by the Council of National Defense to Henry B. Endicott
of the Massachusetts Committee on Public Safety and adjusted by
him. (See Story of the Massachusetts Committee on Public Safety,
page 107.) The report of the Department of Labor for 1917 gives
details of controversies of freight-handlers of the Chicago and Illinois
Railroad in June, 1917; clerks of the Maine Central Railroad, in
August, 1917, and shopmen on a number of roads.

willing to accept arbitration.[1]   The weak financial condition of the railroads, together with the fact that they had been unable to procure an increase in rates, produced a situation in which it seemed impossible for them to meet labor's demands for wage increases as long as the roads remained under private ownership —that is, without a Government subsidy and without independent power to raise rates.   Therefore on December 28, 1917, in order to prevent the occurrence of strikes on the railroads during the war [2] and to make it possible to use them more efficiently for war-making purposes, all of the important railroads of the country were placed under Federal control.

It will be seen from the above that the situation which confronted the Director General of Railroads was a most difficult one.   In fact at this time so dissatisfied were the railroad shopmen—who, it is worth noting, were receiving 40% less than the men engaged in the same trade in the shipyards [3]—that strike votes were being taken in many of the shops in the Middle West, and a meeting had been called at Kansas City for January 14 to arrange for a concerted strike of the men in the railroad shops.

As a result of all these conditions the Director General, in one of the first general orders issued by the Railroad Administration,[4] created a Railroad Wage Commission charged "with the duty of making a general investigation of the compensation of persons in the railroad service; the relation of railroad wages to wages in other industries," and the special emergency created by war con-

[1] President Wilson, in a statement published by the press on November 23, 1917, said that the men representing the brotherhoods "were not inclined to contend after anything which they did not deem necessary to their own maintenance . . . and that they would be willing, in case any critical situation should arise, to consider any proposed solution in a spirit of accommodation and patriotic purpose."

[2] W. F. Willoughby, Government Organization in War Time and After, page 182: "Undoubtedly one of the prime considerations leading to the taking over of the railroads by the Government was the critical situation that existed in respect to railway labor."

[3] Louis B. ·Wehle, in the *Quarterly Journal of Economics*, Volume XXXII, page 361, states that agreements of May and June, 1917 (on a 30-day cancellation basis), established a general scale of wages for machinists in railroad shops east of Chicago from 50 to 52 cents and west of Chicago of from 52 to 56 cents.   Machinists in the shipyards of equal skill had been awarded 72½ cents an hour, with a basic eight-hour day, and time and one-half for overtime.

[4] General Order Number 5, January 18, 1918.   Annual Report of Director General of Railroads, 1918.

ditions and the greatly increased cost of living. The Commission was to report its findings to the Director General and in the meantime it was arranged that the demands of the shopmen and others be held in abeyance, with the understanding that increases in wages would be retroactive as of January 1, 1918.[1]

The task of the Commission was no less than an investigation of the adequacy of the pay of two million men and women, employed in every part of the country, in an industry in which there existed the greatest variety of wage scales and the most complicated methods for wage fixing. These men and women were working for more than 150 of the largest railroads, and included representatives of almost every trade in the country. The Commission held hearings in Washington, and devoted three and a half months to its investigation, in which it had the help of a corps of statisticians and railroad experts. To "reclassify the many hundreds of employments in which the 2,000,000 railroad workers engage would be a task," the Commission decided, "calling for more time, skill, insight, and knowledge than we possess." They therefore determined upon a flat percentage of increase as the method best adapted to meet the exigencies of the situation. And inasmuch as substantial wage increases had been made since December, 1915, and in view of the additional fact that these advances were uneven, some roads increasing one amount, some another, the Commission decided to base its wage adjustments upon the wages received by employees at that date. It found that from December, 1915, to the date of the report the increased cost of living was from 40 to 43% (depending upon income), and it gave to the lowest paid workers an advance equal to its estimate of the entire increased cost of living. Workers receiving more than $50.00 a month were given advances of smaller and smaller percentage until incomes of $250.00 a month were reached, in which cases no increase whatever was made.[2] In addition the

[1] See report of Railroad Wage Commission, reprinted in *Monthly Review*, U. S. Bureau of Labor Statistics, June, 1918, page 26.

[2] The Commission stated that "the War has brought to us all the necessity for sacrifice." No other wage board applied this doctrine in so drastic a manner. In fact, many of them did not act upon it at all. The Commission was not justified in asking workers, who were receiving wages as low as from $50 to $75 per month, to share in the sacrifices of the war by accepting a wage increase less than the increase in living costs. And yet this part of the report received little adverse comment in the newspapers.

report recommended equal pay for equal work without regard to sex or color, and also that permanent wage tribunals be established.

The Director General accepted the recommendations of the Commission, and put them into effect in General Order Number 27, by which he created a permanent wage board known as the Board of Railroad Wages and Working Conditions. He also made a few changes in the recommendations of the Commission by establishing a minimum of 55 cents an hour for machinists, boiler-makers, and other shop mechanics, and by "recognizing the principle" of the basic eight-hour day for all railroad service.

The report of the Commission caused a great deal of dissatisfaction among railroad employees.[1] In the first place, by making the wages of December, 1915, the basis for wage adjustments the inequalities which existed at that time were perpetuated, and the men—especially the shopmen—lost the benefit of whatever standardization they had, in the meantime, been able to bring about. Moreover the actual increases which the men received under the terms of this award were very much less than what they considered just. In the shop trades, for example, many of the men received nothing at all. This resulted from the fact that the new rate was reached by granting a sliding scale of increases over the 1915 standards, and inasmuch as the men, in many instances, had already received this amount of increase, they did not profit at all from the award. Furthermore, even the 55 cent rate, which the men received under General Order Number 27, was far from the $72\frac{1}{2}$ cent rate being paid to the men in the shipyards and in many of the munition plants. This dissatisfaction of the shopmen found expression in a number of strikes and was not allayed until the rate for first class machinists, and other shopmen, was raised to 68 cents.[2]

In addition to the Board of Railroad Wages and Working Conditions, three other boards were created by the Railroad Administration, by agreement between the Administration and the several unions concerned, known as Boards of Adjustment Numbers

---

[1] On the other hand *The Railroad Trainmen*, the organ of the Brotherhood of Railroad Trainmen, for July, 1918, expressed satisfaction with the award. The opposition to it came more largely from the employees not engaged in the actual operation of the trains.

[2] By Supplement Number 4, to General Order Number 27, issued July 25, 1918.

1, 2, and 3. The first of these superseded the Commission of Eight and had jurisdiction over men connected with the movement of trains, the second dealt with the railway shopmen, while the third was charged with adjustments concerning switchmen, telegraphers, and clerks. The jurisdiction of these boards extended over employees who were working under agreements with their respective railroads. Controversies affecting other employees were looked after by a Labor Director, whose duties included general supervision of all labor matters affecting the Railroad Administration.[1]

All of these wage boards, like the Commission of Eight (created to apply the settlement under the Adamson Law), were composed of equal representations of management and men.[2] In this respect they presented a striking contrast with the Railroad Wage Commission, which was a body whose personnel represented only the public. It is a remarkable fact that the Railroad Wage Adjustment boards, created by the Railroad Administration, were before the armistice never deadlocked—on the contrary, their decisions were always by unanimous vote. Speaking in November, 1919, W. N. Doak, Vice-President of the Brotherhood of Railroad Trainmen and a member of Adjustment Board Number 1, stated that his board had settled 1500 disputes.[3] In all, the three boards settled over 3100 controversies without a dissenting vote.

And yet, in spite of the fact that these were large boards, half of the members of which were railroad officials, and in spite of the fact that their decisions were unanimous, the wage adjustments of the Railroad Administration have been very severely criticized. This adverse comment did not come so much from the men (except the shopmen); they were on the whole fairly well satisfied. The bulk of the criticism came from the employers.[4]

The dissatisfaction sprang largely from the extent to which

[1] W. S. Carter, President of the Brotherhood of Firemen and Enginemen appointed February 9, 1918, by Circular Number 1, creating the Division of Labor of the Railroad Administration.
[2] By this method that constant fear of 'prejudiced arbitrators', so pronounced among railway employees, has been entirely removed." W. S. Carter, *Proceedings of the Academy of Political Science*, for February, 1919, page 66.
[3] See *Proceedings of the Academy of Political Science*, for January, 1920, page 180.
[4] W. G. Besler, President of the Central Railroad of New Jersey, *Proceedings of the Academy of Political Science*, January, 1920, page

the process of standardization was carried—a process for which union labor is everywhere contending but to which the railroads have always been opposed. It is a fact that any arbitral wage adjustment is likely to result in standardization; [1] and when the adjustment of wages is being made for almost every member of a given industry in the entire country, it is impossible to avoid creating certain more or less roughly defined classifications, within which all employees will receive the same remuneration. With thousands of cases to handle, involving hundreds of thousands of men, it was inevitable that more or less minor differences in the character of the work and in the advantages of varying localities should be ignored. This same process of equalization took place to a greater or less extent in every industry in the country. There is, however, a widespread opinion that in the railway service it was carried to an extreme,[2] and this opinion is probably correct.

The extent to which the men in railroad shops and other hitherto unorganized parts of the railway service became members of the unions during the period of the war [3] is also a source of irritation among many of the employers. And yet the policy of the Railway Administration in forbidding discharges for union mem-

170, quotes with approval the following editorial from the New York *Sun:*
"As a matter of cold, hard fact the railroads never underpaid their labor and their labor never tried to pillage the railroads until the Government tried to take out of the hands of the railroads the duties and functions which belonged to the railroads.

"As a matter of cold, hard fact the American railway system never mortgaged its body, life and soul to gratify the exactions while stimulating the excesses of labor union leaders. It was the Government itself, after it took the railroads away from their owners, which did that very thing as a gross political gamble." Mr. Besler goes on to characterize the actions of the Railroad Administration as "blundering, bungling incapacity in high places" and he speaks of the "bungling of the wage demands which, because of failure to comprehend the question, resulted in absurd readjustments and the granting of schedules of wages for certain classes without due regard to the character of the service performed, thus establishing inappropriate and extravagant measures of compensation that caused discontent in other classes."

[1] "American arbitration boards (before the war) have been practically unanimous in their approval of the principal of system standardization . . . the boards evidently recognizing the disadvantages attending a wide diversity of rates." J. Noble Stockett, op. cit., page 8.

[2] See William J. Cunningham in the New York *Evening Post*, January 13, 1920.

[3] It is claimed that one million men in the railway service joined labor unions during this period.

bership was identical with that adopted by every war board, and is surely not open to legitimate criticism. Nor can it be said that the total wage increases, large as they were in the aggregate, were more than the circumstances warranted.[1] On the contrary, there were many occupations in which the wage increases, in spite of the scarcity of labor, did not keep pace with the cost of living, nor has the average advance been equal to the increased living cost.[2]

By the methods outlined above, peace was maintained in the operation of the trains during the war period, and there were very few strikes in other branches of the service. In fact it was not until August, 1919, that any very serious stoppage of work took place. Early in that month a strike of the railroad shopmen, unauthorized by the national leaders, occurred in the Middle Western states, spreading to different parts of the country, especially to New England and the South.

This controversy had its roots in the dissatisfaction of the shopmen with the treatment accorded them during the war. We have already discussed the resentment with which they received the award of the Railroad Wage Commission. And although the award of 68 cents an hour which they obtained in July, 1918, partially satisfied them, it did not do so entirely as the increase did not bring their wages up to the standard enjoyed in other industries. But their chief resentment arose from the fact that during the following year, although further increases had been awarded in other industries,[3] their wages remained stationary. In January, 1919, their demands had been referred to the Board of Wages and Working Conditions and hearings had been held, but

[1] G. H. Sines, *Proceedings of the Academy of Political Science,* February, 1919, page 96, enumerates these increases as follows: During 1916 and 1917 the railroads, under private control, had granted increases amounting to about $300,000,000. The award of the Railroad Wage Commission added $300,000,000 more, which was increased another $250,000,000 by supplemental wage orders issued up to the end of 1918. Since then further wage increases have been granted.
[2] G. H. Sines, op. cit., page 98 (speaking in December, 1918): "The average increase in wages will be less than fifty per cent while the increase in living costs is over seventy-five per cent."
[3] Thus, in the shipyards, machinists who were receiving 72½ cents per hour in July, 1918, at the time when the machinists in the railroads were awarded 68 cents, were awarded 80 cents in October, 1918. Navy Yards and Arsenals followed the Shipping Board and many other Government and private plants made wage increases; but the wages of the railroad shopmen remained unchanged.

it was not until July that the board made its report to the Director General. The report showed that the board, which during the war had always been able to reach unanimous decisions, was, now that the pressure of war was released, deadlocked— the three labor representatives recommending an increase to 80 cents an hour, the shipyard rates; the three members representing the management being against this proposal, though favoring a wage readjustment.

Instead of acting one way or the other on this report of the board, Director General Hines, in a letter to the President dated July 30, recommended the creation by Congress of a new commission to consider and pass upon wages in the railway service. The men, who had been waiting since January for a decision on their demands, were bitterly disappointed, and on the following day many of them went out. The national leaders, who had not authorized the strike, urged the men to return to work, and ordered that a strike vote be taken. Nevertheless the walkout continued to spread, and as a result the Director General announced on August 7 that power had been given him by the President to settle the controversy directly with the officers of the men, provided that in the meantime the workers returned to the shops. Even then a great many of the men continued out. Gradually, however, they resumed work, and a conference took place at the White House between the President, the Director General, and the representatives of the men. An offer of a wage increase of four cents an hour, retroactive to May 1, was made and the national leaders decided to submit it to the men, who, by a referendum vote, reluctantly accepted it.[1] It was at the time of this conference that the President made his appeal to the men of the railroads, as well as to all of the other workingmen of the country, to hold in abeyance any demands for wage increases until normal conditions had been restored and until the Government had had an opportunity of prosecuting its campaign for a reduction in the cost of living, which the President said was already showing signs of success.

The feeling of unrest which resulted in the actions of the shopmen found additional expression in another unauthorized strike —this time by the trainmen of California. The trouble started on

[1] The men had demanded an increase of 17 cents an hour, retroactive to January 1, 1919.

August 19, 1919, at Los Angeles, when, in sympathy with the striking employees of the Pacific Electric Railroad and in violation of their agreement with the U. S. Railroad Administration, the trainmen went out. The strike spread quickly from California to Arizona and Nevada in spite of the most explicit orders of the national leaders to the contrary, which was remarkable in so well disciplined organizations as the railroad brotherhoods. (The men claimed that they went out as individuals.) An ultimatum of the Director General [1] backed up the Federal and State Governments and the orders of the officers of the brotherhoods, resulted in a return of the men to work; not, however, until eleven days after the inception of the strike.[2]

During all this time the railroad brotherhoods were urging that the men engaged in the movement of trains be compensated for overtime in the same manner as were the other men in the railroad service and generally in industry; that is to say, by the payment of time and one-half for overtime. As we have seen, the enactment of the Adamson Law, giving the men the eight-hour day, did not carry with it any extra compensation for overtime; nor was this granted by any of the decisions of the Boards thereafter created. In November, 1919, the Director General suggested to the brotherhoods that the men in the freight service receive time and one-half for overtime and that they relinquish certain special allowances which they had for a number of years been receiving. The matter was put to a vote by the brotherhoods and accepted by three of the four. Under their rules it was, therefore, adopted by all of them and on December 15, 1919, the Director General issued an order [3] calling for time and one-half for overtime for the

---

[1] See New York *Times* for August 28, 1919, in which the ultimatum is reprinted in full.

[2] The dissatisfaction of the men with conditions that prevailed after the armistice, the failure of the Government to reduce the cost of living and resentment caused by the delay in the appointment of the Wage Board provided for in the Bill under which the railroads were restored to their private owners, resulted in another unauthorized strike. The firemen, switchmen, yardmen, etc., in many sections of the country went out against the wishes of their national officers and a strike of momentous importance resulted. The freight service was for many months demoralized and an "outlaw" organization has developed which has seriously affected the compactness of the railway unions.

[3] Supplement No. 24 to General Order No. 27, December 15, 1919. Article VII provides that "(a) . . . 100 miles or less, 8 hours or less

freight service and that all "arbitraries" and special allowances applying to freight service, excepting payments for delays at initial and final terminals, be eliminated. The same order provided that yard service was to be paid for at one and one-half times the regular rates and that arbitraries and special allowances be similarly abolished. For the express service also time and one-half for overtime was granted to all the employees who worked the full number of hours per week.[1]

FUEL ADMINISTRATION

One of the causes of anxiety throughout the entire war period was a threatened shortage of coal. Not that the facilities for fuel production were lacking. On the contrary, years of intense competition in the coal mining industry had resulted in the opening up of an unnecessarily large number of mines, especially in the bituminous fields, and the industry had been conducted in a wasteful and almost reckless manner. But bituminous mining also suffered from the tremendous handicap that the coal could not be stored for any length of time at the mines and in large quantities without deterioration. This meant that it had to be shipped as soon as mined. Production was therefore limited at any particular place by the supply of coal cars available at that place.[2] The consumption of coal had in recent years, been rapidly increasing[3] and during the war itself there was a large additional increase due to the tremendous industrial activity which war-making involved. This increase, together with the

. . . shall constitute a days work; miles in excess of 100 will be paid for at the mileage rates provided. . . . (b) On runs of 100 miles or less overtime will begin at the expiration of 8 hours; on runs of over 100 miles overtime will begin when the time on duty exceeds the miles run divided by 12½. Overtime shall be paid for on the minute basis at an hourly rate of three-sixteenths of the daily rate."

[1] By Amendment No. 1 to Supplement No. 19 to General Order No. 27, November 22, 1919. (Employees in the train messenger service were excluded from the operation of the order.)

[2] At a critical time, during the war (December, 1917) the allotment of cars fell as low as 11, 10 and even 7% of normal. See Harry A. Garfield, U. S. Fuel Administrator, in *Proceedings of the Academy of Political Science*, February, 1918, p. 52.

[3] In 1897 the annual production of coal was 200 million net tons. By 1917 it had risen to 630 million tons (of which only 5 to 8% was for export). *Ibid*, p. 51.

shortage of cars and general railroad congestion, brought the nation to a point where a coal famine seemed imminent.

In May, 1917, the Council of National Defense endeavored to meet the situation by the appointment of a Committee on Coal Production. It was soon realized, however, that the powers of the Council were not sufficiently broad to enable it to deal successfully with the difficult problems involved and on August 10, 1917, Congress enacted the famous Lever Act "to provide further for the national security and defense by encouraging the production, conserving the supply and controlling the distribution of food products and fuel." Drastic and far-reaching powers were given to the President under this Act. He could fix prices, take over and operate plants and completely control production, distribution and consumption. In order to administer these powers in relation to fuel, the President on August 23, 1917, by executive order, created the United States Fuel Administration and appointed Harry A. Garfield Fuel Administrator.

In the meantime, serious labor difficulties were threatening in the coal industry as they were in so many other places. In following these occurrences it will be necessary to distinguish between the anthracite and the bituminous industries because their labor histories both before and during the war were quite different. In the bituminous field collective bargaining had been highly developed for a considerable period before the war. Since 1898 the wages of coal miners in the Central Competitive field [1] had been fixed at annual or bi-annual conferences between miners and operators; the result of these conferences was embodied in agreements expiring on April 1 of each year, or of alternate years.[2] In the anthracite field collective bargaining came somewhat later and in a different form. In 1902 the United Mine Workers of America sought a conference with the anthracite operators but were refused. A long and bitterly fought strike followed which led to intervention by President Roosevelt and the appointment by him of the Anthracite Coal Commission. The award of the Commission was embodied in a three-year agreement under which a Board

[1] Indiana, Illinois, Ohio and Western Pennsylvania.
[2] In other parts of the bituminous industry the organization of wage adjustments proceeded much more slowly. The reader is referred, for a detailed account of labor adjustments in the coal industry, to A. E. Suffern, Conciliation and Arbitration in the Coal Industry of America.

of Conciliation was established. This has been renewed from time to time, frequently after the occurrence of a strike, the last renewal before the war having been made in 1916, to run for four years.

Before the appointment of the Fuel Administrator, the Secretary of Labor (a former secretary of the United Mine Workers of America) had been instrumental in averting a number of strikes which, had they occurred, would have seriously interfered with the supply of fuel. Thus in May, 1917, the miners and operators of the Central Pennsylvania districts were unable to agree as to wages and a strike appeared imminent. The Secretary of Labor thereupon conferred in Washington with representatives of both sides and an agreement was reached which was subsequently ratified by the Miners' Convention. In Alabama, in the month of August, 1917, differences between the mine owners and their men had gone so far that a strike order had been issued. In this case the difficulty was intensified by the fact that the operators were unwilling to meet with a committee representing their employees. The Secretary of Labor once more intervened and after a number of conferences, which had to be held separately with each side, succeeded in averting the strike.[1]

At the time that the Fuel Administration was being organized, the operators and miners of the Central Competitive fields were meeting at Indianapolis to consider wage increases. The Fuel Administrator requested that this meeting be adjourned until his office was better organized and until he had time to formulate a policy. In September, at the request of the Administrator, a joint conference was held at Washington. This resulted in the agreement of October 6, 1917, known as the Washington agreement, the terms of which were embodied in contracts by which disputes in other territories were subsequently settled. An important clause of these settlements, especially in the light of post-armistice occurrences, provided for their continuance for the period of the war, but not to exceed two years from April 1, 1918.

The wage increases called for in the Washington agreement were made conditional upon an increase to the coal operators in the selling price of coal, sufficient to cover the increased cost, and on October 27, 1917, the President issued an order making such increase. The Administrator had appointed as advisors on labor

[1] *Annual Report*, Secretary of Labor, 1917, page 13.

matters Mr. Rembrandt Peale, a representative of the operators, and Mr. John P. White, President of the United Mine Workers of America. On July 23, 1918, the Fuel Administrator announced an understanding with the United Mine Workers, setting forth in detail the labor policies [1] which were to govern the Administration for the war period and establishing a bureau of labor with Messrs. Peale and White as joint heads.[2]

Although the joint agreement in the anthracite field did not by its terms expire until 1920, an allowance had been made by the operators in May, 1917, to meet the higher wages which were being paid in other industries. In December, 1917, a supplemental contract was entered into, similar to the Washington agreement, giving the anthracite miners a further wage increase, and toward the end of the war both anthracite and bituminous miners sought additional wage increases at the hands of the Fuel Administration. The miners claimed that the cost of living had advanced in so unprecedented a fashion that more pay had become absolutely essential. The operators themselves realized that, because of the higher wages paid in other industries, the pay of the miners would have to be increased, if the men were to be prevented from drifting away from the mines.[3] Largely on this account, in October, 1918, the anthracite miners were awarded an advance of approximately $1 per day; in the bituminous fields, however, where the competition with other industries was not so keenly felt, no increase was granted, although Mr. Garfield's labor advisors, both the representative of the operators as well as the representative of the men, recommended that such increase be made.

The refusal of the administration to grant to the bituminous workers an advance similar to the one which had been obtained by the men in the anthracite fields led to a great deal of bitter-

---

[1] See *Monthly Labor Review,* Bureau of Labor Statistics, U. S. Dept. of Labor, September, 1918.

[2] Warren Pippen, an officer of the Miners' Union, succeeded to the position held by Mr. White in the Labor Bureau.

[3] It was stated before the Conference Committee of National Labor Adjustment Agencies that, whereas there were 180,000 men normally employed in the anthracite fields, this number had dropped to 144,000. It was urged that any further depletion would be a matter of very grave concern. Contract miners (one of the two classes into which men at the mines are divided) had not only to be skilled men but were working under a state certificate which required two years experience in the mines to qualify the worker.

ness, and when the cost of living kept on increasing after the armistice had been signed, the men became more and more insistent that their wages be increased. It will be remembered that the agreement for the Central Competitive fields was to continue for the duration of the war but not later than April, 1920. The men claimed, in the fall of 1919, that the war had come to an end and that the agreement was, therefore, not operative. A convention of the miners was held which adopted a series of demands, among other things for a 60% increase in wages,[1] a six-hour day, a five-day week, and the abolition of all penalty clauses. These demands were rejected by the operators and it was every day becoming more apparent that unless something were immediately done, a strike could not be averted. The Government had permitted the Fuel Administration to disband, and although it had been perfectly apparent for months before matters reached a crisis that conditions in the coal industry needed radical readjustment, things were allowed to drift until it was too late to effectively correct them. On October 16, 1919, in an effort to avert the impending strike, Secretary Wilson brought about a conference in Washington between the representatives of both sides. At this time a strike order for November 1 had already been issued and the operators refused to enter into negotiations for a new schedule until the order was rescinded. The representatives of the miners, on the other hand, said they had no power to call off the strike and the conference broke up without having accomplished anything. The feeling of the men was very much embittered by the statement which the President issued October 20, 1919, in which he referred to the proposed action of the miners as an abrogation of their agreement and said that the strike was not only unjustifiable but unlawful. Referring to the efforts of the Administration to reduce the cost of living he sought to persuade the miners to remain at work. But the President himself had long before said that the war had come to an end and the miners felt that an effort was being made, because of the *technical* continuance of the war, to hold them to a contract which so far as the intention of the parties to it was concerned had expired and

[1] See C. F. Stoddard in *Monthly Labor Review*, U. S. Bureau of Labor Statistics, December, 1919, page 61. See note at page 182 of this book for an explanation of the miners' demand for the 30-hour week.

which was no longer a fair contract. The President was entirely unsuccessful in his appeal to the men and when it appeared that nothing further could be done to prevent the occurrence of the strike, the Attorney General, at the request of the President, procured from a Federal Judge at Indianapolis an order restraining the union officials and all other persons from taking steps to put the strike order into effect. This injunction not only deprived the strikers of any assistance from their national and local officers but the funds of the unions were tied up so as to prevent the payment of strike benefits, which the union had counted upon to prevent suffering among the strikers. The injunction, however, absolutely failed to prevent the men from going out and the strike which followed resulted in a tie-up of the greater part of the bituminous fields and involved more than 400,000 miners. A week later, Federal Judge Anderson, who had issued the original restraining order, granted a temporary injunction, including therein a most unusual provision—a direction to the officials of the miners that the strike orders be withdrawn. On November 11 the miners' officials obeyed the mandate of the court and recalled the strike order. But the Government was now to learn that the recalling of a strike order was not, under these circumstances, equivalent to the settlement of a strike. The men paid no attention to the action of their leaders and continued their refusal to work.

Conferences were now resumed between the operators and the miners in which the Government took part. The Secretary of Labor felt that the miners were entitled to an increase of 31%; Mr. Garfield, whom the President on October 30[1] had asked to resume his duties as Fuel Administrator, did not think that so large an increase was warranted. He favored the granting of 14% (which he claimed could be paid by the operators without increasing the cost of coal to the consumer). But the men were absolutely unwilling to accept so small an increase and after additional conferences, the President, going over the Fuel Administrator's head, offered to the men a reference of the issues in controversy to a commission with broad powers if they would return to work on an immediate increase of 14%; the question of further increases to be determined by the commission.[2] This

[1] One of Mr. Garfield's first acts on his resumption of the duties of Fuel Administrator was to restore war time regulation of coal prices.
[2] The Commission, consisting of Messrs. Peale and White, Mr. Gar-

offer was accepted by the men who had remained out on strike all this time, and work was resumed.

An examination of the labor policies of the Fuel Administration will show that, in the main, they were the same as those applied by other agencies. The most important difference was the adoption of the so-called penalty clause. In order to avoid stoppages of work at the mines, the Fuel Administrator insisted that in every agreement made between operators and men it be provided that, if the men should strike without bringing their grievances to the Fuel Administrator for settlement, each man be fined $1 a day; the fine to be collected automatically by the employer and paid over by him to the Red Cross. A lockout by the employer would be similarly punished by a fine of $1 per day for every worker affected. A great deal of difficulty was experienced in inducing the workers to accept this penalty clause but the Fuel Administrator insisted upon its acceptance and wage increases were made dependent upon its adoption. This resulted, in the fall of 1917, in a strike in the Kansas field, caused by the refusal of Mr. Garfield to sanction an agreement which gave the men an increase but which did not contain the penalty clause. President Howatt, of the Kansas miners, who had at first refused to agree to the penalty, finally ordered the men to return to work and, after protracted negotiations, the penalty clause was accepted.

The eight-hour day, which prevailed in the mines before our entry into the war, was not the basic eight-hour day obtaining in most industries, but an actual one; that is to say, no work was done after the expiration of the eight hours. And it is claimed by labor representatives that this policy was most successful and that a greater amount of work was done by a smaller number of miners than ever before in the country's history.

field's former labor advisors, and Mr. Henry M. Robinson was unable to come to a unanimous decision. The chairman and the representative of the employers united in an award which gave the men an average wage increase of 27%. They found that, from 1913, tonnage wages had advanced on the average 48% for machine and 35% for pick workers whereas for day men, the increase had been 76%. Their award was a 31% increase for tonnage, and a 20% increase for day men. These advances are both in excess of the rise in the cost of living and brought the increase since 1913 in the wages of tonnage workers to 88% and of day workers to 111%. The commission refused to make any change in the eight-hour day. For majority and minority reports see Awards and Recommendations of U. S. Bituminous Coal Commission, 1920.

In July, 1918, at the time of the organization of the Bureau of Labor of the Fuel Administration, Mr. Garfield announced the text of an understanding which he had reached with the Secretary of Labor and with the United Mine Workers of America.[1] The principles contained in this statement are consistent with those enforced by other war labor agencies. The election of mine committees was encouraged and it was provided that in the first instance disputes should be referred by such committees to mine officials; if they could not be adjusted in this way, they were to be referred to an umpire[2] with right of appeal to the Administrator.

Convinced that the payment of bonuses disturbed wage conditions and caused shifting of men from mine to mine, a determined effort was made by the Fuel Administrator to abolish these payments and Mr. Garfield went so far as to declare that in any case where the operator paid a bonus, this would be considered an admission that such operator did not need the increase in selling price which had been allowed by the Fuel Administration, and the operator would be compelled to sell fuel at the old price. It would have seemed that, armed with the absolute right to control prices, it would have been comparatively easy for the Administrator to have insisted upon the abolition of bonuses; such,

[1] The text of this understanding is given in the *Monthly Labor Review*, U. S. Bureau of Labor Statistics, for September, 1918, and can be summarized as follows:
  (a) No strike pending settlement of controversies until dispute has been reviewed and decided by Fuel Administrator.
  (b) Recognition of union not to be exacted where union was not then organized, but if fields are already organized, any future adjustment shall recognize the United Mine Workers of America.
  (c) No recourse to be had to Fuel Administration until other methods of mediation, provided for in agreements, were exhausted.
  (d) No discharge because of affiliation with union.
  (e) No change from open to closed shop or vice versa during the war.
  (f) The provisions of the Maryland and Potomac agreement were held applicable in any cases in which the Fuel Administration intervened. This agreement provided for mine committees and their protection against discharge, for the appointment of check weigh men, semi-monthly pay days, and the right of peaceful assemblage.
[2] Prof. Jacob Hollander was appointed umpire for the Maryland and upper Potomac district.

however, was not the case and the desire of certain operators to make these extra payments was so strong that the Administrator found it impossible to prevent them. As the labor shortage increased, and it became more difficult to keep the men, the tendency of the operators to increase rates by premiums and bonuses became more pronounced and resulted in an appeal by the operators' association to Washington to put a stop to this practice. The employers realized that to prevent the men from going into other industries a further wage increase was necessary and they are said to have encouraged the miners in the fall of 1918 to ask for a wage increase.

In the mines, as elsewhere, immunity from discharge for union affiliation resulted in a large increase in the membership of the unions and it is stated that locals were established during the war in fields which had, until then, successfully resisted the efforts of the organizer.[1]

The war experience and the crisis that succeeded the armistice have brought into prominence the chaotic conditions that surrounded the bituminous mining industry. In spite of the obvious dependence of the United States upon an abundant supply of coal at a fair price, the Government has consistently failed to take any action that would remedy the outstanding evils surrounding coal production. The first of these is tendency to overproduction of coal and the second our failure to devise a method of keeping the mines going six days a week. It appears from the records of the United States Geological Survey that from 1910 to 1918 the number of days worked by the miners ranged from 195 to 214. Since the armistice and through October, 1919, only $62\frac{1}{2}\%$ of full time capacity was employed, and a week's work consisted on an average of thirty hours.[2] If we are to successfully meet the nation's industrial problems. wasteful conditions of this kind will have to be eliminated.

[1] James Lord, President of the Mining Department of the A. F. of L. in the *Report of the Executive Council,* to the 39th Annual Convention, June, 1919, page 143, says "The United Mine Workers of America have made a gain of 447 local unions and the average paid up membership is 406,089. . . . The organization has been extended into fields hitherto considered impregnable, local unions having been established in the Fairmont field of West Virginia, the Georges Creek field of Maryland, Eastern Kentucky, Nova Scotia and Utah."
[2] These figures are quoted by W. L. Chenery in the *Survey* of November 22, 1919, page 152.

FOOD ADMINISTRATION

The Food Administration organized its own labor bureau,[1] but did not directly handle the mediation of industrial disputes. These were referred to the Labor Department. Although the Federal Food Administrators of California and Massachusetts occasionally acted as mediators, such action on their part was not directly a function of the Food Administration.

Perhaps the most acute situation which confronted the Administration was a strike in August, 1917, in the canning industry of the San Jose district of California, led by a newly formed organization known as "The Toilers of the World."[2] Rioting took place, resulting in one death and in a number of injuries, and troops were called out. The Governor of California appointed Mr. Harris Weinstock, State Market Director (a former member of the United States Industrial Commission), to represent the State of California, and Mr. Ralph B. Merritt, Federal Food Administrator, was asked to act on behalf of the Federal Government.

The two mediators stipulated that troops should be withdrawn and that all municipal, state and federal authority should be vested in them. These conditions were complied with and the mediators held conferences with the parties in interest. They requested the workers to clear the streets, and this having been done, meetings were held and, upon the assurance that their wage demands would be investigated and considered, the strikers returned to work. Within a few days uniform wage scales were established, with the acquiescence of both sides, and the canning industry proceeded without further interruption.

Mr. Merritt was also appointed to act as mediator in additional disputes involving food production—fishermen, employees of milk distributors and others. In 1919 the operators in canneries and dried fruit plants petitioned the Governor to appoint a representa-

[1] Prof. M. B. Hammond, of the Ohio State University, was labor director and representative of the Food Administration on the War Labor Policies Board.

[2] In spite of the similarity of names the "Toilers of the World" do not seem to have been connected with the I. W. W. and made application for affiliation with the American Federation of Labor; it did not, however, become affiliated with that body. It appears from evidence at the Chicago trial of members of the I. W. W. that the strike was in part at least, due to that organization.

tive who should establish the wage to be paid to employees in canneries and dried fruit plants in the state. Mr. Merritt served in this capacity and, after conferences with the parties involved, rendered decisions which were posted in every cannery of the state and which proved satisfactory to both sides.

Before the appointment of the Food Administration and in the first days of the war, quite a serious strike occurred among the Gloucester and Boston fishermen which was settled through the activities of the Labor Department.[1]

Strikes in the packing industry were handled either by state mediators or, as we have seen in previous chapters, by the President's Mediation Commission, or its representatives.

[1] See Fifth Annual Report, Secretary of Labor, page 26.

CHAPTER IX

Telegraph and Telephone

IN order to understand the situation which developed in these industries during the war a brief explanation of pre-war conditions will be necessary. In making this explanation we must bear in mind that we are dealing with two separate industries—easily confused because of similarity of name and function.

The telegraph industry has, for many years, been in the absolute control of two large national companies, the Western Union and the Postal Telegraph. These corporations are competitive, but both have adopted similar labor policies as well as the policy of central rather than diffused organization. The Western Union Company, by far the larger of the two, has always taken an attitude of open opposition to the membership of any of its "essential employees, especially those working the wires," in any labor unions which would subject them to "a strike order either for their own benefit or sympathetically for the benefit of others." [1]

As contrasted with the telegraph, the telephone industries were not so centrally organized. The dominant corporation in this field is the American Telephone and Telegraph Company (the name is a misnomer, inasmuch as the company's business is confined to the operation of Bell *telephone* systems). In some districts there are independent competing companies, all of which, however, operate in restricted territories. The A. T. & T. Company had resulted from the amalgamation of a number of local companies, most of which have been retained as separate corporations. The stock of these companies is to a varying extent held by the parent company, but the separate companies each keep their own individual organization, and to a large degree determine their own labor policies. [2]

[1] Statement of "The Company's Position" issued by the Western Union Telegraph Company, 1918.
[2] Annual Report of the A. T. & T. Company for 1918, page 4: "There are in the United States approximately 11,000 separate tele-

106

Unlike the telegraph companies, most of whose employees are skilled, telephone work is largely done by girls of little skill. Some of the local companies, affiliated with the Bell System, dealt collectively with labor organizations but many of them have, like the telegraph companies, been hostile to unions and have discriminated against their members.

In pursuance of its long-established policy, the Western Union Telegraph Company made it a practice to discharge any of its employees who joined the Commercial Telegraphers' Union of America (which was affiliated with the American Federation of Labor). As might have been expected, however, upon the announcement of the principles of the Taft-Walsh Board, permitting employees to join trade unions of their choice without interference by the employer, redoubled efforts were made by the union to extend its membership among Western Union employees. One hundred and forty men responded to the union's call; attended an organization meeting, joined the union and were thereupon promptly discharged.[1] This led to complaints to the National War Labor Board, and an endeavor by the joint chairmen to adjust the grievances of the discharged men. A compromise was suggested to the company, which would have permitted the men to join the union, but with an agreement not to strike during the period of the war, and to leave all grievances to the adjustment of the board. The company rejected this offer, insisting upon its right

phone companies. Of them 36 are Bell companies, 9,338 independent companies whose telephone systems connect with the Bell System, and about 1,600 independent companies whose telephone systems do not connect with the Bell System. There are also a large number of rural lines and systems which connect with the telephone systems of these companies, 26,055 of which are connected with the Bell System."

[1] This is the figure given by the Western Union Company; the union states that a very much larger number of men were discharged. It is interesting to note that this meeting took place in Seattle, where as we have seen labor was especially well organized and radical in temper. The incident led to the introduction of several resolutions in the Minneapolis convention of the American Federation of Labor in June, 1918. The one adopted called upon the President and Congress immediately to take over the wires. One of the resolutions that was proposed by the representative of the Central Labor Council of Seattle, contained language which amounted to the suggestion of a general strike. This feature of the resolution was opposed on the floor of the convention and the resolution was defeated. See *Proceedings* Convention American Federation of Labor, June, 1918, p. 204.

to discharge men for union affiliation.[1] This led on June 11, 1918, to a letter from the President of the United States to both the Western Union and Postal Telegraph Companies in which the President stated that "It is imperatively necessary in the national interest that decisions of the National War Labor Board should be accepted by both parties to labor disputes," and asked for the coöperation of the companies and their acquiescence in the Government's labor policies. The Postal Telegraph was willing to accede to the President's request, but the Western Union remained obdurate. Thereupon the Government took over the wires of both companies,[2] and their administration was placed in the hands of the Post Office Department.

The hostile attitude of the Post Office Department toward labor unions—and especially of its chief, Mr. Burleson—was well known, and had been clearly stated by him in his report for 1917.[3] For this reason the action of the Government in placing the telegraph wires under the control of the Postmaster General was much more welcome to the employers than it was to the workers.

Simultaneously with the Government's taking over of the telegraph wires, control was also taken of the telephone system of the country. In order to handle the problems of management, the Post Office Department vested this function in a Wire Control Board, consisting of three Government officials.[4] The late Mr.

[1] See discussion of worker's right to organize into trade unions in Chapter XIII, where statement of the President of the Western Union Telegraph Company, on this point, is quoted.

[2] The President was authorized to do so by joint resolution of Congress, approved July 16, 1918.

[3] On page 33 of this report Mr. Burleson says: "The advisability of permitting Government employees to affiliate with an outside organization and use the strike and boycott as a last resort to enforce their demands is seriously questioned by those interested in the public welfare. Postal employees have become bold because of this affiliation and have within recent years threatened to strike, and in one case actually did so by tendering their resignations and leaving the service in a body. In this case they were promptly indicted and prosecuted in the Federal Courts. While strikes in the Postal Service may be averted for the time being, yet they will inevitably come, and the public will then be brought face to face with a most serious situation —one which will be a menace to our Government. . . . The conduct of these organizations at this time is incompatible with the principles of civil service and with good administration of the Postal Service."

[4] John C. Koons, First Assistant Postmaster General; D. J. Lewis, U. S. Tariff Commission; W. H. Lamar, Solicitor of the Post Office Department.

T. N. Vail, President of the A. T. and T. Company, was appointed advisor to the Wire Control Board. There was also appointed an Operating Board, consisting of four telephone and telegraph officials.[1]

When we come to examine the Post Office Department's labor policy, as distinguished from its methods of management, we will find the greatest confusion. The most vital question—that is, the location of authority to deal with labor disputes and to adjust wages and working conditions, was not settled until many months later. In the meantime the actions of the department were inconsistent in the extreme, and if a deliberate attempt had been made to evade the issues, what actually took place would not have been markedly different.

The first step of the department was on the surface an excellent one. It appointed a committee "to investigate the working conditions and wages paid to employees of the telegraph and telephone companies." [2] But the fact is that this committee [3] almost completely failed to function. According to its name, it might have been a board like the Railroad Wage Commission. This board, it will be remembered, made a thorough investigation of wages and working conditions, and subsequent Railroad Adjustment boards were based upon its report. In sharp contrast to this, the wage committee for the telephone and telegraph industries was never given either the funds or the authority to make a similar investigation, and it seems to have accomplished nothing whatsoever.

Although it had no authority to adjust grievances, and although it had no connection with the Wire Control Board, in which this authority was afterwards discovered to be located, a number of

[1] U. N. Bethel (Chairman), Vice President of the A. T. and T. Company; F. A. Stevenson, of the Bell System; C. M. Yorks, of the Western Union Telegraph Company; A. F. Adams, representing independent telephone companies.
[2] Order Number 2005, September 13, 1918.
[3] The Chairman was an official of the Post Office Department; of its other members two represented the employers, one the Labor Department, and one the employees, e. g.—W. S. Ryan, Assistant Superintendent Division of Post Office Service; U. N. Bethal, Vice President of the A. T. and T. Co., and F. B. MacKinnon of the Independent Telephone Association; John B. Colpoys, Special Agent of the Department of Labor; and Miss Julia S. O'Connor, President of the Telephone Operators Department of the International Brotherhood of Electrical Workers.

wage complaints were nevertheless sent to the committee. In June, 1919, almost a year after the assumption of Government control, an order was issued by the Postmaster General directing each telephone company to designate an officer to whom such complaints might be presented. But nothing was said as to the authority of local companies to make adjustments, nor what was to become of.controversies, if the action of the local companies was unsatisfactory to the workers. To make the confusion worse, many of these local officials refused to undertake the adjustment of serious grievances, claiming that they had no authority to do so.

At a later date the Postmaster General stated [1] that the operating officials had been instructed to receive committees of their own employees and to transmit recommendations as to wages and conditions to the Wire Control Board for final review and action. This procedure had certainly not been clearly established nor were the previous actions of the Department consistent with it. But in any event the statement is remarkable in that it completely ignored the Wage Committee. Moreover, the Wire Control Board, in which authority for wage adjustments was thus apparently placed, consisted of Mr. Burleson's first assistant, the Solicitor of the Post Office Department, and a third representative of the Government, with the President of the A. T. and T. Company an official adviser, and no representative whatever of labor —nor was labor represented, for that matter, on the Operating Board, closely associated with the Wire Control Board, all four of which were officials of the telegraph and telephone companies.

Under all these circumstances it is not strange that a condition of unrest and dissatisfaction should have prevailed. The workers had hoped that Government control would result in the removal of grievances; instead, its only effect was that company officials who had been fighting the demands of the men were thereby changed into officers of the Government whose wishes it was just that much harder for the workers to oppose. The policy of discriminating against members and officers of the union was, the employees claimed, more vigorously pursued under Government

[1] In a letter to the Secretary of Labor, in answer to criticism on his labor policies and administration contained in a report by Felix Frankfurter.

than under private control; [1] this in spite of the fact that on August 15, 1918, the Postmaster General had issued an order forbidding discharges solely because of union affiliation.

As to the telegraph industry, it will be remembered that it was the Western Union Company's persistence in discriminatory discharges in spite of the Government's policy to the contrary which led to the taking over of the wires. The action of the Post Office Department in not preventing the continuance of this practice was therefore particularly irritating.[2] The exasperation of the workers was further increased by the manner in which the Post Office Department handled a wage increase that the Western Union Company had, just prior to the assumption of Government control, agreed to. This increase was to be of 5, 10 and 15%, depending on seniority and retroactive from August 1, 1918. After the Government had taken over the wires, a demand for this increase was presented to the Wage Committee, which held hearings and recommended its adoption. The Post Office Department, however, did not accept this recommendation, but reduced the maximum increase to 10%, and later the entire wage advance from January 1, 1919, instead of from August 1, 1918.

During the entire period of Government control there was the greatest dissatisfaction on the part of the Commercial Telegraphers' Union with the actions of the Post Office Department. The union was vigorously attempting to extend its membership among the employees of the two telegraph companies, and was incensed at the persistence with which, it claimed, discharges for union affiliation continued to be made. Finally, as the time approached for the return of the wires to their private owners a strike was called on June 11, 1919. The men's demands included an increase of wages, collective bargaining, and the right to join the union, together with reinstatement of the men who had been discharged on this account.

The strike affected both companies, in fact the Postal Telegraph more severely than the Western Union. In some sections of the country, especially in the South, the service was for a time badly crippled. In most places, however, very few of the

---

[1] The Western Union Telegraph Company had, as we have seen, relentlessly followed this practice. Many of the telephone companies did the same.

[2] In the meantime, the Company was fostering the growth of a company union.

men went out, and in a short time the union, completely beaten, was compelled to call the strike off. This was one of the very few cases in which the employer's boast that their men would not go out on strike proved to be well founded.[1]

Returning now to the telephone industry, here too the claim of discriminatory discharges was a cause of unrest and in some cases of strikes. Such a discharge resulted in a strike of telephone operators at Wichita, Kansas. At St. Paul and Minneapolis the inability of the workers to secure a wage increase resulted in a walk-out. Without passing on the merits of these controversies, the outstanding fact is that the Post Office Department had failed to provide any adequate machinery for determining the justice of the workers' claims. In both strikes, however, the Department was successful—that is to say, it was able to dictate the terms upon which work was to be resumed.

But this was not to be the case in a very much larger strike of the New England telephone operators; and so unpopular had Mr. Burleson become with all classes of the community that the defeat which he suffered in this case was a matter of almost universal satisfaction.

The New England Telephone Company operates the Bell System in Massachusetts, New Hampshire, Vermont and Maine. Some years before the war it had agreed with the telephone girls' union—the Telephone Operators' Department of the International Brotherhood of Electrical Workers—upon the organization of a board of labor adjustment with equal representation of the company and the employees. Up to the time of the taking over of the telephone wires by the Government this board had had a useful career and seems to have functioned very well indeed.[2]

The agreement under which the board was constituted expired

[1] See discussion of this position, so frequently taken by employers, in the first section of Chapter XVI.

[2] In describing its work, a circular issued by the union states that: "Although established primarily as machinery for adjusting individual and personal grievances, it became the medium of all relations between the company and the operating force. . . . It has reduced the working day one and one-quarter to two hours. Requirements for promotions, selections of hours, seniority rights, transfers, penalties for poor tests, adjustment of tricks, in short, every phase of an operator's life and activity has been made the subject of rulings by the Adjustment Board." A similar labor policy was followed by the Providence Telephone Company, operating in the State of Rhode Island.

in December, 1918, and efforts to renew it had failed—the officers of the New England T. and T. Company claiming that they had no authority to act.[1] In November, 1918, the same answer had been received by the telephone operators in reply to demands for a general wage increase. These demands were then taken to the Wage Commission at Washington. Miss O'Connor, President of the Telephone Operators' Department, herself a member of the Commission, states that she was assured by Mr. Ryan, its chairman (an important official in the Post Office Department), that the Commission had jurisdiction and that it would recommend a wage increase. In the meantime Miss O'Connor and Mr. Colpoys, a member of the Wage Commission, submitted to the Chairman of the Wage Commission a report in which they made two important recommendations—that the Commission enunciate the principles of the National War Labor Board and that wage adjustment machinery be established for the telephone and telegraph service similar to that which had been created in the Railroad Administration. At the request of the Chairman of the Commission, this report was submitted to the office of the Postmaster General, and then to his first assistant, Mr. Koons. Almost immediately thereafter Miss O'Connor, who had continued as an employee of the New England T. and T. Company, was asked to resign unless she limited her absences from duty to the call of Government officials. Miss O'Connor thereupon severed her connection with the company, and on January 28, 1919, withdrew from membership on the Wage Commission.

No further action having been taken by any Government body relative to the workers' demands, a strike vote was ordered for February. The following month a committee visited Mr. Burleson who, it is claimed, in the presence of the committee, directed Mr. Koons to have the Wire Control Board consider the matter. On April 7 the secretary of the union received a letter from Mr. Koons promising a speedy decision by the Wire Control Board, but a few days later Mr. Burleson himself telegraphed, asking why the demands had not been presented to the superintendent of the local company. After additional conferences the workers, thoroughly incensed at the treatment which they had received, ordered a strike for April 15, and insisted on their demands being met—

[1] The Adjustment Board continued to function in relation to personal and general grievances but was not permitted to handle wage questions,

not only the demand for wage increases but also for the restoration of the wage adjustment functions of the Adjustment Board, which, under Mr. Burleson's administration, had been abandoned by the Government. Mr. Burleson's answer to the strikers' demands was not to deny their justice, but to blame the workers for not having followed the procedure which he claimed had been established. He used the advantage, which the inconvenience caused by a strike in a public utility would naturally give him, for the purpose of alienating sympathy from the strikers. And yet public opinion seems to have been on their side.

The strike lasted six days, spread throughout New England, and completely tied up the telephone system all over that area. Mr. Burleson, who in former strikes had been able to send ultimata to the workers and upon their failure to accede to his terms to replace them with others, found himself in this instance in quite another position. He was forced to send his representative to Boston, who, after conferences with the union leaders, reached a settlement with them. The workers received substantial wage increases (although not as much as they had demanded) retroactive to January 1, 1919; and the machinery for collective wage bargaining was restored.[1]

In the period that followed the New England strike, a number of walkouts occurred in other parts of the country due to claims of discrimination.[2] The union of the telephone girls was a new one and apparently it was bitterly fought by most of the telephone companies. Many of the strikes commenced without the authorization of the national officers but were afterwards supported by them.

By the summer of 1919, the resentment of the telephone operators had become so great that a general strike of all the workers in the industry was decided upon. Just before the date set for this strike a committee, appointed by the A. F. of L., waited upon the Postmaster General[3] and succeeded in getting from him a statement which satisfied the workers and averted the trouble.

[1] As a part of the settlement all of the strikers were restored to their positions, as though no break had occurred in the continuity of their service. In the other two strikes mentioned in this chapter the workers who came back lost the advantages of long service, having been, not reinstated, but "reëmployed."

[2] At Jacksonville, Florida, and Atlanta, Ga.

[3] Proceedings 39th Annual Convention, A. F. of L., p. 307.

This statement embodied in Order No. 3209 of the Post Office Department, dated June 14, 1919, gave the employees of telephone companies the right to bargain collectively through committees chosen by them and provided that, "Where, prior to Government control, a company dealt with representatives, chosen by the employees to act for them, who were not in the employ of the company, they shall thereafter do so. The telephone company shall designate one or more of its officials who shall be authorized to deal with such individuals or representatives in matters of better conditions of labor, hours of employment, etc." The former order of the Postmaster General, forbidding discriminatory discharges, was also reiterated.

It is claimed, however, that this order did not put a stop to the discriminations which had led to the threatened general strike and shortly thereafter walkouts occurred at Cleveland and Youngstown, Ohio, in California, Michigan, Virginia and elsewhere, unauthorized by the leaders but usually successful in securing considerable increases in wages.

CHAPTER X

The National War Labor Board

MANY kinds of industrial activities were not covered by the special boards previously discussed. The President's Mediation Commission, the only war labor board the jurisdiction of which was not confined to one department or industry, had ceased to function upon its return from the Pacific Coast to Washington in January, 1918. The Administrators, whom it appointed for the copper mines, the packing plants and elsewhere, continued their activities, but otherwise the work of the Commission came to an end with the filing of its reports.

Meanwhile, hundreds of strikes were occurring all over the country in industries vital to the war, yet industries which were not covered by any of the existing boards. It was realized that, because the nation's economic needs and because a successful outcome of the war to a great extent depended upon the prosperity and happiness of the people, there were practically no occupations in which strikes could be viewed with indifference. Under the strain of war, the nation was forced to realize its responsibility for the avoidance of industrial strife in a way in which it had never done—and never does—in time of peace.

One of the national industries upon the peaceable operation of which so much depended was the street railways. In most cases, operating companies had been overcapitalized and many of them were in a weak financial condition even prior to our participation in the war. Street railway employees had always been underpaid, and in many places there was the bitterest feeling between the management and the men. The Amalgamated Association of Street Railway Employees, the dominant union (A. F. of L.), was seeking wage betterments, recognition, and the closed shop. The railway companies were opposed to their employees becoming members of this union, frequently practicing discrimination against men who joined it, and in some cases they went as far as to insist upon their employees signing contracts not to join any labor organization. The fact that street railway fares were in most cases fixed, and the fact that all operating costs were mounting month by month made it next to impossible for the street railways, often near the point of a receivership, to keep pace in wages with the increased cost of living. As might have been expected, strikes were occurring all over the country, of a nature most difficult to cope with, and no agency existed capable of dealing satisfactorily with the situation.

There were also many other industries which did not fall within the jurisdiction of any of the wage boards in which unrest threatened at any moment to develop into stoppages of work.

Fully to understand the circumstances under which the National War Labor Board was organized, it will be necessary to examine briefly the steps which led to placing in the hands of the Secretary of Labor the task of developing a War Labor Administration. From the time of our entrance into the war there were some (although few) far-sighted advisors of the President and of the Council of National Defense, who realized the necessity of a more unified labor administration, able to cope with the thousands of perplexing labor problems which the war had either produced or magnified.[1] A suggestion in the Council of National Defense, for instance, for a central labor administration was defeated in August, 1917, by only one vote (a unanimous vote being required for adoption). Many valuable months were lost during which various suggestions were made; finally an Interdepartmental Committee was appointed, consisting of representatives of those departments and boards chiefly interested in finding a solution of the labor problem. This committee reported to the Council of National Defense on December 20, 1917, outlining steps to be taken and machinery to be provided, "to allay industrial unrest and to create a spirit of real coöperation between labor and capital during the war," and suggesting six functions [2] which would have to be in-

[1] An excellent account of war labor conditions and the need for a central administration was written during the war by Professor L. C. Marshall. May, 1918, *Journal of Political Economy*, Volume XXVI, page 425.

[2] These functions were: (a) Furnishing an adequate supply of labor; (b) machinery for the adjustment of disputes; (c) machinery for safeguarding condition of labor in the production of war essentials; (d) machinery for safeguarding conditions of living; (e) fact gathering body; (f) Publicity and Educational Division.

cluded in any comprehensive plan, one of which was, "machinery which will provide for the immediate and equitable adjustment of disputes."

The President approved the program and on January 4, 1918, asked the Secretary of Labor to organize a labor administration along the lines of the six functions recommended in the report. Thereupon the Secretary of Labor called together an advisory council to assist him with suggestions of plans and personnel. Professor Leon Marshall, who was the secretary to this council, had been in charge of the Industrial Service Section of the Council of National Defense, and had been an active member of the Interdepartmental Committee. In describing the work of the Council, Professor Marshall says, "On January 19, three days after they began their work, the Council presented to the Secretary of Labor the following memorandum:

"The Advisory Council recommends to the Secretary of Labor that he call a conference of twelve persons representing employers' organizations, employees' organizations, and the public, for the purpose of negotiating agreements for the period of the war, having in view the establishment of principles and policies which will enable the prosecution of production without stoppage of work.

"The Advisory Council recommends that this Conference body of twelve be composed as follows: Employers' organizations, as represented by the National Industrial Conference Board,[1] are to name five employers, and these five are to select a person representing the general public. Employees' organizations, as repre-

[1] The National Industrial Conference Board consists of 17 National Employers' Associations representing 50,000 employers. At the invitation of the Council of National Defense, it had, on September 6, 1917, presented to that body a series of recommendations to prevent interruption of industry by labor disputes and had recommended the creation of a board, constituted equally of representatives of employers, employees, and the Government. . . . It is interesting to note that this is one of the organizations of employers to which the President turned when in October, 1919, he organized his first Industrial Conference. The position taken at this later conference by employers is in strange contrast to the remarkably liberal position taken by them in September, 1917. At this later conference not only had their attitude become more conservative, but it was even more conservative than the attitude of those employers who were members of the "Public" group. It was precisely this stubbornly reactionary stand of the employers' group which led to the withdrawal from the conference of the representatives of the employees, i.e., of "Labor."

sented by the American Federation of Labor, are to name five representatives of labor, and these five are to select another representative of the general public."

This recommendation having been approved by the Secretary of Labor, a War Labor Conference Board was summoned which made its report to the Secretary on March 29, 1918, recommending the appointment of a National War Labor Board and outlining its powers and functions and the "principles and policies to govern workers and employers on war industries for the duration of the war." On April 9, 1918, the President created the National War Labor Board, adopting the principles recommended by the War Labor Conference Board and appointing its members as members of the National War Labor Board.

In this manner, one year after our entry into the war, a tribunal for the adjustment of labor difficulties was organized which soon became a Supreme Court for the determination of war labor disputes. It achieved this position because of the representative character of its personnel, the ability and standing of its joint chairmen, the fact that the Board had the prestige of having been appointed by the President of the United States and that its principles were promulgated by him, and, finally, because the President could—and did—employ his great war powers in enforcing the decisions of the Board in those cases where the exercise of those powers became necessary.

It should be noted that the National War Labor Board did not oust any of the existing wage boards from their jurisdiction; on the contrary, its own activities were expressly limited to disputes for the adjustment of which there did not exist "by agreement or Federal law a means of settlement which had not been invoked." Subject to this limitation, the Board's powers extended to "fields of production necessary for the effective conduct of the war, or in other fields of national activity, delays and obstructions in which might in the opinion of the National Board affect detrimentally such production." The Board was also prepared to hear appeals from decisions of existing boards in those cases where the principles contained in the President's proclamation had been violated or where either party to an award had refused to abide by it. It also determined questions of jurisdiction between Government boards.[1]

[1] The appellate powers of the board were seldom invoked, and it is

Congress took no part in the creation of the Board, made no appropriations for its support and conferred no authority upon it. The Board never possessed any legal power to compel either employer or employee to submit any matter in dispute to its arbitral determination, or legal power to compel either side, which had not submitted to its jurisdiction, to follow its recommendations or findings. In such cases, the duties of the Board were limited to conciliation and mediation (accompanied by the right to summon witnesses). Its arbitral determination of wages and other matters of disagreement depended upon the voluntary submission to the Board—by both parties—of the matter in controversy. The rules of the Board provided that upon the joint submission of a dispute a unanimous decision was necessary, and if a unanimous agreement could not be reached, the case was referred to a single umpire whose decision was final. This procedure was adopted in the Bridgeport case and in a number of others of lesser importance. If a complaint of either party was heard without the agreement of the other side to abide by the decision of the Board, unanimity was not required in the "findings" or "recommendations" which in such cases were made.

In spite of the limitation of its power, the National War Labor Board came to be regarded by the public as by far the most important agency for the maintenance of continuous war production. In the public mind it embodied the Government policy that industry should not be interrupted by strikes, and public opinion with its accompanying war psychology was in most cases sufficiently strong, before the signing of the armistice, to compel both sides to submit to the jurisdiction of the Board rather than allow disputes to result in stoppages of work. If an employer refused to submit to its jurisdiction, the President had the power, during the war, to take over the plant,[1] and in two cases refusal of em-

difficult to say how far the right of appeal could have been insisted upon. The most important case in which an appeal was taken was stated by W. Jett Lauck, Secretary of the War Labor Board, in his memorandum report, to have been that of the New York harbor workers. The appellate jurisdiction of the board was also exercised in the case of the Commonwealth Steel Company, Granite City, Illinois, which had been decided by a representative of the Industrial Service Section of the Ordnance Department (in which the decision of the Ordnance Department was sustained).

[1] It was also possible for the Government to exert pressure through such agencies as the War Industries Board and the Fuel Administra-

ployers were considered of sufficient importance to justify this action.[1] On the other hand, in one case, the failure of the employees to abide by the decision of an umpire, appointed by the War Labor Board, led to a request by the President to the men —the machinists of Bridgeport—to return to work.[2] It is significant to note that the Government did not have any legal powers of compulsion over the men commensurate with its right to commandeer the plant of the employer. Its compulsive powers were limited to the withdrawal of draft exemptions which had been granted on occupational grounds to those men who were within the draft age, and to the refusal of assistance from the United States Employment Service to any worker who had violated the Government's recommendations, and, in fact, a threat to make use of both of these means was contained in the President's appeal to the Bridgeport workers. Other cases than those referred to, of refusal by either or both employer or employee to submit to the National War Labor Board, occurred even before the signing of the armistice, but they did not receive much publicity and were not considered sufficiently important to justify drastic action.

After the armistice was signed quite a different spirit prevailed. There were very many cases in which both employers and employees disregarded complaints to the Board and refused to submit to its jurisdiction and to carry out its findings and recommendations.[3] Shortly after the armistice the Board decided not to entertain complaints after December 5, 1918, unless both sides agreed to abide by its award or unless the President, through the Secretary of Labor, specially requested the Board to hear the case. In

tion. Thus the Government could deprive an offending or recalcitrant employer of priorities or could completely shut off his supply of raw materials of most kinds.

[1] *I.e.*, in the cases of Smith & Wesson of Springfield, Massachusetts, and of the Western Union Telegraph Company. See Chapters VII and IX.

[2] See Chapter VII.

[3] The change of spirit which followed the armistice is well illustrated by the case of the Cleveland and Erie Traction Co., Girard, Pa., National War Labor Board, Docket No. 631. Employer and employee had jointly agreed to submit the controversy to the Board, but before a hearing could be held the armistice had been signed. The employer now refused to go on with the case claiming that conditions had changed and that the signing of the armistice had ousted the Board of jurisdiction. The Board held however that the company could not withdraw "from an obligation and agreement made in good faith with the men."

the absence of the extreme pressure for uninterrupted production, which had accompanied the war, the influence of the Board grew less and less until finally on June 25, 1919, the Board by resolution decided to receive no more new cases or applications, to finish up its work, and to transfer its records and files to the Department of Labor. On August 12, the Board took formal action terminating its existence.[1]

In the short period of its official life, the work of the National War Labor Board took it into almost every state in the Union and covered a wide range of industries, including those closely related to the conduct of the war, such as machine shops, foundries, shell and munition plants, and including, indeed, so diversified a list as moving picture studios, the manufacture of coffins, the printing industry, laundries, the building trades, and numerous others. The Board was called upon to fix the wages of almost every important street railway in the country.[2] Wage adjustments were indeed asked for by municipal employees; and although in one of these cases, on complaint of the firemen of the city of Omaha, the Board held that it had no jurisdiction,[3] in another, it *recommended to* the city of Pittsburgh [4] that it increase the wages paid to its fire fighters.

The decisions of the Board were courageous and statesmanlike, and embodied the most progressive views concerning industry that had found sufficiently general approval to have justified their use during the war. At the same time they were sound and conservative and although, as was inevitable, some of them provoked a good deal of criticism at the time they were made, there seems very little doubt that their justice and soundness will become increasingly apparent when the history of war labor administration is studied from a more detached angle than is possible at the present time.

The President's proclamation, creating the Board, adopted and

[1] N. Y. *Times* for August 13, 1919.
[2] To May 31, 1919, 169 Street Railway cases were considered by the Board resulting as follows: 91 awards and findings; 17 cases dismissed after hearing; 28 cases dismissed after agreement; 18 cases referred to Department of Labor; 7 cases pending. Report of Secretary National War Labor Board to the Secretary of Labor for the 12 Months Ending May 31, 1919.
[3] Docket Number 780.
[4] Docket Number 226.

set forth the principles which were to govern its decision.[1] The minimum wage was more fully recognized in the awards of the Board than it had ever been before, and the eight-hour day, although not universally applied, was granted in many cases. Wherever possible, collective bargaining was insisted upon, and to the newly created committees was often assigned the task of establishing wage rates and of adjusting conditions, with the right to appeal to the National War Labor Board.

As the activities of the Board expanded a large organization was built up, as many as 250 men and women having been employed at the time of its greatest activity. In spite of the Board's practice of dividing its membership into sections (usually consisting of one employer and one employee member each), the number of complaints was so large that it soon became necessary to delegate to examiners the taking of testimony. This method was followed in more than half of the cases heard by the Board. There was also developed the practice of assigning representatives to administer awards and to see that their provisions were followed by both sides.[2] A staff of expert advisers on matters of economics and finance was also developed, and reports prepared on the cost of living, the eight-hour day, and similar questions affecting the decisions of the Board. In this manner, in the comparatively short time of the Board's existence, an incredibly large number of complaints were heard and awards handed down.

Nor was the influence of the Board confined to the cases which it heard and decided. From the time of the enunciation of its principles and policies, these liberal and wisely conceived doctrines were adopted by all other wage boards,[3] and they formed a Magna Charter of war labor rights, satisfying the workers' sense of justice, and yet not seriously alienating the loyalty of the employers. Although neither side was satisfied, there is no doubt that labor was much better pleased with the working of the Board

[1] These are given in full in Appendix No. VII and will be discussed in greater detail in a subsequent chapter.

[2] Up to May 31, 1919, 180 awards and findings had been administered by the Board's agents, administrators having been present in person in 128 cases.—Memorandum Report of Secretary Lauck.

[3] The principles did not vary much, from those already being applied, except in emphasis, clarity, and the publicity which they received. These factors, however, were very important and resulted in the applications of the principles over a wider area than would otherwise have been possible.

than was capital. Yet upon the termination of the war both sides seemed to desire its abolition.

The reason for this desire was that at the close of the war both sides chafed under the restriction imposed upon them by the existence of the Board. On the part of the workers, this feeling was due to the fact that the American Federation of Labor has traditionally been opposed to anything resembling compulsory arbitration. It has always favored collective bargaining between capital and labor, and the conclusion of joint agreements between employers and unions, but it has opposed the interference of outside agencies. To be sure, it has favored mediation of the type which has been for the last few years carried on by the Department of Labor. This has consisted of efforts by Government representatives to encourage the "getting together" of the two sides, without any obligations being imposed on either, and without the exercise of any arbitral functions by the Government. (The National War Labor Board was, we must remember, an agency which, if it was to function properly, had to have the right, either as a result of public opinion or otherwise, to intervene in and to decide industrial disputes.)

Another reason which made the workers willing to have the War Labor Board dissolved was their desire, now that the war was over, to attain ends more favorable to them than were sanctioned by the principles of the Board and by its decisions. Thus they sought union recognition even in cases where there had been none before the war. They desired reductions in hours of work more radical than those which had been awarded by the Board. They felt that they had the power to compel employers to grant these changes, and did not wish to be hampered in the exercise of this power by the existence and authority of the National War Labor Board. On the other hand, the employers had never been reconciled to the employees' immunity from discharge (because of union membership), which had been one of the cardinal principles of the Board. They desired, in many cases, to resume their former discriminatory practices and they felt that with respect to any demands of labor they were strong enough to fight them out successfully in open industrial conflict. They were anxious to have the National War Labor Board dissolved because they did not wish to be placed in the dilemma of either submitting to arbitration before an existing tribunal, in which case they felt they would be sacrificing their new peace-time power, or of refusing to submit, in which case the mere existence of the Board, together with the prestige which it had acquired, would have prejudiced public opinion against them. The soundness of this feeling, from their own point of view, can be seen in the case of the steel strike. Public opinion does not seem to have condemned the refusal of the Steel Company to arbitrate, whereas, had the War Labor Board been in existence and had it offered its good offices—as undoubtedly it would have done—this refusal would have met with general condemnation.

All these reasons make it easy to see why both sides welcomed the dissolution of the National War Labor Board with something almost akin to relief.

CHAPTER XI

War Labor Policies Board and Conference Committee of Labor Adjustment Agencies

WAR LABOR POLICIES BOARD

WE have seen in a previous chapter that in an effort to coördinate the work of the different labor boards and to strengthen and unify the labor program, the President on January 4, 1919, accepting the report of the Inter-departmental Committee, directed the Secretary of Labor to organize a Labor Administration. One of the final steps taken to carry out this order was the organization of the War Labor Policies Board on May 7, 1918. It was composed of representatives of all Government agencies interested in production and vitally concerned in finding a proper solution of the labor problem. The board was intended to be a planning body, to study problems and map out methods for their solution, and to formulate the policies by which other branches of the Government should be guided. By locating this function in a board composed of the labor administrators of the different branches of the Government it was hoped that the new body would serve to unify all Governmental labor policies and to coördinate and develop war labor activities in a unified, orderly, efficient manner, and that the collective "voice of all the industrial agencies of the Government" would supply vision and foresight in charting the course to be pursued.

So far as the activities of the War Labor Policies Board relate to the subject matter of this book—labor disputes—they consisted mainly in drafting uniform labor clauses for introduction in contracts for war production [1] and in attempting to standardize wages for all war industry. This latter was a stupendous undertaking, involving the consideration of wage scales in thousands of localities and in hundreds of different occupations. The board never

[1] These included a clause on Adjustment of Labor Disputes, and are set forth in Appendix X.

accomplished its purpose, but its efforts to do so had two results. In the first place the Emergency Construction Commission, which had only one industry to deal with, and which, at the request of the Secretary of War, had made considerable progress in preparation for standardizing wages in the building industry, was directed to discontinue this work and to give its material to the War Labor Policies Board. A resolution was also adopted by the Policies Board urgently requesting "the departments and boards represented to refrain from making changes in present standards pending the standardization now under consideration." This resolution was put into effect by departmental orders. It prevented Government adjusters from making any changes in wages pending action by the Policies Board, and as time went on without such action being taken, very embarrassing situations developed.[1]

Thus in the building industry under the Baker-Gompers agreement it was understood that there would be put into effect on Government work wage scales adopted jointly by unions and employers' associations. But such new wage scales were frequently interpreted by the Emergency Construction Commission to amount to "changes in standards," and under the orders of the War Department they could not be adopted, because to have done so would have been contrary to the resolution of the Labor Policies Board. For several months the hands of labor administrators were tied, and it was impossible under the circumstances to reach adjustments which otherwise would have readily been made, and to grant wage increases to which the workers were obviously entitled. It was almost impossible to make the men understand why decisions should be so long delayed, and inevitably a great deal of unnecessary unrest and a number of strikes resulted. Eventually this restriction was withdrawn, and the adjusters were allowed to make decisions without waiting for definite action by the Policies Board, and as a matter of fact the war ended before this standardization had been achieved.

The board also adopted the principles of the National War Labor Board; indorsed excellent regulations in regard to the employment of women at night; [2] and established a policy for the

---

[1] To a certain extent, these situations were relieved by the fact that the rule referred to wage *Standards* and not to actual wages, thereby giving a degree of latitude to the Government adjusters.

[2] Prepared by the Women in Industry Service of the Department of Labor of which Miss Mary Van Kleeck was the head.

United States Employment Service for those cases where an employer, whose employees were on strike, requested Government assistance.[1] Shortly before the signing of the armistice the Policies Board also negotiated agreements between employers and workers for the formation of a Metal Trades Board and a Building Trades Board. Had the war lasted longer both of these would probably have become very important agencies for unifying the work of Government wage adjustment. Although from this description, the sum of actual accomplishment of the War Labor Policies Board may seem slight, it must be remembered that its main activities were in other fields than mediation, that it was organized very late in the war and that the tasks which it undertook involved study and investigation, and were necessarily slow of accomplishment. Nevertheless there can be no doubt that if such a board were permanently organized and continuously functioning it would prove of inestimable value.

CONFERENCE COMMITTEE

In September, 1918, there was also organized the Conference Committee of Labor Adjusting Agencies of which Mr. Frankfurter, Chairman of the Labor Policies Board, was likewise the head. The personnel of the committee consisted of those in charge of all war labor adjustment agencies. In most cases the departments represented on the War Labor Policies Board were also represented on the Conference Committee (and by the same individuals). But this was not entirely the case—thus the Department of Agriculture and the Food Administration having no wage adjustment boards of their own, were not represented on the Conference Committee, whereas the National War Labor Board, which was not a part of the Labor Policies Board, was, however, represented on this Committee. The purpose of the Committee was to prevent the adoption of decisions by one agency which would upset the work of others. Experience had shown that, inasmuch as each board was acting practically independently of every other

[1] The representative of the U. S. Employment Service was to arrange for the resumption of work pending arbitration—if the employer refused, he was to receive no assistance from the Employment Service; if the employees were unwilling to return to work and arbitrate, the Service was to supply the employer with men to take the places of the men on strike.

board, decisions were being made which awarded higher wages to some workers in an industry than were being awarded to other workers in identically the same industry—and sometimes even in the same locality. Naturally this conduced to increase dissatisfaction among the workers. It was to eliminate these inequalities that the Shipbuilding Labor Adjustment Board appealed to President Wilson to create some agency which would be in a better position to cope with this problem than was the Labor Policies Board. The President thereupon requested the Secretary of Labor to carry out this suggestion and the Conference Committee was organized. Before awards were thereafter to become effective they were to be submitted to this Committee for its approval.

The Conference Committee was organized so short a time before the signing of the armistice that it had little opportunity to function. A number of awards were, however, submitted to it before they were promulgated, notably those in October, 1918, of the Fuel Administrator, of the Shipbuilding Labor Adjustment Board, and of the Marine and Dock Industrial Relations Division. But at the time of their submission they represented *faits accomplis*. Inasmuch as they were the result of negotiations between employer and employee and inasmuch as these awards had been virtually promised in advance, it would have been exceedingly inexpedient for the Conference Committee to have either delayed or changed them. What it did was to listen to, and discuss the proposed awards, and after a short time give its approval.

It soon became apparent that if the Committee was to have any real power and was not merely to be a rubber-stamp for decisions already made, agreements like that under which the Emergency Construction Wage Adjustment Commission operated would have to be completely revised,[1] and all of the agreements would have had to contain a clause lodging in the Conference Committee more or less definite powers of revision. Yet even if the original agreements had been changed the exercise of the Com-

---

[1] This agreement required the adoption of *prevailing rates* of wages for each locality. But the rates of a particular locality might—and often did—conflict with the rates in force elsewhere. Sometimes, in fact, wages in a particular trade would be fixed at an amount greatly in excess of the wages for the same trade in the immediate neighborhood. Here it can be clearly seen that if the Conference Committee was to function at all the prevailing rate of a particular locality could no longer be used as a standard for wage adjustment.

mittee's functions would still have involved an inherent difficulty of great magnitude. The adjustment agencies were, in almost all cases, composed of an equal number of representatives of both employer and employee, with or without the representation of the public. And the awards arrived at were usually the outcome of compromise between the desires of each side which the adjusters sought to reconcile. On the other hand the membership of the Conference Committee was not equally divided between capital and labor; most of its members were Government officials.[1] Consequently if industrial peace was to be maintained, it was extremely inexpedient to submit to a board of this type the conclusions reached by a bargaining process between the immediate parties in interest, each of whom was familiar with the special problems of the trade in question—problems of which the members of the Conference Committee could not possibly have as intimate a knowledge. The adjustments made by each board were frequently the result of patient investigation of all the peculiar circumstances affecting a particular industry, and were reached in many cases only after both sides had consulted their constituents and to a greater or lesser degree persuaded them of the fairness of the award. When after all of this effort awards were finally arrived at, the boards were extremely reluctant to have the questions reopened.

The element of time was likewise of the utmost importance in the settlement of labor disputes, and presented another difficulty in the successful operation of the Conference Committee. All of the boards were overworked and were having the greatest trouble in keeping up with their calendars; obviously it was impossible to go before the Conference Committee until an award was pretty well agreed upon and decisions were usually not reached by the adjustment boards until weeks and often months after the presentation of the controversy. Therefore to have submitted awards to the Conference Committee and to have waited for its decision would of course have meant more delay—which delay would have been much increased had changes been demanded and had the award been sent back to the agency of original jurisdiction.

Nevertheless, in spite of all these difficulties the need for greater uniformity was so keenly felt that, had the war continued, and

[1] The personnel of the Conference Committee is set forth in Appendix IX.

had the Committee been given a better opportunity to function, some method would have been found to accomplish the desired result. The Committee would probably have developed, not so much into a court of appeals for the review of decisions after they had been made, as into a body which, by bringing the representatives of the different boards into frequent consultation with each other, would have afforded them an opportunity to keep in touch with the actions which each board was contemplating and thus to reconcile their decisions as they were being formulated.

The other important work of the Conference Committee was the preparation of a document setting forth labor standards as the basis for a National War Labor Policy to be promulgated by the President of the United States. In a comparatively short time the Committee agreed upon a set of recommendations which were submitted to the President. These recommendations stated that the principles of the National War Labor Board, previously announced by the President, were not to be superseded, and that the War Labor Board was the final arbiter if differences arose as to the application of the principles. It also provided "for the maintenance of proper standards of living—such standards as are appropriate to American citizens devoting their energies to the successful prosecution of a righteous war." It stated that: "Changes in the cost of living, therefore, call for adjustment in wages . . . no alteration of the national policy as to American standards should occur until the government has announced the necessity for the reduction of standards of all classes to meet the exigencies of the war. In the interests of stability revision of wage scales based upon changes in the cost of living, as herein provided, should be made semi-annually." The eight-hour day was reaffirmed for Government work (direct or sublet), with Saturday in June, July and August, a half holiday (four hours).[1]

Another clause provided for the recognition of differentials in favor of shipyard and other emergency war workers. In order to overcome the poor working conditions in the yards and their disadvantageous locations it had been the practice of the Shipbuilding Labor Adjustment Board to give them a higher wage than prevailed in other industries. Although the clause in question was not as clear and unequivocal as was desired by representatives of

---

[1] These provisions were inserted against the wishes of the Railroad Administration.

the Shipping Board, the proclamation of the President would have put upon this arrangement the sanction of the highest authority in the land. Heretofore when an award had been made to the shipyards giving the shipyard workers of a particular industry a higher rate of wages than they received elsewhere in the same industry, immediately there had naturally followed an effort by the other mechanics employed in this industry to obtain for themselves a wage equal to that paid to their fellow craftsmen in the shipyards. It was hoped that the Presidential proclamation sanctioning the giving to the shipyard workers a preferential would reconcile the workers in other industries to receiving a smaller wage.

In one respect the statement was weak. The abuse of overtime, which badly needed definite curbing, was vaguely dealt with. The declaration of principles failed to make sufficiently definite provisions for limiting this evil—merely stating that, "All government authorities are urged to put a stop to the abuse of overtime as extra compensation," and, "No government work on Sundays or holidays except in an emergency and then to be paid for at double," and so on.

The draft of the Conference Committee's declaration of policy did not reach the President until some weeks before the end of the war, and was delayed by his preoccupation with diplomatic affairs so that the armistice was signed before this proclamation was forthcoming. Nothing further was done.

CHAPTER XII

United States Labor Department and State Boards

PRE-WAR labor adjustment activities of the Labor Department of the Federal Government and the labor bureaus of the several states have been discussed in a previous chapter. It is now proposed to briefly examine the war-time activities of these boards. We have seen that in the years immediately preceding our participation in the war, the work of the Bureau of Mediation of the U. S. Labor Department had been steadily increasing in volume and in importance. This increased activity was maintained during the entire war period.[1] The work of the Department was especially important during the time which intervened between our entry into the war and the organization of the various special boards described in the previous chapters.

UNITED STATES LABOR DEPARTMENT

Thus the Secretary of Labor was able to prevent the occurrence of several large mining strikes which threatened during the spring and summer of 1917, before the Fuel Administration was prepared to act in these matters.

A list of the industries in which the mediators of the Labor Department intervened would cover most of the industrial life of the country and would include practically every trade in which war labor boards were subsequently created. Shipyards, packing houses, copper mines, munition plants, the building trades, street cars, the mechanical and clerical departments of the railroads, and many others could be mentioned. The number of workers stated by the Department to have been affected by these adjust-

[1] In June, 1917, the Department was handicapped by lack of funds, and had to dispense with the services of many of its conciliators. On July 1, the commencement of a new fiscal year, the new appropriation became available and in September Congress made an additional appropriation for the work of the Department. (See Fifth Annual Report, Secretary of Labor.)

ments is very impressive. Its reports for 1917, 1918 and 1919 show that from our entry into the war to June 20, 1919—a little less than twenty-seven months—2,180,652 workers were directly and in addition 2,762,480 indirectly affected by these activities, in all very nearly five million men and women! Although these figures are based on labor controversies in the adjustment of many of which the Department played only a minor rôle, it is nevertheless true that its mediators contributed substantially to the maintenance of industrial peace during the war and that a very large number of workers were affected by their efforts.

The Department had no authority to insist upon its mediators being heard. Moreover its policy was not to attempt arbitration, but merely to try to bring the two parties together in conference or, if they could not be persuaded to meet each other face to face, then to act as mediator between them.

The Department has the absolute confidence of the vast majority of the workers, especially those affiliated with the American Federation of Labor. It has, however, been unable to inspire this feeling among very many of the employers, especially the largest, who are bitterly opposed to labor unions. After the armistice the difficulties which all the special war boards encountered in securing the coöperation of employers were as keenly felt by the Labor Department.

There can be no doubt that its mediation service is utterly inadequate to meet the country's requirements; it is loosely organized, and suffers from the fact that its personnel is insufficient both in numbers and in industrial representation.

BUREAU OF INDUSTRIAL HOUSING, U. S. LABOR DEPARTMENT

As we have seen in a previous chapter the war labor policy of the Government included the erection of workingmen's houses in many of the overcrowded war-production centers. To carry out this work (with the exception of the houses erected by the Shipping Board—Emergency Fleet Corporation), a Bureau was created under the jurisdiction of the Department of Labor and for administrative purposes a company was organized known as the United States Housing Corporation. Although Congress had failed to appropriate the necessary funds until the summer of 1918, the Bureau undertook and completed the erection of thousands of houses in places like Bridgeport, Conn.; Erie and Bethlehem, Pa., and Rock Island, Ill. It was a vast construction program which involved the employment of thousands of skilled mechanics and common laborers at a time of greatest labor shortage. To get the necessary workers, and to meet the problems of labor adjustment, the Housing Bureau organized an Industrial Relations Division,[1] independent of other Government bodies. The Bureau was not limited by the adjustments of the Emergency Construction Wage Adjustment Board and could pay any wages to mechanics engaged upon its enterprises which it saw fit. Its policy is stated in the Report of the Housing Corporation to have been to ascertain "the rates of wages and working time in any particular locality from the examiner in charge of the nearest branch of the United States Employment Service and not to vary from these established rates and conditions without instructions from the division." Attention has already been called to the chaos which attended the fixing of rates in the building industry because of the number of different agencies which exercised independent authority in this field. The Report points out these conditions by continuing as follows: "But in few localities were the established rates being observed, and the Industrial Relations Division soon found itself involved in a contest of wage increases. In only two instances, so far as the manager of the Division is aware, were the contractors of the Housing Corporation the first to vary from the established rates."

As to hours the Housing Bureau claims to have tried to confine work on its projects to ten hours a day, overtime on Saturday afternoon and not on Sunday, except in cases of real emergency. It was no doubt easier for it to do this than for some of the other Government departments because of its freedom to meet competition as to wage rates on account of its independent wage adjustment authority. This independent power was exercised after the armistice, when as a result of the stoppage of overtime, strikes threatened in many places. The Housing Bureau met this emergency by wage increases in order to partially compensate the men for the reduction in their income which the elimination of

[1] See Report of United States Housing Corporation, December 3, 1918. Otto M. Eidlitz was Director of the Bureau and President of the Corporation; Frank J. Warne was Manager of the Industrial Relations Division.

overtime involved.[1] Many other questions arose, requiring the services of a labor adjuster in order to keep the men at their jobs; they were similar, however, to those we have considered elsewhere in this book and therefore need not be given special attention.

STATE BOARDS

A large number of individual states are still without any provision whatever for governmental aid in the adjustment of labor controversies, although some of them have been the scene of violent labor conflicts. A few are not even provided with a properly organized labor department and in many cases, where provision is made for such a department, no authority is given for the conciliation of labor disputes,[2] athough in some cases the reports of these departments contain short accounts of strikes which occurred during the period of the report.[3]

In most of the jurisdictions in which provision had been made for conciliation and arbitration by state boards, these agencies continue to function during the war in much the same manner as they had previously.[4] It will not, therefore, be necessary to give

---

[1] It has been pointed out in a previous chapter that partly because of overtime payment, wages in the building industry had not nearly kept pace with increased living costs. The increases above referred to can therefore be justified as fair and proper.

[2] The following states were not provided with any machinery for the conciliation of labor disputes:

Arizona	Kansas	North Carolina	South Dakota
California	Kentucky	New Mexico	Texas
Delaware	Michigan	North Dakota	Virginia
Georgia	Mississippi	Oklahoma	Washington
Indiana	Montana	Oregon	Wyoming
Idaho	New Jersey	Rhode Island	

[3] The Report of the Missouri Bureau of Labor Statistics, from which it appears that the state itself did not act in the mediation of labor disputes, contains short accounts of a number of important strikes. The 1917 controversy, involving the Kansas City street railroad men, is worth mentioning. It seems that during the strike, men were brought to Kansas City to run the cars and violence resulted. Forty-three policemen refused to act as guards on the street cars and were dismissed from the police force.

[4] Among these can be mentioned,

Colorado	Minnesota	New York
Illinois	Nebraska	Ohio
Iowa	Nevada	Pennsylvania
Massachusetts	New Hampshire	Utah

separate treatment to the activities of each of these boards but only to explain the work of those of Massachusetts and New York.

Two other states should be separately mentioned because of special labor legislation enacted by them during the war—Minnesota and New Hampshire. The first of these possessed one of the oldest mediation boards in the country although the services of this board had not been very often called into use. Shortly after the outbreak of the war, however, a Public Safety Commission was created with large powers. This Commission on April 30, 1918, issued an order which, in effect, gave the Board of Arbitration compulsory powers to settle labor controversies on the basis of an agreement which, at the direction of the Governor of the State, the board had brought about between the Minnesota Employers' Association and the principal representatives of labor organizations. Under this new law the activity of the board increased very much [1] although the most important controversy was not settled by the state board but by the National War Labor Board.

In New Hampshire a law was passed in the first days of the war prohibiting strikes in plants doing war work.[2] Not being an industrial community nor one in which there were likely to be many strikes, the passage of this law is mentioned more as a matter of historical interest than because of its influence on war production. The enactment of this legislation seems to have attracted very little attention.

MASSACHUSETTS

The State Board of Conciliation and Arbitration had for a number of years been the most active of the boards functioning in the different states and continued so during the war. Besides its

The following states have boards of mediation but they do not seem to have been active during the war period.

| Connecticut | Maine | Vermont· |

[1] The Report of the board for a period from September 1, 1917, to December 1, 1918, shows that a total number of 45 cases were handled, involving 600 firms and 7,000 employees, that 6 of these disputes were settled by arbitration, 31 by conciliation and the others were either withdrawn, referred to other bodies or pending at the time of the submission of the Report.

[2] Chapter 146, page 48, The Compiled Labor Laws of the State of New Hampshire, 1917.

duties as mediator the Massachusetts Board arbitrated a large number of controversies, principally in the shoe industry but also in the building and paper trade, the street railroads and elsewhere.

In addition to the activities of the State Board, some of the most important strikes occurring within the Commonwealth during the war were settled through the service of the late Henry B. Endicott, Executive Manager of the Massachusetts Committee on Public Safety.[1] Those affecting railroads and shipyards have been referred to in earlier chapters of this book. To Mr. Endicott's decision as arbitrator was also left the adjustment of a large number of controversies in other fields—fisheries, street railroads, trucking and others.

In May, 1918, a most serious strike occurred in many of the textile mills of Massachusetts and Rhode Island. Fifteen thousand men and women quit work and the entire industry of about 350,000 employees was affected.[2] The supply of cloth for uniforms for men in the service was interfered with and the Secretary of War telegraphed to Mr. Endicott requesting him to endeavor to restore production. Mr. Endicott's intervention was successful and an agreement, by which he was given power to arbitrate the matters in dispute, terminated the controversy. A few months later, in July, 1918, 1800 weavers in certain mills of the American Woolen Company struck for the abolition of the premium system. The Secretary of War once more asked Mr. Endicott to use his good offices and he was able to bring about an agreement whereby the premium system, which had for a long time been a source of dissatisfaction, was abolished, a wage increase granted, and other contested points settled.[3]

The successful adjustment of these two textile strikes was, however, not to be duplicated in the very severe conflict which broke

[1] See Part 2. Story of the Massachusetts Committee on Public Safety by George H. Lyman.

[2] Ibid., page 32.

[3] In a statement by President W. M. Wood of the American Woolen Company, quoted in The Story of the Massachusetts Committee on Public Safety at page 138, he said: "The settlement of the Lawrence strike by Mr. Endicott was such as to be perfectly satisfactory to both sides. The premium system was a source of irritation to the weavers and no great benefit to us. We have had a splendid opportunity to compare figures on efficiency between our mills in which the premium system was used and our other mills, and have arrived at the conclusion that it did not promote efficiency."

out in Lawrence three months after the signing of the armistice. In January, 1919, the United Textile Workers of America—affiliated with the A. F. of L.—presented demands to textile mills all over the country for a reduction of working hours to forty-eight per week. Nothing, however, was said as to wages, and this meant that the demands if granted would be accompanied by a reduction in weekly earnings.

The employers decided upon a reduction of hours from fifty-four, as they prevailed in most places, to forty-eight as demanded by the unions. The officers of the union were, therefore, satisfied and refused to sanction any further demands. But the unorganized workers, especially the foreigners, objected to the reduction in their pay which this cutting down of the hours involved, and demanded fifty-four hours' pay for forty-eight hours' work. The employers, having met the demands of the union for shorter hours and resenting the radicalism which prevailed among the ranks of the unorganized and foreign workers, refused this increase in wages and a walkout of more than twenty thousand workers began on February 3. The strike lasted three months and was one of the bitterest of a period in our history which has been marked by many bitter strikes. It soon spread to other cities in Massachusetts and elsewhere, so that a large part of the industry was involved in the demand for the shorter week without reduction of pay.

The men who had walked out were largely foreigners, many of them radical socialists, and the strike attracted a number of other radicals to Lawrence. Just about this time the general strike was taking place at Seattle and feeling all over the country was running high. The conservative press contained sensational stories of the doings and purposes of the strikers and the police of Lawrence, as well as other city officials, embarked upon a career of suppression and violence of very much the same kind which six months later accompanied the steel strike.[1]

---

[1] In an account of the Lawrence strike, published in so. conservative a paper as the New York *Times* on Sunday, May 25th, the following appeared: "The newspapers in Lawrence were alarmed at the spread of radicalism and advocated the formation of vigilantes, or an organization similar to the old-fashioned Ku-Klux Klan of the South. Some of the citizens, identity unknown, decided to follow this advice. On May 5th they went to one propagandist's hotel about midnight, called him to the door, seized him, blackjacked him, and carried him half

Efforts by the Massachusetts State Board to arbitrate were refused by the employers who also rejected the suggestion of the Governor that Mr. Endicott act as arbitrator. The strike was finally ended by the decision of the companies to grant an increase in wages which not only equaled the amount for which the strikers had originally asked, but was a little in excess of their demands, and the men and women who had been out for over three months returned to work.[1]

conscious to a waiting automobile. They drove several miles into the country, stopped near a tree, fished out a rope from beneath the automobile seat, and started to hold a little private lynching bee. By this time he had recovered his senses and resisted with all his might. In the mêlée he was badly beaten and, according to his statement, he would have been hung had it not been that an approaching automobile frightened the vigilantes away. As they left, they shouted to him: 'Keep out of Lawrence; you will not escape next time!'" It seems perfectly clear, from the evidence, that the police indulged in brutal assaults on peaceable citizens whose only offense was their connection with the strike and that the right of free assemblage was unjustifiably interfered with. The attitude of the city government of Lawrence is best shown in the following quotation from a letter of the Commissioner of Public Safety, Peter Carr, to whom the strikers had applied for permission to parade, reprinted in part in the *Survey* for April 5, 1919: "All those who seek to exploit the fair name of Lawrence are those who care nothing for our City, our State or our Union. Bolshevism, the enemy of democracy, the destroyer of property rights, the breeder of anarchy, will get no foothold in Lawrence. A parade under present conditions will encourage bolshevism; there will be no parade."

[1] While the strike was in progress a conference of textile strikers from different parts of the country was held and a new and more radical union formed, known as the Amalgamated Textile Workers of America. The organizers of this union had the assistance of the Amalgamated Clothing Workers and the union was organized on industrial lines, attempting to include in its membership all of the workers in the textile mills, no matter what their craft. In the period of a little more than one year which has elapsed since the formation of this union it has had a most phenomenal growth and in May, 1920, it claimed a membership of over 50,000 workers. It soon spread to the silk industry and took a leading part in the fight for the 44-hour week in the silk mills. Its growth was hastened by the expulsion of a number of Locals of the United Textile Workers' Union because of their refusal to obey their national officers and their insistence on a reduction of the working hours to 44. It is stated that the Amalgamated controls the silk weavers in several important manufacturing centers, including New York and Bergen County, N. J. In New York the new union has recently concluded an agreement with four leading manufacturers by which strikes are prohibited and provisions made for an Impartial Chairman to decide all controversies between the weavers and their employers. The agreement is designed not only to protect the workers but also to stimulate production.

There were also many strikes in the shoe industry. In the most important of these—the Lynn strike of 1917—both the State Board and the Committee on Public Safety participated in bringing about a settlement. Prior to April, 1917, conditions in this industry in the city of Lynn seem to have been chaotic. The factories had been unable to keep their workers steadily employed and although rates of pay were the highest in the United States, the actual earnings of the workers over a period of several months were inadequate. At the expiration of their contract with the union, in April, 1917, the members of the Manufacturers' Association closed down all their plants. Unofficially they stated that this action was due to high prices of leather and uncertain market conditions, but it was generally believed that the manufacturers sought a wage reduction and a modification of union shop rules. The lockout or strike that followed lasted over five months during which time the industry at this important shoe-making center— and in spite of the needs of the army—was almost entirely shut down. The Massachusetts State Board endeavored to effect a settlement, held hearings and suggested an award but could not get the parties to agree. The unions were willing to submit to arbitration by Mr. Endicott, but for a time the employers refused. Finally Mr. Endicott called a meeting of the two sides and induced them both to accept a settlement by which the men were immediately to return to work and be paid the wage and bonus they had been receiving in April; there were to be no strikes for three years, future controversies being left to the decision of the State Board; and Mr. Endicott was to settle the wages to be paid to the workers from the time of their resumption of work. His decision, announced some months later, left wages where they were when the lockout occurred except slight advances to women in a few occupations. The award was accepted by both sides, very reluctantly by the men, and in 1918 a number of strikes occurred, in which there seems to have been a failure on the part of the workers to respect their agreement to arbitrate. The manufacturers thereupon succeeded in obtaining an injunction against the United Shoe Workers of America, restraining them from participating in any strikes against the members of the Manufacturers' Association. The bitterness engendered by these controversies was increased by the fact that there are two rival unions in the shoe industry. The more conservative, the Boot and Shoe Workers

Union, is affiliated with the A. F. of L.; the more radical, the United Shoe Workers of America, is not. The two unions have been engaged in a bitter contest for supremacy. During the Lynn controversy in 1917 it was alleged that the Manufacturers' Association sought to induce their workers, many of whom were members of the United, to join the more conservative organization. The rivalry between the two unions resulted in 1918 in a number of strikes, notably in Brockton.[1]

But although not adjusted by the State Board, this account would be incomplete without mention of one of the most serious strikes of the post-armistice period—that of the Boston police. The rising living costs had been most oppressively felt by men and women in public employment, teachers, office assistants, firemen, policemen. In these occupations salaries were fixed by law and during all the time that the cost of living had been increasing to well-nigh double its former level, the earnings of the men and women in these Government positions had increased but little. Mechanics and laborers had by means of their unions and as a result of competition among employers obtained wages more or less in keeping with rising living costs. But the teachers and the policemen were asked to continue their work on salaries which were never liberal and which owing to the lessened purchasing power of money had become shockingly inadequate.

The unrest which prevailed everywhere among large bodies of Municipal and Federal employees and which during the war had found expression in a number of strikes of firemen,[2] resulted during the fall of 1919 in the formation in Boston of a policemen's union, affiliated with the A. F. of L.[3] The Boston police had in June, 1919, received a substantial increase, but not commensurate with increased living costs. And in addition to low wages there

[1] This strike was taken up by the National War Labor Board but referred back by it to the Massachusetts State Board.
[2] See Chapter X.
[3] The Charter issued by the A. F. of L. to policemen forbids the use of the strike. For many years no policemen's locals were organized by the A. F. of L. At its June, 1919, Convention, however, a resolution was adopted which favored the granting of such charters (Report of Proceedings 39th Annual Convention, page 302). Mr. Gompers stated in a speech in Boston (reprinted in *American Federationist*, February, 1920, p. 135) that "in less than four weeks there were 35 organizations of policemen which had sent in their applications for charters—never so many from one class of workers in the same period in the history of the Federation."

were apparently many other causes of complaint in the working conditions of the police force. The Police Commissioner (who strangely enough is an appointee of the Governor of the State and not of the Mayor) placed on trial nineteen men, prominent in the union, for violation of a police rule forbidding membership in any organization that affiliated with any group save war veterans. During the course of the trial efforts were made by a committee appointed by the Mayor to find some way out of the threatened difficulty; for it was realized that, if these men were discharged, a strike of the entire police force might follow. Attempts at adjustment were unsuccessful; the nineteen men were dismissed and on September 9, 1919, the entire police force left their posts. In this emergency the authorities, who had had ample warning of this contemplated action and who had stated that they had the situation well in hand, failed to provide State Guards to preserve order.[1]

As might have been expected, in the absence of the police and with no adequate substitute, the criminal elements of the community took advantage of the situation to commit acts of theft and violence, with fatal results in several cases. The spectacle of the City of Boston left by its police force to the mercy of the lawless filled the columns of the country's press and aroused the greatest indignation. Public opinion was everywhere against the strikers, and although Mr. Gompers and others leaders of the A. F. of L. issued statements defending them, their action was generally condemned.

Efforts to settle the strike and to have the police reinstated were met by an uncompromising attitude on the part of Governor Coolidge and his Police Commissioner. The Governor declared that the actions of the police had shown a "deliberate intention to intimidate and coerce the Government," that the success of the strike meant anarchy and that he was unwilling "to place the maintenance of the public security in the hands of a body of men who have attempted to destroy it."

The strike was a most unfortunate one in its effect upon public opinion and is an important link in the chain of events which

---

[1] The report of the Mayor's Committee of which extracts are given in the New York *Times* for October 4, 1919, states that the Committee, concerned for the safety of the city, had suggested that troops be immediately called in, but the Police Commissioner stated "that he did not need or want the State Guard."

have led to the present reactionary and intolerant attitude on the part of many of those in positions of authority.

NEW YORK

In the State of New York the responsibility for the prevention and conciliation of industrial disputes is vested in the Bureau of Mediation and Arbitration of the Industrial Commission. Although this Bureau has served a useful purpose, it is entirely inadequate to meet the needs of the largest industrial state of the Union. Out of the many hundreds of strikes which occurred in 1917 and 1918, requests for intervention (in most instances by only one side) were received in twenty-five controversies in 1917 and twenty-four in 1918; and the Bureau seems to have intervened sixty-nine times in 1917 and eighty-eight times in 1918 and to have been successful in thirty-nine cases in the first year of the war and fifty-six in the second.[1] The war mediating agencies of the National Government, owing to their connection with the Federal production departments, exercised far greater authority than any state board could have done, and, as in other jurisdictions, the work of the New York Bureau of Mediation became less important after the creation of these National agencies.

In one of the most bitterly fought strikes in New York State of the post-armistice period, the State Board made excellent use of its powers of investigation and public inquiry. A strike had occurred in May, 1919, of the employees of the brass and copper mills of Rome, N. Y., several thousand workers being involved. The strike was for the eight-hour day and against the abolition of a 10% war bonus in wages. For ten weeks, during which the strike continued, the employers refused the offers of the state mediators and members of the State Industrial Commission to bring about a conference with their striking employees. The Commission thereupon, in August, instituted a public inquiry [2] and was

[1] Annual Reports of New York State Industrial Commission, 1917 and 1918. The period covered by these reports is from July 1st of the previous year to June 30th of the year of the report. Many of the strikes referred to in the report for 1917 occurred before our entry into the war. It appears that only two disputes were settled by arbitration in 1917 and one in 1918.

[2] See *The Bulletin* (issued by the New York State Industrial Commission) August, 1919, for an account of the strike and extracts of the testimony given at the public hearings.

about to publish its findings, when a settlement was arranged between the employers and their men and work was resumed.

In the fall of 1919 Governor Smith, at the suggestion of his reconstruction commission, called a conference to consider the best means of avoiding the serious disturbances which were occurring in the post-armistice period. As a result of this conference, he appointed a Labor Board, consisting of nine members, three representing the public, three representing employers and three representing labor.[1] This board had no statutory power but merely the prestige which the fact of its appointment by the Governor gave it. Since its creation it has intervened in only a few of the many disputes that have arisen but has done successful work in one or two cases.[2]

KANSAS

The strike of the soft coal miners of the winter 1919, affecting as it did practically every bituminous field in the country, operated also to tie up completely the coal mines of Kansas. An acute coal shortage ensued which necessitated the closing up of schools and factories and, it is claimed, threatened the continued use of hospitals. The State of Kansas thereupon took over the mines and asked for volunteers to operate them. Governor Allen called a special session of the legislature and urged upon it the

[1] The membership of the Board was as follows:

Representing the Public:	Lieutenant Governor Harry C. Walker
	Superintendent of Public Works Edward S. Walsh
	Adj. General Berry
Representing Employer:	Wm. Baldwin of the Otis Elevator Company
	Saul Singer, Cloak, Suit and Skirt Manufacturers' Protective Assoc.
	E. J. Barcalo, of Buffalo
Representing Labor:	James P. Holland, President of the New York State Federation of Labor
	Hugh Frayne, representing the American Federation of Labor
	F. M. Guerin, Vice-president State Federation

[2] To settle a very serious controversy in the Cloak, Suit and Skirt Industry of New York City, the Governor appointed a special board whose good offices were accepted by both sides. The board held hearings and made an award which seems to have successfully settled the dispute and reëstablished harmonious relations.

enactment of a law which he thought would make the recurrence of such an emergency impossible. The legislature thereupon passed a bill which has, since its enactment, been the storm center of acrimonious discussion all over the country. It creates a Court of Industrial Relations composed of three members,[1] which may intervene in any industrial controversy in the State in "any industry affected with a public interest." [2] Strikes are forbidden as are also suspensions of operation by the employer for the purpose of affecting wages or commodity prices, and severe penalties are provided for violations of the law. The Court is given the power to fix wages and the new rates may be made retroactive to the date when the Court took jurisdiction of the controversy. It is provided that wages shall be "fair" and that capital invested in an enterprise shall be entitled to a "fair" return. It will thus be seen that the Government through the agency of three appointed judges is given the power of fixing the wages of all workers, as well as large powers over the use of capital, in certain essential industries.[3] Employers are forbidden to discharge employees because of testimony given before the Court but no immunity is provided for discharge on account of union membership or activity, and inasmuch as strikes are forbidden, it would seem as though the workers were without any protection against the

[1] The first appointments to the Court were W. L. Huggins, an attorney, chairman; and Clyde M. Reed and William Allen White, newspaper men. Mr. White declined to serve, and George N. Wark, a law school graduate and a member of the American Expeditionary Forces, was appointed in his place.

[2] The manufacture or preparation of food products from their natural state to a condition to be used as food; the manufacture of wearing apparel in common use by the people; fuel mining and public utilities.

[3] The political philosophy of Governor Allen is set forth as follows in a speech made by him before the League for Industrial Rights and published in *Law and Labor*, April, 1920, page 88: "There is only one place in which justice may reside, only one guarantee of it, only one standardization of it, and that is in government. And so in Kansas, government has merely taken under its jurisdiction offenses against the public welfare committed in the name of Industrial Warfare; has taken under her jurisdiction the same right to govern them as she has to govern recognized crime. You say it cannot be done. My friends, if moral principles do not exist in American institutions to meet this emergency, then American institutions are doomed to failure, because the issue here is government and nothing but government."

breaking up of their unions by systematic discriminatory discharges.

The enactment of this law was vigorously opposed both by organized labor and by many employers and since its passage labor unions all over the country have made it the target for bitter attacks. President Howatt of the Kansas miners and a number of his associates were imprisoned because of their refusal to testify before the Court, and both the enactment of the law as well as the imprisonment of Mr. Howatt resulted in strikes of the miners, although it is claimed that these strikes were not at all serious. Governor Allen toured the country explaining the nature of the new Court and urging other states to adopt similar measures, and bills patterned after the Kansas statute have been introduced in the legislatures of a number of states. Too short a time has intervened since the passage of this law to say from experience how it is going to work. The Governor claims that great things have already been accomplished and that greater ones are to be expected.[1]

[1] Willard A. Atkins in *The Journal of Political Economy* for April, 1920, p. 343, says: "It is obvious that the Act is colored with the impatient thought of the present post-war period. Indeed under more tranquil conditions it is difficult to conceive of similar legislation evolving for some time to come."

PART TWO
PRINCIPLES

CHAPTER XIII

General Principles

THE policies adopted by Government labor boards were of the utmost importance in determining the treatment accorded to the workers during the war, because sooner or later all branches of industry came into contact with them. The course adopted by the Government was the resultant of many forces pulling in different directions. One of the most important of these forces was the American Federation of Labor, the influence of which, because of the skill and high degree of organization of its membership, was far greater than the relation of its size to the working population of the country would seem to have warranted. Its coöperation with the Government was essential—so also was that of the financial and manufacturing interests.

Obviously it was difficult to satisfy both sides. And in arriving at a policy the Government seems to have disregarded the extremists in each camp—the labor radicals, including the left wing of the Federation of Labor, and the most reactionary of the capitalists. The task was to find a policy which would satisfy the large body of labor, without alienating the financial and employing interests any more than was unavoidable. War psychology induced each side to compromise during the war period. Labor waived certain basic peace-time demands—insistence upon which, as we have seen, has increased in intensity as the period between the armistice and the present time has lengthened. Capital also was willing during the war to accept certain principles which in peace time it would in many cases actively have fought. Recent history, for example the story of the President's First Industrial Conference in Washington and the action of countless individual employers, confirms the correctness of this statement.

Many employers are under the impression that the Government truckled to labor during the war, and gave it everything it asked. A more careful study of just what labor did receive has confirmed and strengthened the opinion formed by the writer during the war that this was not in any sense the case, and that the Government did not, except in isolated cases, give to labor any concessions which were not demanded both by justice and expediency.[1] It will also be realized that, taking into account the power which the abnormal economic conditions and the needs of the hour placed in labor's hands, its conduct was both conservative and patriotic.

Early in our participation in the war, two ideas found expression:

(1) The demand for a relaxation of labor safeguards.

(2) The demand for the maintenance of the *status quo*—that is to say, that neither side was to attempt to change the conditions and principles then prevailing in industry.

As to the first demand, our knowledge of the mistakes England had made in throwing down all the barriers which had been erected to protect the workers, helped us to avoid a similar error (although war hysteria brought about the advocacy of this course by a substantial part of public opinion, including even some labor bodies).

As to the second demand, as far as the maintenance of the *status quo* applied to the retention of labor safeguards, it was a most salutary one. In the early statements of the Council of National Defense,[2] however, and in their amplification by the Secretary of Labor, this doctrine was used not merely to protect established labor standards, but also to discourage labor from making any effort—during the war—to obtain amelioration of those conditions in a particular industry which it had not been able to effect in peace-time (even the twelve-hour day, which was expressly mentioned in this statement). On the other hand, the employer was similarly urged not to depress conditions of labor. The tone of these early statements, in which the leaders of the American Federation of Labor concurred, is in sharp contrast with the still earlier resolutions adopted at a conference of the leaders of the Federation, at Washington on March 12, 1917, in which they said, "War has never put a stop to the necessity for struggle to establish and maintain industrial rights. Wage-earners in war times must, as has been said, keep one eye on the exploiters at

[1] See however discussion of overtime evil in the two succeeding chapters.
[2] *Monthly Review,* U. S. Bureau of Labor Statistics, June, 1917.

home and the other upon the enemy threatening the national government."[1] This remarkable change of attitude illustrates the effect of the patriotic motive during the first hysterical months of the war, when labor seemed willing to waive claims for even such improvements as were clearly demanded by public policy. This attitude, however, soon gave place to a more rational one, and later still to one of demanding thoroughgoing reforms.

The position taken by large manufacturers, as reflected in these statements of the Council of National Defense, resulted partly from their fear of an endeavor to extend the closed shop. In other respects also the employers were desirous of maintaining the *status quo,* as was shown by the statement of the Industrial Conference Board, submitted to the Council of National Defense on September 6, 1917.[2]

This insistence upon the maintenance of the *status quo,* held throughout the war by the employers, but soon abandoned by labor, was not the position finally adopted by the Government—except on the question of the open and closed shop. On the contrary, the various mediating agencies (especially the National War Labor Board) in many cases changed pre-war standards, awarding shorter hours, and wages which, in spite of the increased cost of living, more nearly approximated a living wage. They likewise failed to adhere to the pre-war status by insisting upon the extension of collective bargaining.

Statements of the Government's war labor principles find expression in three places: (1) Resolutions or executive orders of officers of the Government or of labor adjusting agencies; (2) Agreements between Government departments or boards on the one hand, and groups of employers and labor unions on the other; (3) Decisions of boards of adjustment.

[1] *American Federationist* for April, 1917, Volume XXIV, page 277.
[2] In this statement emphasis is laid on the maintenance of the open shop, but employers also demanded an "unambiguous interpretation" of the Council's recommendations (that standards be not changed) with respect to wages and hours, proposing
"(b) Applied to wages, demands shall be tested by the prevailing local standard of the establishment in effect at the beginning of the war with such modification as may be shown to be necessary to meet any demonstrated advance in the cost of living.
"(c) Applied to hours, the standard shall be those established by statute or prevailing in the establishment at the beginning of the war subject to change only when in the opinion of the Council of Defense it is necessary to meet the requirements of the Government."

The most comprehensive statement of principles was that of the National War Labor Board, contained in the President's Proclamation of April 9, 1918. These policies and principles came to be regarded as the highest labor law of the land, and were adopted by the War Labor Policies Board and accepted by every other agency, although many differences arose in their interpretation and application. In this chapter it is proposed to examine the principles that were applied by the different agencies and to consider the results upon industry which followed the Government's action.

NO STRIKES OR LOCKOUTS DURING THE WAR

The first principle enunciated by the National War Labor Board was that there should be no strikes or lockouts during the war. European countries had prohibited strikes in war time, but these legal prohibitions (especially among the Allies) had not been effective. With us, strikes were not legally prohibited; at any rate both the Government on the one hand and capital and labor on the other acted on this assumption. At the most critical periods of the war strikes of great magnitude occurred in the shipyards, the copper and coal mines, the lumber camps, and in munition plants (even in those engaged in the manufacture of the Browning machine gun, which at that particular time was a vital need of our army). And yet no attempt was made to prevent these strikes by means of legal prohibitions. It was not until a year after the signing of the armistice that the Government sought by force to put a stop to an important strike—the Lever Act, a purely war emergency measure (although never used for this purpose during the war itself) being made the justification for the issuance of a Federal injunction at the request of the Attorney General, speaking for the National Government.[1]

[1] On several occasions injunctions were issued by state and Federal Courts to prevent strikes and picketing under circumstances in which such relief might not have been granted except for the existence of the national emergency. These strikes were not important and the injunctions in question did not receive prominence. It was not until the issuance of the injunction under the Lever Act above referred to that any serious attempt was made on the part of the Government to prevent the occurrence of strikes by court action. In N. Y. State a lower court (Judge Scudder—Supreme Court, Trial Term, Queens Co., Oct., 1918) held in the case of Rosenwasser Bros. vs. Pepper (reported in 104 Misc. 457) that the plaintiff was entitled to in-

When machinery for the adjustment of disputes was established in the various branches of war production, there was a general

junctive relief by reason of the fact that 80% of its output of shoes, etc., was being manufactured for the U. S. Government. After stating in his opinion (p. 475) that "the life of our nation is dependent upon an uninterrupted production of the things needed to successfully carry on the war in which our country is engaged" an injunction was granted not merely against repetition of acts of violence and disorder, but also providing (p. 475): "Strikes for any cause whatsoever to be enjoined for the duration of the war." This decision was adversely criticized in the *Harvard Law Review* (Vol. XXXII, p. 837, May, 1919) as unsound on the ground that it is the function of legislative or administrative authorities and not of the judiciary to determine whether acts otherwise lawful are to be deemed unlawful because of national necessities created by the war.

The U. S. District Court for the Eastern District of Missouri (Wagner Mfg. Co. vs. District Lodge No. 9, International Association of Machinists, June, 1918, 252 Fed. Rep. 597) held that the fact that the plaintiff was engaged in manufacturing munitions for the United States and had been supplied by the Government with materials and property rendered it, to all intents and purposes, an agency of the Government itself; and that in the exercise of such duties, a Federal question was involved which conferred jurisdiction on the Federal courts—and subsequently an injunction issued from the court, not, however, unusually broad in its terms.

In the case of Kroger Grocery & Baking Co. vs. Retail Clerks International Protective Association (250 Fed. Rep. 890), also decided by the U. S. District Court for the Eastern District of Missouri (March, 1918), the Food Conservation Act of Congress (Aug. 10, 1917, Chap. 53, Sec. 4) was invoked by the court to justify an injunction against picketing, etc., considerably broader in its terms than would otherwise have been permissible under the Clayton Act—holding that during the war emergency the owner of perishable food products is entitled to the aid of a court of equity to restrain acts which would cause great destruction of food and that in such case "it would be wholly immaterial whether it was done by violence, threats, intimidation or otherwise."

In U. S. vs. Hayes—decided on Nov. 8, 1919, Judge A. B. Anderson issued a restraining order in connection with the coal strike which probably went further than any court of the United States had theretofore deemed proper. Under the authority of the Lever Act, the injunction issued not only prohibited the defendants from acts in furtherance of the coal strike, but also enjoined them from permitting the strike order to remain in effect and directed them to issue a withdrawal and cancellation of the order. The conduct of the Government in invoking the Lever Act for this purpose seems to have been in violation of distinct pledges made at the time of its passage that it would not be applied in cases where workers were endeavoring to secure improved working conditions; moreover a mandatory injunction in the form issued by Judge Anderson appears to have been unprecedented. The Executive Council of the American Federation of Labor denounced the decision as unwarranted, unparalleled and autocratic, stating "Never in the history of our country

understanding that in these industries strikes were not to take place. As a matter of fact this understanding was expressly incorporated in only two of the contracts under which the adjustment boards were created.[1] In several cases an agreement not to strike at least until controversies had been reviewed, was implicit in the terms of the contracts, and in all cases the boards took the position that there should be no cessation of industry during the war. In fact, the prevention of any stoppage of work was the main function of these boards. The avoidance of strikes was also one of the objects sought to be attained by the April, 1917, declarations of the Council of National Defense, already referred to, and great prominence was given to this principle by the President's proclamation creating the War Labor Board.

Inasmuch as the general principle of "no strikes in war time" was adopted almost unanimously by all parties to labor controversies, it might reasonably have been expected that very few strikes would have occurred during the war. Yet the facts were the precise opposite; more strikes did occur at this time than during any previous period of similar length in the history of the United States.[2] This is so extraordinary that it merits close inquiry and detailed explanation of the factors which were responsible for these dangerous and abnormally frequent stoppages of production. What were some of the more important of these factors?

In the first place, the workers usually had legitimate grievances. Their situation at the outbreak of the war, as we have seen in an earlier chapter, was frequently such as to deserve immediate bet-

---

has any such mandatory order been obtained or even applied for by the Government or by any person, company or corporation."

In addition to the occasional use of injunctions, already referred to, a number of State Governments sought to prevent individuals from remaining idle, during the national emergency, by the use of so-called "work or fight" laws.

[1] *I.e.*, Harness and Saddlery Adjustment Commission. The Fuel Administration announced an "understanding" on July 23, 1918 (agreed to by the workers), "That no strike shall take place pending the settlement of any controversy until the dispute has been reviewed by him" (the Fuel Administrator). See *Monthly Labor Review*, United States Bureau of Labor Statistics, for September, 1918. The agreement, signed by the workers for the creation of the New York Harbor Wage Adjustment Commission, provided that no strikes were to take place pending arbitration. *Monthly Labor Review*, September, 1918.

[2] See Appendix No. 1.

terment; in these cases the increase in the cost of living made their situation intolerable. In other industries where the previous rate of wages was a fair one the increasing living costs made revisions imperative, if the wage during the war was to remain the equivalent of the wage before the war.[1] To make matters worse the attitude of the employers was frequently provocative, particularly in the manner in which they discriminated against unionism, foolishly selecting members of shop committees for discharge immediately after their election to office, and in other similarly irritating actions.

In spite of these genuine grievances the workers in many industries—for the first year of the war—had no means of securing redress other than the strike. For a long time there was in many occupations absolutely no adequate machinery for the adjustment of disputes, and even later when mediation machinery of universal application was created there were many cases in which it was unworkable. Even the National War Labor Board, which was regarded as the most effective instrument for adjusting disputes, had no legal power to compel either side to submit to its jurisdiction, and there were a substantial number of cases in which employers refused to arbitrate and left to the workers the choice of either submitting or striking. All labor adjustment agencies, especially the National War Labor Board, were also overcrowded with work and necessarily slow in hearing grievances and making awards. They acted much more quickly if a strike was imminent or if the men were on the street[2] and production actually stopped. Unable to give prompt attention to every complaint that was made, the most urgent cases were taken up first, and a premium was thus put upon strikes and strike threats.

Unfortunately, moreover, the persistent tendency of the public and especially of the press[3] to condemn the workers on the

---

[1] Other grievances have been discussed in the first chapter and elsewhere.

[2] The National War Labor Board, as well as other wage adjustment boards, insisted that men return to work before it would take jurisdiction. In a number of cases, however, where the men were out, they were induced to return to work and submit their grievances to the Board only on its promise of *immediate* action. And these cases were heard and decided long ahead of cases where submissions were made in the regular way. There were also cases in which the National War Labor Board held hearings with the men out and upon the men going back, went definitely into the case.

[3] This will be more fully discussed in Chapter XVIII.

occurrence during the war of any and all strikes acted as an additional cause of irritation. The public did not realize that in many cases the men had no other way of securing redress or even a hearing.

The facts above set forth explain a large proportion of the strikes which occurred during the war. There can, however, be no doubt that after making all allowances there were hundreds of strikes which should not have occurred and that herein lay the greatest failure of the workers to conform to the Government's war labor policy. Many strikes took place in industries where machinery did exist for the peaceable adjustment of the workers' demands, without any adequate effort by the men to secure such adjustment. In many other cases the men stopped work without sufficient reason for so doing,[1] or in order to force compliance with demands not sanctioned by the Government's war labor policy.[2]

Some strikes were the result of the failure of one side or the other to comply with Government awards. These cases were, however, of infrequent occurrence. Many of the strikes in which the men acted without sufficient cause took place against the wishes of the national officers and sometimes even without the sanction of the local leaders. In very few cases, however, did the unions mete out any punishment to the locals or to their individual members because of these unauthorized strikes. The

[1] A case in point was the strike of machinists employed by the General Electric Company (Schenectady Works) in June, 1917, the cause of which was the employment by the company of a negro student to operate a drill press. The company employed very few negroes, and disclaimed any intention of supplanting its skilled men by negro employees. It made a practice, however, of employing a number of college students during the summer vacation, and among those recommended was the negro in question, whom the company refused to discharge or segregate. After about a week, the men returned to work. Many other examples could be given.

[2] The demand for the extension of the closed shop, more fully discussed subsequently in this chapter, was the cause of a large number of strikes, in violation of the Government's labor policies, as were some of the demands in relation to wages and to hours. A strike of a particularly irritating kind was reported from Jacksonville, Fla. Plasterers employed on a housing operation of the Emergency Fleet Corporation quit work because, they claimed, the foreman was driving them. He pointed out to the men that this was not the case—that they were not doing nearly as much work as they ordinarily did for a private contractor. They are reported to have replied: "We don't have to. It's Uncle Sam's money."

unions consequently cannot escape blame.[1] Nor can there be
any doubt that although at times the men took matters in their
own hands and walked out against the wishes of national as well
as local leaders, there were also many cases in which the leaders
remained passive and allowed the men to strike for the enforcement of demands which they knew were not sanctioned by the
Government. Occasionally, they even encouraged them to do so.

During the second year of the war, after the organization of the
National War Labor Board, the development of the Government's
labor administration, and the extension of the work of labor adjustment to practically all production departments, strikes became less frequent, although there were still many more than
could be justified. Had the war continued, they would undoubtedly have decreased more and more.[2]

Looking back over the entire war period, we cannot escape the
conclusion that strikes were the cause of very substantial losses
in production, for which both sides were at one time or another
to blame. In the aggregate, nevertheless, these losses were not
serious. Indeed it seems certain that the fear of stoppages of
work made both Government and employer more eager than they
would otherwise have been to eliminate grievances by fair adjustment of wages, by improving sanitary and housing conditions,
and by removing all other causes of unrest. If strikes contributed
substantially to the improvement of the condition of the workers
—which the writer is sure they often did—they were well worth
what they cost. At a time of social upheaval and world-wide unrest, when, moreover, the need for workers far exceeded the
supply, it was absolutely indispensable that reasonable demands
of the men be satisfied. Unquestionably, strikes and fear of
strikes were the chief causes for that amelioration of conditions
which strengthened morale and increased efficiency.[3] Nor has the
writer any doubt whatever that bad as industrial conditions now

[1] The Administrator of Labor Standards in Army Clothing, in an
effort to prevent strikes, which he said were happening entirely too
often in the clothing industry, refused to reinstate five workers who
had instigated a strike, without any effort being made to bring to
his attention for adjustment the grievances of the men. (Pohl, Hoyt
Company.—Brooklyn, New York.)

[2] See Appendix 1 for statistics relative to the number of strikes,
men involved, and so on.

[3] We shall see in a later chapter that, in spite of the above, morale
and efficiency were none too good.

are—recognizing fully the extent of present-day unrest and the lowered efficiency of the workers—they would be infinitely worse, if labor had been treated with less consideration during the war.

COLLECTIVE BARGAINING

This is the right of the men not only to deal with the employers as individuals but also to delegate to a few the right to bargain on behalf of the many. Collective bargaining need not involve unionism, and would do so only if the representatives of the men were not in the employ of the firm, or if, although in such employ they were elected as representatives of the union. Collective bargaining, then, may be simply defined as the right of the workers to choose representatives to deal with the employer on their behalf, and to present grievances, and to negotiate for changes in wages and working conditions. And it seems incredible that in a country which has for many years boasted of its political democracy so many employers should have insistently denied the same principle of democracy when applied to industry.[1]

It was realized by Government mediators that the task which confronted the nation was not only to settle a particular controversy and secure the return to work of men who were on strike, but that a stronger sense of loyalty and an increased willingness to give the best that one has must also be promoted. Every active Government labor board therefore realized the desirability of collective bargaining—which gave the workers a sense of responsibility—as the strongest factor in such promotion of morale,[2] the

[1] The attitude of many employers is illustrated by the testimony of Vice President Lewis of the Bethlehem Steel Company, at the hearings before the National War Labor Board of the complaints of the employees against the company. Mr. Lewis was asked if the company (this was in the summer of 1918) received complaints from committees on behalf of the men. He answered that it did not. He said that if anything was wrong with a man's working conditions he was to complain to his foreman or superintendent. Pressed for an answer as to whether the company would receive a committee consisting of its own employees (not a committee of the union) he said: "I don't think, at this time, we would be prepared to allow that practice . . . we don't employ a committee, we employ a particular individual, and naturally we are always willing to listen to what he has to say and make corrections."

[2] The Post Office Department seems to have been the only exception. In its administration of the telephone service, it not only failed to promote collective bargaining, but actually prevented existing machinery for this purpose from functioning.

boards differing only in the extent to which they gave it practical application. Consequently not only did the Government protect existing forms of collective bargaining, but it also fostered the development of new machinery for the purpose.[1]

The President's Mediation Commission, the National War Labor Board, the Shipbuilding Labor Adjustment Board, and the Administrator for Army Clothing, were all active in setting up systems of this kind. General Order Number 13 of the Ordnance Department recommended collective bargaining, and the Industrial Service Section of the Ordnance and Aircraft Departments actively encouraged its introduction in manufacturing plants. On the railroads, it already existed in many places, and its extension was fostered. In fact, throughout all industry in the entire country the war period witnessed a phenomenal broadening out of this principle.

Collective bargaining can be practiced in many different ways. The method usually adopted by the Government was through the medium of shop committees, elected by all the workers in the plant.[2] But in the installation of these committees and in the Government's efforts to get them to function properly great difficulties were encountered. In the first place, many employers were hostile to any form of collective action on the part of their employees; they had to be coerced into establishing any type of employee representation whatsoever. Inasmuch as shop committees could not possibly function without the exercise of a spirit of coöperation by both parties, this was a very unfortunate beginning. A second difficulty came from the other side. Most plants were partially but not wholly organized, and the leaders of labor unions were frequently opposed to shop committees which they could not control. In case the shop was completely organized this objection did not hold, because the shop committees would be composed of men who were members of and in sympathy with the union. If, however, the shop was only partially organized, and this was the condition in many, if not most, of the plants doing war work, these committees might contain men who were not members of the union and who might be hostile to it. Since the Government made it a fixed policy not to influence

[1] It is interesting to note that the British Commission on Industrial Unrest recommended collective bargaining for immediate adoption.
[2] In most cases three or six months' service was necessary to qualify the worker as a voter.

the worker in regard to joining any union, and therefore would not force the complete organization of a shop, the Government was powerless to overcome this objection of the men.[1]

The difficulty resulting from the partial organization of the shops was also illustrated by the friction which in some cases accompanied the election of shop committees. In order to prevent employers from controlling these elections and from making impossible the free choice of union members, and, on the other hand, to prevent a minority of union men from improprely securing the election of members of their organization, the Government boards found it desirable to insist that the voting take place under the supervision of Government representatives. It was even necessary to exercise care in the choice of a polling place; elections held at union headquarters were set aside by both the Shipbuilding Labor Adjustment Board and the National War Labor Board because it was believed that all the workers had not had an opportunity freely to express their choice. And, similarly, one election was set aside by the National War Labor Board because it had been held in the company's office. Further difficulty arose as to what the proper constituencies of the shop committees ought to be. Employers usually preferred representation according to physical divisions of the plant, i.e., by shops or floors, whereas the employees favored representation according to craft. This was natural enough, since the organizations which the men had previously built up were along craft lines, and the men wished to preserve this structure. On the other hand, just because the existing or hoped-for organizations of the men were along craft lines, the employers, in their opposition to unionism, preferred to have committees which represented the individual shops,[2] rather than entire crafts. There were also a few cases in which the employers, although willing to deal with shop committees, objected to committees representing the entire plant.

[1] It might also have been possible for the Government to have satisfied the unions, if they had compelled employers to deal with union committees. But if, at the outbreak of the war, the employer had not previously made a practice of so doing, it was an invariable rule that he would not be made to do so during the war. (This is more fully discussed in a later part of this chapter.)

[2] The plans for the organization of shop committees, used by the Shipbuilding Labor Adjustment Board, provide for representation according to craft.

Even under ideal conditions, systems of collective bargaining, to be successful, are of slow growth. It is therefore not to be wondered at that all of these new shop committees did not function successfully; as a matter of fact, in some cases where shop committees were installed during the war strikes have occurred since the signing of the armistice, and the committees have been abandoned.[1] Information as to the actual workings of these committees is difficult to get, and there is likely in any event to be a great deal of difference of opinion. In many cases, they undoubtedly did excellent work; as we have seen, the Taft-Walsh Board entrusted them with the application of wage scales throughout large plants, with the classification of employees, the enforcement of rules relative to hours of work and with other important functions. In December, 1918, thirty-six shipyards reported to the Shipping Board that their shop committees were working well.[2] In other industries also these committees are reported to be functioning satisfactorily.[3]

For several years previous this movement had been gathering force, and although given a decided impetus by the events of the war, it would undoubtedly have been developed in any case.[4] In spite of their abandonment in some places, employers everywhere are manifesting keen interest in shop committees and in the gen-

[1] As an example, the Pittsfield, Mass., plant of the General Electric Company. On the other hand although strikes occurred at the same time at other General Electric Company shops, the men at Lynn, Mass., did not go on strike. Here a shop committee plan installed under the direction of the National War Labor Board was working excellently and has been continued, as have shop committee plans in some of the other plants of the company.

[2] Works Committees—A. B. Wolfe.

[3] Works Councils in the United States, Research Report No. 21, October, 1919, published by the National Industrial Conference Board quotes from replies to a questionnaire sent out by it to a large number of firms which had installed shop committees under the direction of the National War Labor Board. In some cases they were reported as working very well, in other cases it was stated that they had been abandoned.

[4] In England a number of National Commissions have recommended workers representation and the findings of some of them go very much farther. Thus the Whitley Committee recommends not only shop committees for individual establishments but also District and National Councils.

eral subject of employee representation.[1] Many, perhaps, because they see in some of its forms a weapon with which to fight unionism; they realize that representation of the workers in industry is bound to come sooner or later in some form or other and they prefer shop committees to "outside" unions.[2] Some more farsighted employers realize that representation in industry is demanded by social justice and that with the spread of education among the workers they will insist upon getting a larger share of control over industry and participation in its management.

RIGHT TO ORGANIZE

In the statement of principles of the National War Labor Board at the same time that the right of the workers to bargain collectively was recognized, their right to organize in trade unions and engage in legitimate trade union activity without interference by the employer was affirmed.[3] The first official pronouncement

---

[1] In Works Councils in the United States, The National Industrial Conference Board, it is stated that practically all of the 225 Works Councils, or shop committees reported upon were formed since January 1, 1918; 86 were created as a result of awards of the National War Labor Board, 31 of the Shipbuilding Labor Adjustment Board, 3 are war time "Government Committees" and 105 were voluntarily instituted.

[2] The opposition of unions to forms of workers' representation known as "company" or "household" unions, i. e., shop committee plans for workers of a particular plant, not affiliated with the unions of the entire trade, was shown at the 39th Annual Convention, A. F. of L., June, 1919, by the adoption of a resolution condemning the "Rockefeller" plan of industrial representation and all so-called "company" unions and demanding the right to bargain collectively through trade unions. It is also of interest to note that in the steel strike the abolition of "company" unions was one of the demands of the strike.

[3] The one exception to this otherwise universal rule occurred in the State of Minnesota where the right to organize was denied during the war period. Immediately after the declaration of war by the United States the legislature of Minnesota passed an act (April 18) creating a Public Safety Commission. A year later the State Board of Arbitration brought about an agreement between the Minnesota Employers' Association and the Minnesota Federation of Labor, agreeing upon certain principles as basic in the relation between employer and employee during the war. Among them was the provision that if an employer, before the war, had refused to employ or continue in his employ any member of a trade union, the continuation of this practice, during the war, would not constitute a ground of complaint. The Commission of Public Safety issued an Order on April 30, 1917, under war powers given to it, which vested in the

of this principle was that of Secretary Wilson, who, after a conference with representatives of the Council of National Defense and of organized labor, issued a statement on April 23, 1917, explanatory of two statements previously issued by the Council of National Defense on April 7 and April 16.[1] Secretary Wilson referred to the right to organize into trade unions as a "burning question," and said "my own attitude is this, that capital has no right to interfere with working men organizing labor any more than the working man has a right to interfere with capitalists organizing capital." [2] This was the position taken with great unanimity by all labor adjustment boards, although the agreements creating the boards did not, for the first year of the war, expressly mention it except in one case.[3] In practice, however, the boards consistently acted upon this principle.

This feature of the Government's war labor program—the granting to the workers of the right to organize into trade unions —was the one big concession made to labor by the employers, and indeed many of the largest among them were never reconciled to it. On this point the feeling of the employers was well expressed by Newcombe Carlton of the Western Union Company when in explanation of the position taken by his company in refusing to reinstate a number of employees at the request of the War Labor Board he issued a statement in which he said, "if these principles are interpreted as compelling this company and others in like situation to abandon their settled policies, and leaving outside organizations free to work as they may see fit among their employees, then the hands of the employers are tied and the principles of the War Labor Board furnish a cloak behind which a

Board of Arbitration, "compulsory powers to bring about arbitration on the conditions set forth in the agreement." This conflict between the rule adopted by the State of Minnesota and the principles of the National War Labor Board resulted in a good deal of confusion. In one case, the Twin City Rapid Transit Company, the right to organize was one of the vital issues. The War Labor Board assumed jurisdiction, and gave the men the right to organize which the State Board would have denied them.

[1] *Monthly Review,* Bureau of Labor Statistics, June, 1917, page 807.
[2] *Monthly Review,* Bureau of Labor Statistics, June, 1917, page 809.
[3] The "understanding" of the Fuel Administration, issued on July 23, 1918 (*Monthly Review,* Bureau of Labor Statistics, September, 1918), contains express provision against discrimination, as does the agreement creating one of the earlier boards, to wit, The New York Harbor Adjustment Commission.

propaganda for the unionizing of labor in every industry may be carried on without hindrance." Although this deep resentment at the fact that they were forced to allow their men to organize was shared by most employers,[1] few—and the Western Union Company was one of them—ventured to go to the length of openly refusing to accept this definite rule of the Government. But in many instances they covertly violated it.

The importance of the Government's recognition of the right to organize can be appreciated when we recall the fact that the employers' denial of this right[2] had been one of the chief causes of industrial unrest. In fact, the testimony of the labor adjustment boards evidences innumerable cases in which before the war union members were consistently discriminated against. As an example the use of the so-called "rustling card" (and of central employment offices) on the Great Lakes and the Pacific Coast was shown to have been largely for the purpose of controlling, if not eliminating, the employment of members of unions; and discrimination was likewise revealed as common in the street railway service, the metal trades, lumber camps, and in hundreds of other places.

In spite of the fact that discrimination of this kind was forbidden during the war by Government policy, the workers constantly complained that it was, nevertheless, being continued. Nor

---

[1] Nor was the resentment of the employers lessened by the fact that the rule adopted by the Government's Labor Administration was directly contrary to that which had previously been adopted by the Supreme Court of the United States. Practices of discrimination on account of union membership had gone so far that employees were compelled, upon entering upon the employment of certain firms, to sign agreements not to join a labor union or to give up their jobs if they did so. The State of Kansas had forbidden the requirement of these contracts. In the case of Coppage vs. Kansas, 236 U. S. 1, this law was declared unconstitutional and in Hitchman Coal and Coke Company vs. Mitchell, 245 U. S. 232, an injunction was upheld which restrained the officers of a union from securing secret promises to join the union from employees who had agreed to give up their employment if they joined it. In Adair vs. United States, 208 U. S. 161, an Act of Congress which forbade interstate carriers from discharging because of union membership was held unconstitutional.

In spite of these decisions by the U. S. Supreme Court, the National War Labor Board refused to permit discrimination in any form and in a number of cases ordered contracts of the type above referred to abolished.

[2] The metal trades of Bridgeport and practically all of New England are cases in point.

can there be any question that in many instances the workers' complaints were justified by the facts—in other words, that flagrant violations of the Government's policy were frequently taking place. This persistence in the practice of discriminating against members of unions constituted the most serious violation of the Government's war labor principles by employers, just as the persistent calling of strikes by the workers constituted their most serious violation.

The justice of this statement can be shown by the testimony before the wage boards, which contains many examples revealing how widespread was the practice and how great was the bitterness which it caused among the men. In their attempt to decide whether or not a discharge was justified the Government boards were embarrassed by the fact that their decision involved the necessity of determining the employers' motives. Unfortunately it was very easy for the employer to find a pretext, and the board had to decide whether the reason assigned for the decision was genuine. This difficulty was increased by the fact that, in view of the danger of enemy propaganda and violence, it was essential to employ secret service agents, who reported to the firm every form of agitation among the men. These detectives did not distinguish between routine trade union activity and agitation for radical industrial changes. They made no effort to confine their reports to actions which could be even remotely construed as sympathetic toward the enemy, calling attention to action so harmless as using the lunch hour for soliciting union membership.

Even before the war many employers had made it a practice to spy upon the activities of the unions. Never warranted in time of peace, this practice might have been justified during the war if it had been limited to an effort to prevent the unions from becoming instruments for furthering enemy purposes. As a matter of fact, however, it was used in many cases to discover employees who were active members or organizers of the unions. These men were thereupon marked for immediate discharge, or a pretext might be waited for until the worker who had been active in his organization could be plausibly dismissed.[1]

[1] There were cases in which, in order to prevent the spread of unionism in their shops, firms discharged men who had been in their employ for over 30 years. The writer knows of one instance where, for this purpose, the following procedure was adopted. The general

In order to determine whether or not a discharge was justified it frequently became necessary to determine what was "legitimate trade union activity," as distinguished from practices which were clearly not allowable, such as collection of dues during shop hours. These questions were sometimes extremely difficult to answer,[1] but it was always held that during shop hours solicitation for union membership and other union activity were illegitimate.

As a result of the immunity from discharge for union membership or activity, granted by the Government, a most active campaign was carried on by the men to increase the membership of their organizations. On the railways alone it is claimed that union membership was increased during the war period by one million men and it is stated that another million joined the unions

manager, hearing that an effort was being made to organize the men, came to Newark, where the shop is located, and after ascertaining the prevailing rate of wages, determined upon a scale which he was willing to pay. The new rate, although higher than that which was then prevailing in Newark, was lower than the rate demanded by the unions, and the men in this shop were working nine hours whereas the union demand was eight. The foreman was instructed to go to every man, to tell him his new rate, and then to ask him whether or not he was satisfied with conditions. If he answered "No" he was summarily discharged, irrespective of the length of time that he had been in the employ of the firm; some of the men who were thus discharged had been with the firm for over 25 years. Inasmuch as every member of the union would certainly answer in the negative, this proved a convenient method of getting rid of the union men without it too openly appearing that they were being discharged for union membership.

[1] A curious case was decided by Professor Ripley, Administrator of Labor Standards in Army Clothing. The employer (A. B. Kirschbaum Company of Philadelphia) at the instigation of the Administrator, had entered into an agreement with its employees for the introduction of a system of collective bargaining in conformity with the practice of the National War Labor Board—the shop committees having no connection with any outside organization. An employee, after warning, persisted during the lunch hour in distributing leaflets announcing a shop meeting of the Amalgamated Clothing Workers of America. For this action the worker was discharged. The Administrator had some difficulty in deciding whether or not this was "legitimate trade union activity." He decided that it was not because ". . . the leaflets announcing the meeting remained scattered all over the floor during the rest of the day. These leaflets constitute in a sense a trespass upon the employer's premises and strongly tend to build up the outside union regardless of the effect upon the 'household' union set up within its gates." The reinstatement of the discharged employee was therefore refused.

in other industries.[1] It cannot be said that the protection afforded by the Government from discriminatory discharges was entirely responsible for this increase. Professor Commons[2] and others have pointed out that the growth of unions usually takes place when prices and profits are rising. It is more than likely that in any event a large growth would have taken place, but undoubtedly this growth would have been much smaller without the protection which the Government afforded.

COERCION

The rules of the Taft-Walsh Board also prohibited the use of "coercive measure of any kind to induce persons to join their organization" or "to induce employers to bargain or deal therewith." Reinstatement was always refused where it was found that a discharged employee had violated this rule. But whether this rule had as a matter of fact been violated was always difficult to determine, as definite proof of acts of coercion was frequently lacking and what proof there was, was contradictory.

The commonest forms of coercion were the spoiling of work of men who refused to join the unions, ostracizing them, and pestering them during the lunch hour and to and from the shop. How difficult it was to establish the facts of coercion is shown, for example, in the case of spoiled work; sometimes the damage was clearly deliberate, in other cases it might appear to have been the carelessness of the worker himself, but in all cases it was almost impossible to prove who actually did the harm.

There can be no doubt that coercion was, and is to-day, frequently practiced; indeed, during the war, material urgently needed for its successful prosecution was deliberately destroyed just in order to increase union membership. Although the leaders

[1] The American Federation of Labor—History, Encyclopedia and Reference Book, 1919, page 63, publishes a chart showing flunctuations in union membership from 1881 to 1919. It appears that from 1905 to 1910 (inclusive) membership remained stationary at approximately 1,500,000. It then rose gradually to 2,000,000 in 1914 and stayed at practically this level during 1915 and 1916. But in 1917 (our first year of the war) it rose over a quarter of a million and in 1918 almost half a million to nearly 2,750,000. In 1919 it passed the 3,000,000 mark. The Railroad Brotherhoods, as well as unions in the clothing, textile, and other trades, which also grew rapidly during the war, are not included in these figures.
[2] John R. Commons; Industrial Goodwill, page 171.

did not encourage these vicious practices, on the other hand they did not vigorously oppose them.

NO CHANGE FROM UNION TO OPEN SHOP OR VICE VERSA

At the outbreak of the war the biggest industrial issue confronting the country was the issue of unionism and especially of the open versus the closed shop. Most large employers, even though they permitted union men to remain in their shops, were unalterably opposed to the exclusive employment of union men; and they anticipated an attempt on the part of the unions to take advantage of the abnormal conditions accompanying the war by compelling them to adopt the closed shop. It was in answer to these fears that Secretary Wilson, in his statement of April 23, 1917, declared "that where either the employer or the employee has been unable under normal conditions to change the standards to their own liking, they should not take advantage of the present abnormal conditions to establish new standards." This was regarded as a statement of the Government's general policy, and was interpreted by the Secretary of War to mean specifically that the Government did not intend to compel the extension of the closed shop.[1] This rule was adopted by all other boards,[2] except the Emergency Construction Wage Adjustment Commission.[3]

[1] In its instructions to bidders, issued by the War Department, Purchase Section, Gun Division, dated September 25, 1917, there appeared the following explanation of the "labor disputes clause": "In order to obviate any misunderstanding with respect to the intent of this clause or the policy of the Government in inserting the same, the Secretary of War designates that contractors be advised of the fact that by the foregoing statement (that of Secretary Wilson quoted in the text) the Government has emphatically renounced any suggestion of introducing the closed shop, under cover of settling disputes in plants doing Government work."

[2] *I.e.*, by the National War Labor Board (See Appendix VII); by Fuel Administration when, in an "understanding," it stated that recognition of unions was not to be exacted where they were not now recognized; in most other cases there was no express provision in the agreements creating the boards but this rule was followed. In the special case of the New York Harbor Wage Adjustment Board the agreement in fact stipulated that the Board "shall have no authority to pass upon the question of the open or closed shop. (See *Monthly Labor Review*, United States Bureau of Labor Statistics, September, 1918, page 4.)

[3] This board was organized for the express purpose of permitting the utilization by building contractors (engaged in the construction of

The relinquishment by the unions of the demand for the closed shop (together with the demand for union recognition, the next point discussed in this chapter) was the most important concession made by labor during the war. And from the standpoint of efficient production it was absolutely necessary that the Government procure this concession; without it, strikes would probably have been disastrously widespread and severe, because it is certain that many large employers would have fought the demand for the closed shop to the last ditch. In fact, the granting of the right to organize was in part the result of the Government's effort to reconcile labor to this concession.

Yet the adoption by the Government of the principle that the closed shop should not be insisted upon during the war did not entirely put a stop to this demand. In the first place it was not generally known until later in the war that the Government had adopted this policy. And even after it was known there were many cases in which the principle was violated. Sometimes the demand for the closed shop was used merely as a bargaining point, to be withdrawn as soon as negotiations had proceeded any distance; at other times it was a genuine demand, seriously made— but in many of these cases to be withdrawn as soon as it was pointed out that the change to the closed shop was not sanctioned by the Government. A few of the International Unions, such as the Amalgamated Association of Street and Electric Railway Employees and the Brotherhood of Carpenters, persisted in their efforts to obtain the closed shop. The latter, indeed, as we have seen in a previous chapter, went so far as to refuse to become a party to the agreement creating the Shipbuilding Labor Adjustment Board because to have done so would have meant the abandonment of the demand for the closed shop. For the same

quarters in which to house and drill the newly formed American Army) of all the building mechanics in the country, whether or not members of trade unions. Although the agreement did not expressly state that members of the unions would work with non-union men, this was the understanding under which the board was created. And in many cases building constructors, who before the war had closed union shops, exercised the right—when engaged on cantonment work —to employ any one at all, whether union members or not. Much later, however, after the announcement by the President of the principles of the National War Labor Board, this rule of no change from open to closed shops was, at the direction of the Secretary of War, adopted by the Emergency Construction Wage Adjustment Commission.

reason the carpenters also had constant friction with the Emergency Construction Wage Adjustment Board.[1] In no case, however, did any Government agency compel an employer to change from the open to the closed shop.

Quite a number of small vexatious strikes took place, all of them revolving around the same dispute. Usually these strikes were called against the wishes of the national officers and frequently without the sanction of even the local leaders. Thus in the New York machine shops there were almost constant walkouts because of the presence of non-union men or of members of a rival union. These establishments, although they had never been closed shops, were in many cases almost 100% organized. It seemed almost impossible to get the men back to work and to restore harmony, if the non-union men were not discharged. Although the Government always took the position that the shop should remain open, the employers, who were anxious to see production resumed in their plant rather than waste time over a few men, preferred to drop the non-union men, even if they did not formally agree to the closed shop. Ordinarily, as has been stated earlier, the employers—and especially the larger ones—would have fought this closed shop demand to the bitter end. But these last mentioned cases were special and more or less unimportant.

UNION RECOGNITION

This is frequently confused with the closed shop, although the two are entirely distinct. If an employer deals with union officials, who are not his own employees, and discusses with them conditions in his shop, this would constitute a "recognition" of the union in the sense in which this term is ordinarily used. Employers who are hostile to labor organizations have been afraid that to negotiate about working conditions in their own plants with union leaders—not members of their own establishment—would so

[1] The carpenters' strike on the Navy Training Station at Pelham Bay in the summer of 1917, involved as its chief issue the closed shop. This was before the jurisdiction of the Emergency Construction Wage Commission was extended to navy work. As a matter of fact, in this case the carpenters were successful. Upon the organization of the National War Labor Board, Mr. Hutcheson, the Brotherhood's President, became a member of it, and hence was committed to its principles by his official position. Irrespective of this, his organization continued to make this demand.

strengthen the union in the eyes of their workers that it was bad policy for them to do so. In fact, they seem in such cases to have feared that such dealings with union representatives would inevitably lead directly to the closed shop.[1]

The Government's rule in regard to recognition of the union was identical with that governing the extension of the closed shop —to wit, that no change was to be made during the war, and that no employer would be forced to recognize a union where such had not been his practice before the war. The principles of the National War Labor Board, although, as we have seen, insisting upon collective bargaining, expressly provide that "in establishments where . . . the employer meets only with employees or representatives engaged in said establishments, the continuance of such conditions shall not be deemed a grievance." This rule was generally applied by all Government boards.[2]

Like the giving up of the demand for the closed shop, the giving up of the demand for union recognition was an important concession on the part of labor.[3] Like it also, the demand for union recognition was frequently one of several, but was usually not insisted upon, especially towards the end of the war when the

---

[1] In the recent steel strike in which the walkout of the men was precipitated by Mr. Gary's refusal to see a committee representing the A. F. of L. and to discuss with it the grievances of his men, the steel company went so far as to say that the closed shop was the real issue in the strike, implying that to recognize the union would inevitably lead to the closed shop. In explaining his position to the Steel Institute, Mr. Gary makes the closed shop synonymous with "collective bargaining through labor union leaders." (See *Review of Reviews* for November, 1919.) The press in its news accounts and editorial discussion of the strike assumed that the closed shop was actually the issue. Yet, as a matter of fact, the men were not demanding the closed shop at all; they merely wanted the right to negotiate with their employers through men who were officers of international unions.

[2] An exception to this general application was the ruling of John Lind, ex-Governor of Minnesota, as Umpire of the National War Labor Board in the case of the Bement-Niles-Pond Co. Docket No. 339.

[3] The importance of this concession can be best realized by recalling the strength of this demand shortly after the armistice was signed. In the steel industry, for instance, it would have been inconceivable that a demand for union recognition—on a nation-wide scale—should have been seriously put forward during the war, for the reason that such a demand would have been contrary to the Government's war labor principles, to which the leaders of the A. F. of L. had subscribed.

principle of "no change" became better known and more generally acceded to.

There can be no doubt that the refusal of the employers to deal with union representatives was—and is—the cause of a great deal of bitterness among the men. One of the reasons for this is that the men feel that union leaders who devote all their time to the business of the organization are in a better position to represent them and to look after their interest than are the men in the shops. The men's attitude toward these leaders is somewhat akin of the attitude of employers toward attorneys whom the employers engage to represent them (sometimes, indeed, even in labor disputes). The men also feel that outside union leaders who are not dependent for their livelihood upon the employer will be more fearless in their bargaining. A more obscure but none the less real cause for this resentment springs from the fact that refusal to meet their representatives (for many of whom they have a high regard) is frequently taken by the men as a personal insult. These leaders are, after all, the heads of an organization to which the men in question belong and to which they attach the utmost importance. Unwillingness even to meet these leaders implies an attitude of contempt toward the whole organization. Yet although the abandonment of the men's demand for union recognition often resulted in bitterness and unrest,[1] the Government's mediators invariably [2] enforced the rule that when a union

[1] The Amalgamated Association of Street and Electric Railway Employees always made recognition of the unions one of their demands, in cities in which the union was not already recognized; and a number of very bitter strikes took place (at times accompanied by violence) in which this demand was pressed. At Dayton, Ohio, the men were out on strike and at first refused to go back, pending the adjudication of the National War Labor Board, unless their union was first recognized. They claimed that so bitter was the opposition that if they went back, the union would be destroyed while they were waiting for the decision of the Board. The matter was finally submitted to the National War Labor Board (Docket No. 150), where recognition of the union was denied.

[2] The case of the telephone girls on the Pacific Coast, adjudicated by the President's Mediation Commission, is a very interesting one, because it is said to have been the first time that a men's union struck to secure recognition for a women's union. The commission granted recognition to the union, which might appear inconsistent with the above statement. But this decision was made in the early days of the war before the rule was generally promulgated. It was also based upon the fact that the company had previously recognized the girls' union in some other parts of the country. (See Report of President's Mediation Commission, page 12.)

had not been previously recognized, it would not demand such recognition during the war.

MAINTENANCE OF ESTABLISHED STANDARDS

Reference has already been made to the attempt in the first days of the war to break down the laws and customs which had been built up by painful effort for the protection of the workers, especially of women and children. Unlike similar attempts in Europe which were successful, with us, these attempts met with prompt defeat in the legislatures of the different states. Wage boards also took the position that established safeguards should not be relaxed. General Order Number 13 of the Ordnance Department expressly provided for the maintenance of standards of health and comfort, as did the principles of the National War Labor Board. In some cases the Government went so far as to insist that clauses, protecting standards of health, be inserted in contracts for the manufacture of war materials. Thus contracts for army clothing provided against the employment of children under 16 years of age, compelled compliance with local factory laws, and contained provision intended to eliminate the sweat-shop system of manufacturing.[1]

The War Labor Policies Board gave thorough consideration to the standardization of these labor clauses to be inserted in contracts of the War and Navy Departments, the Emergency Fleet Corporation, and the United States Housing Corporation.[2] Standards for safeguarding women, who were entering industry by the hundreds and thousands, were worked out by the newly created Women in Industry Service of the Department of Labor, indorsed by the War Labor Policies Board, and applied by the different labor adjustment agencies. These regulations were particularly useful in preventing the night work of women except under ex-

[1] *Monthly Review*, Bureau of Labor Statistics, October, 1917, page 31.
[2] These clauses require that "all work . . . shall be performed in full compliance with the State, Territory, or District of Columbia, where such work is performed; provided that the contractor shall not employ in the performance of this contract any minor under the age of 14 years or permit any minor between the ages of 14 and 16 years to work more than 8 hours in any one day, more than 6 days in any one week, or before 6 A. M. or after 7 P. M." Also provisions against convict labor and for the observance of the Federal Eight-Hour Law.

traordinary circumstances, and in providing for the maintenance of proper sanitary conditions and for proper limitations of the hours of work and for rest periods. It is a remarkable fact that in spite of the pressure for war production the Government should at this particular time have gone out of its way not only to protect existing labor standards but also to initiate new ones. Instead of the war period having been one of retrogression it was on the contrary a period during which attention was directed to the necessity for these standards as it never was before.

EQUAL PAY FOR EQUAL WORK

Until fairly recently this principle was almost unknown. The movement for its application especially in public work had been gathering force as women gained increased political power. It has also been one of the demands of the labor unions—not so much as a matter of justice to women as to protect the wage standards of men.

The emergencies of war production made it imperative that millions of women should be introduced into industry to take the places of the men at the front. The wage-earners, union men especially, feared that this would result in a lowering of wage standards, and they consequently from the outset demanded that the women receive the same pay as the men for the same work.[1] This demand having been adopted by all the war labor boards the unions were reconciled to this dilution of their trades.

The adoption of this principle was a wholesome measure, even though its adoption was easier than its enforcement. It provided for equal pay *for equal work;* but the difficulty was to determine whether or not the work was equal, and if unequal, to what degree.[2] For some jobs women were used exclusively, and here it was particularly difficult to enforce the rule. Even where men and women were engaged in exactly the same work there were elements which a strict enforcement of the rule made it necessary to take into consideration. Thus women might require a

[1] See the March 12, 1917, statement of the A. F. of L. (*American Federationist* for April, 1917, page 279): "In any eventuality when women may be employed, we insist that equal pay for equal work shall prevail without regard to sex."
[2] See G. D. H. Cole in *The Dial,* July 26, 1919, for discussion of English controversy on this subject.

greater amount of supervision; they might be less adaptable to other work and therefore less valuable in a factory; they might have to call upon the assistance of men to do heavy lifting which men could do by themselves. In the application of the rule there can be no doubt that women in many cases did not receive quite as much as men would have for the same work. But it is nevertheless true that on the whole there was a substantial approximation to equality, and as a result women's wages advanced during the war much more rapidly than they would have if this rule had not existed. Speaking generally, women were during the war period very well paid.[1] This is in marked contrast to the conditions which prevailed during the Civil War, when in spite of large increases in the cost of living the pay of women advanced very little, and in some cases actually declined, although the wages of men uniformly advanced.[2]

---

[1] The aëroplane factories paid women 40 cents an hour while learning to become machinists, and very much higher wages when they became proficient.

[2] E. D. Fite in his Social and Industrial Conditions in the North during the Civil War, page 186, after referring to the increase in prices which he states advanced approximately 100%, says: "The low wages of women were a special grievance. When it was known in the winter of 1863-1864 that these had practically made no advance, general sympathy was aroused; and when, a year later, it appeared that only a paltry advance of twenty-five per cent had been achieved, less than half that for men, the sympathy was increased. In some lines of women's work no advance at all was made by the latter date, but on the contrary an actual decline. This seems scarcely credible, and yet the evidence is overwhelming. The most pitiable case was that of the seamstresses, thousands of whom were employed in making army clothing, some hired directly by the Government, some by contractors under a vicious system of contracting and sub-contracting. In the Philadelphia Armory in 1861 women were paid by the Government seventeen and one-half cents for making a shirt, three years later, at the very time when prices themselves were highest, only fifteen cents, and at this latter date the contractors were paying only eight cents. A small advance by the Government toward the close of the war was of little real benefit, since most of the work was then being given over to the contractors whose prices grew lower and lower. Protests in public meetings, the most harrowing tales in the newspapers, and petitions to the Secretary of War and to the President appeared useless, and the poor victims were left to their fate, undoubtedly the greatest sufferers of any class from the war; they suffered even more than the clerks in mercantile pursuits and college teachers. . . . An average week's wage paid by the contractors in 1865 was $1.54."

CHAPTER XIV

Hours

THE establishment of the eight-hour day is one of the few industrial questions about which it can be said that there has been a national policy, favored by a fair preponderance of public opinion.[1] It had been established by law—both Federal and, in many cases, State—for all public work. Before the United States entered the war the movement for the eight-hour day had been gaining throughout all industry, and had reached a high point, when by means of the Adamson law it was extended to the railroads.[2]

In any discussion of this question the distinction must be made between the absolute eight-hour day, by which the hours of the working day were strictly limited to eight, and the basic eight-hour day, by which the normal number of working hours is fixed at eight, but additional hours are not prohibited, although they must be paid for extra, usually at a higher rate. Owing to the emergency, the absolute eight-hour day in Government work was changed by Presidential order to the basic eight-hour day [3] of the usual type, that is to say, with a higher rate of pay for overtime. During the war period, therefore, the absolute eight-hour day was not usually observed.[4]

[1] It is interesting to note that the American Federation of Labor adopted the demand for the international establishment of the eight-hour day in the peace terms. (Report of Executive Council Buffalo Convention, June, 1918.) It was also one of the proposals of the delegates of the American Federation of Labor to the inter-allied Labor Conference at London in September, 1918.

[2] In a "Memorandum on the Eight-hour Day," submitted to the National War Labor Board by its Secretary, a list of employees is given whose work-day had been reduced to eight hours; in 1915, 171,978; in 1916, 342,138; in the first six months of 1917, 512,587; (including 400,000 men on the railroads).

[3] *Monthly Review,* Bureau of Labor Statistics, July, 1917.

[4] It prevailed in the coal industry. In one case Justice Clark, as umpire for the National War Labor Board, insisted upon the ab-

Yet in spite of the tendency toward its general adoption and the public opinion in its favor, the demand for the basic eight-hour day was the principal cause of a number of the most important strikes of the war period and one of the causes of quite a few others. Thus in the lumber disputes of the Pacific Northwest, while there were other causes involved, there seemed very little doubt that the principal one was the eight-hour day and that its concession would at any time have terminated the strike. Not merely was the lumber industry tied up but as a protest against "Ten-hour lumber," the strike spread to the shipyards of the Pacific Coast, and resulted in a tie-up of important shipbuilding plants for a period of several months.[1] So bitter was the opposition of the Pacific Coast employers to the eight-hour day that they went as far as to bind members of their association to discriminate against any employer who would grant this concession.

Except when required by existing law, the National War Labor Board did not in its principles adopt the eight-hour day. But it stated that, "The question of hours shall be settled with due regard to governmental necessities and the welfare, health, and proper comfort of the workers." And in practice the board usually awarded the eight-hour day. Such also was the practice of the other boards. General Order Number 13 of the Ordnance Department stated that "the drift in the industrial world is toward the eight-hour day as an efficiency measure" and all of the War Department's labor adjusting agencies made awards of the eight-hour day. And for the shipyards, the railroads, telegraph and telephone, in the Government building trades, the stockyards, and packing industry, in coal mines, the Western lumber camps— in all these places the eight-hour day became practically universal. It was also very much extended in the metal trades, in the steel

solute as distinguished from the basic eight-hour day. He provided, however, for a plant committee, consisting of two representatives of the employer and two of employees, with power to permit overtime if an emergency justifying it existed. Three votes were necessary in order to empower the committee to allow overtime. The umpire called attention to the heat and fumes to which the workers in the industry in question were subjected, quoting testimony to the effect that the lives of molders working nine and ten hours a day, average only fourteen years. See Molders vs. Wheeling Mold and Foundry Co., National War Labor Board, Docket No. 37 b.

[1] The New York Harbor Strike of the fall of 1918 had the eight-hour day as one of its principal demands.

plants, the metal mines, the street railroads, and in numerous other industries. And toward the end of the war the War Labor Policies Board adopted a form for an eight-hour labor clause to be inserted in the contracts of a number of the departments and boards.[1]

For longshore work customs at different points varied greatly; the early decisions of the National Adjustment Commission granted a nine- and in some cases a ten-hour day. In October, 1918, however, wages and hours for longshore work on the North Atlantic coast were standardized and not only was the eight-hour day awarded,[2] but Saturday was made a half holiday. An eight-hour day was also awarded the longshoremen at many of the Pacific ports.[3] On the other hand, decisions of the Shipping Board for deep-sea and coastwise shipping did not award the eight-hour day, nor was this granted to harbor marine employees.[4] It is interesting to note, however, that San Francisco, the one important port in the United States in which the Shipping Board's system of labor adjustment was not in force (because of the opposition of the employers to dealing with the International Longshoremen's Association), was the first Pacific port to introduce the eight-hour day.[5]

Both before and during the war, the eight-hour day meant in almost all industries—other than building—the forty-eight hour week. When the Saturday half holiday was observed, an agreement was usually made whereby five hours were worked on Saturdays and the lost three hours were divided equally among the other five days of the week, thus making eight hours and thirty-six minutes the actual week-day time.

Some demands for the forty-four hour week occurred before the

[1] The Board of Control for Army Clothing had early in the war recommended that the provisions of the Federal Eight-hour Law be included in contracts for army clothing. *Monthly Review*, Bureau of Labor Statistics, October, 1917, p. 31.

[2] Chairman's Report, National Adjustment Commission for period ending December 31, 1918, page 146. But in Southern Atlantic ports, where the ten-hour day generally prevailed, the decision of the Commission of December 2, 1918, made no change in this respect. Page 168 of the same report.

[3] Same report, pages 158 and 164.

[4] The Railroad Administration, however, did grant the eight-hour day to the Harbor Marine employees in its service. See Chapter VIII.

[5] Report of Director of Marine and Dock Industrial Relations Division, December 31, 1918, p. 163.

signing of the armistice,[1] but they usually were not pressed, and did not give rise to any important controversy, except in the clothing industry, which, in New York City, was tied up by this demand.[2]

Before the armistice no Government award except that of the National Adjustment Commission had allowed the Saturday half holiday (in industries where it had not prevailed before) except during June, July and August, unless compensated for by additional week-day work. After the armistice, as a result of widespread strikes, the forty-four-hour week was conceded by many private employers, especially in the clothing industry, and the other needle trades, and the National War Labor Board took cognizance of this spread of the forty-four-hour week and awarded it to the textile workers of Paterson. The painters of New York in the fall of 1919 went so far as to demand a forty-hour week and the jewelers a thirty-nine-hour week and a bitterly fought strike followed in each case. These demands would have been unthinkable during the war period. The painters were successful but the jewelry workers obtained the thirty-nine-hour week in only a very small proportion of the New York shops.[3]

[1] The National War Labor Board, regarding the 48-hour week as the normal one for shop work, refused to grant a 44-hour week to painters engaged in the woodworking shops of Philadelphia although they allowed the shorter week to painters doing outside work in accordance with agreements between the Master Painters and the Brotherhood—National War Labor Board, Docket No. 230.

[2] Even in this case the strike, as we have seen, was confined to the manufacture of clothing for private use and did not affect Government work.

[3] The stubborn resistance with which the jewelry workers' demands for the 39-hour week was met is an indication that the movement for so great a curtailment in the hours of factory workers will not for some time to come meet with success. A substantial number of the strikers returned to the jewelry shops on the conditions prevailing before the strike and the manufacturers seem determined not to make any concessions in regard to the shorter week and are training men and women to take the place of their former employees. On the other hand, in the building trades, the 40-hour week had been making progress before the strike of the New York painters. Bulletin No. 259, U. S. Department of Labor, giving the union scales of wages and hours, May 15, 1918, name the following branches of the building industry which had up to that time established a 40-hour week: The carpenters of Boston and Bridgeport, lathers of Boston and Seattle, painters of Boston and Seattle, plasterers of Boston, San Francisco and Seattle, the Borough of Queens in the City of New York, Philadelphia and Providence, the plasterers, labor-

In relation to the rate of payment for overtime, there were great variations in the practice of the adjustment boards. The rule most generally adopted was time and one-half for week-day overtime and double time for Sundays and holidays. When higher rates prevailed, they were not interfered with by the Government. In the building trades, for instance, the usual practice was double time for overtime. But to the railroad men no overtime rate has ever been paid to the men engaged in the actual movement of trains in the passenger service and it was not until a year after the armistice that extra compensation for overtime was paid to those in the freight service.[1] In most cases where the rate for week-day overtime was time and a half the workers, as we have seen, were usually paid double for Sundays and holidays; but even here there were some variations, the National Adjustment Commission, for instance, awarding the same rate for all overtime, no matter when performed. President Wilson in his Proclamation of March 24, 1917, suspending the operation of the eight-hour day for Government work and permitting a greater number of hours, provided that at least time and one-half should be paid therefore. The Conference Committee of Labor Adjustment Agencies also recommended the same rate except where a higher overtime rate has already been established. But they recommended that in no case should more than double be paid.

In some cases the men demanded extra compensation for haz-

ers in Boston and Philadelphia and the tile layers in Boston. Since the armistice the 44-hour week has been established in the textile and shoe industries in many places and has been conceded to the printers to become effective in the near future. In the textile industry, in some large centers, the weekly hours have been reduced from 54 to 48 and in other places, where the eight-hour day was not granted during the war, efforts have been successfully made to establish it since that time. The demand of the bituminous miners in their recent strike for the six-hour day impressed the public as a most extreme and unwise example of the tendency toward a shorter working day. It was not generally realized that, because of the peculiar conditions surrounding the mining and transportation of soft soal, the miners had seldom if ever averaged 6 hours of steady work a day; in fact Acting President Lewis of the United Mine Workers of America is quoted in the New York *Times* of January 19, 1920, as stating that the demand of the miners was not for a maximum but for a minimum working day of six hours.

[1] See Chapter VIII for detailed statement of the effect of the Adamson Law of 1916 and the final adoption for the freight service of time and one-half for overtime by the U. S. Railroad Administration on December 15, 1919.

ardous or disagreeable work, claiming that these additions should supplement the normal increases for overtime and that each successive extra compensation should be pyramided upon each preceding one. Thus the longshoremen demanded double rates for handling barbed wire and other commodities involving possible physical injury or danger to health, such as cement in bags or wheat in the bottom of the hold, where the dust was likely to be excessive. They also demanded double when working downstream or when loading explosives.[1]

In fact, the remarkable extent to which overtime developed as a regular industrial practice during 1917 and 1918 was a war phenomenon. It became the custom even in industries which normally made use of overtime only under exceptional circumstances (such as the building industry) to work ten and sometimes even twelve hours a day.

The beginning of overtime can be traced directly to cost-plus contracts, particularly those for the construction of cantonments. The Government found it necessary to do a large part of its work on a cost-plus basis; in the building industry practically all of it.[2] In these cases the contractor's personal interest was not in keeping down costs. On the contrary, if his compensation was in the form of percentage of cost (rather than a fixed fee)[3] it was directly to his financial advantage to have the cost run high. Furthermore, the contractor's standing with Government officials was largely determined by the speed with which he executed his contracts. In his desire for speed—unhampered by any considerations of economy—his first impulse was to have the men work long hours. In the beginning this impulse sprang from the feeling that long hours meant increased production. But intelligent employers soon realized that as a matter of fact long hours advanced

---

[1] One of the employers calculated that if all of the demands of the men were granted and pyramided, longshoremen engaged in extra-hazardous work, down stream on Sunday, working during the lunch hour, would receive $105 for the day's work.

[2] The principal reason for this was speed. In the first place, time was saved in the letting of contracts, because, with work on this basis, it was unnecessary to wait for completed specifications and plans and estimates thereon. In the second place, it usually costs more to do a piece of work quickly than to do it slowly; therefore there was danger that if the contractor had to do the work for a definite price, he would look for economy rather than speed—and speed was the all-essential thing for the Government.

[3] The Government gave out contracts of both kinds.

production little if any. Yet they continued the practice of over-time—in spite of the fact that it did not mean increased pro-duction—because they wished to add to their labor force. And since the hourly rates of pay in many industries were limited by trade custom or by the Government, it they wanted to attract men by increased wage the only method they had was by giving the men overtime, with the result that competition for workers took the form of offering excessive overtime.

Thus in the building industry, where overtime was paid double the normal hourly rates, it was the universal practice to work at least two extra hours a day on Government work. This meant compensation for four extra hours, and as an example, steam fitters, plumbers, or electricians, whose compensation was in many localities $0.75 an hour, were thus paid $9.00 every week day. In some cases, in order to get men away from one job to another, a contractor would offer four hours of overtime, thus bringing the pay of these mechanics to $12.00 a day. The pay was too large and the hours entirely too long. Unfortunately the large earnings due to overtime made the workers of certain industries (particularly the building industry) content with an hourly rate which remained practically stationary. Considering the increased cost of living, $0.75 an hour was not an adequate rate for these skilled men. It would have been fairer if hourly rates had been reason-ably increased. And this was keenly realized by the men them-selves when, upon the signing of the armistice, orders were issued in all departments prohibiting overtime.[1]

Not only did overtime have an unfortunate effect upon the hourly rates of some of the workers, but it was undoubtedly in-jurious to their health.[2] Furthermore, from the Government's point of view, it was unnecessarily wasteful. Inasmuch as the extra hours did not materially increase production (for it is now

---

[1] In most cases the men found their earnings reduced one-third; in some cases cut in half. A number of strikes against the abolition of overtime followed, some of a very serious nature, notably that at Nitro, Va. The housing work of the Shipping Board and of the Labor Department was tied up in many places, and wages in a number of trades were increased to enable the men to earn a fair amount in the normal working day of eight hours.

[2] See for English experience on this point, Final Report of Health of Munition Workers' Committee, 1918. For a criticism of this report from the employers' point of view, see Research Report, No. 2, National Industrial Conference Board.

generally recognized that over considerable periods of time the human body is capable of only a definite amount of certain kinds of industrial work) the large payroll which resulted from long overtime at abnormally high rates represented almost that much loss in dollars and cents. The wastefulness of this practice was further increased by irregularity of attendance due to the way in which overtime affected the men. In the first place, they often made so much money in a few days that they felt like taking frequent vacations.[1] In the second place, the long hours, made much worse by bad transportation, resulted in a working day of such extreme length that the men felt it absolutely necessary at times to absent themselves from the shop in order to get much needed rest. Still another practice developed in many places of staying away Mondays but working Sundays in order to get the increased pay.

From the standpoint of the community also the practice of excessive overtime had unfortunate social consequences. Large numbers of men were earning from $75 to $100 a week who before the war had earned less than half that much. The sudden increase in their earnings frequently resulted in foolish extravagance and sometimes in intemperance. There was a general expectation that these high earnings would continue, and some of the excesses which have characterized the present unrest undoubtedly have their origin in disappointment that the excessive earnings which resulted from the war practice of overtime have not been continued.

For all the reasons given above it will be readily seen how great an evil was the undue practice of overtime. The question naturally arises, why did not the Government place an effective curb upon it? The reason cannot be said to have been a failure to recognize the evil, for the Government did recognize it. In General Order Number 13 of the Ordnance Department (a similar order was issued for the Quartermaster Corps) the statement is made, referring to overtime: "There is no industrial abuse which needs closer watching in time of war." Similar utterances were made by other Government officials. And yet in spite of the recognition of the evil of overtime work no general rule was adopted

---

[1] This was particularly true of negroes, whose pay was increased in an even larger proportion than that of whites, although it affected all of the workers.

to cover the entire country until after the armistice was signed. One of the reasons for this failure was the length of time which elapsed before an adequate war labor administration was organized. As we have seen, it was not until May, 1918 (over a year after the war began), that final steps were taken to complete this organization by the creation of the War Labor Policies Board. A national rule coming from that body would have been of the greatest help, and had the war lasted longer, it is quite likely that some definite action would have been taken. The fact that this was not done during the six months in which the board functioned prior to the armistice was due in part to its preoccupation with other matters, and probably in part to the lack of agreement among those responsible for the production programs of the different departments; in part, also, to the difficulty of enforcing any common rule upon those in charge of work of such emergency character, where it might have been necessary to create innumerable exceptions.

Nevertheless, some of the individual boards did adopt rules which limited the amount of overtime in the industry over which they had jurisdiction.[1] Thus the National Harness and Saddlery Board in 1918 limited weekly hours in June, July, August, and September to fifty-five, and from October to May to fifty-eight, except upon certificate of extreme urgency. The Emergency Construction Commission confined its overtime to two hours every day, although in practice this rule was not very rigidly enforced. The Shipbuilding Labor Adjustment Board for all districts except the Pacific Coast "prescribed a maximum working day of twelve hours and a maximum sixty-hour working week, except at the order of the Fleet Corporation or Navy Department."[2]

In some cases the National War Labor Board, in order to re-

---

[1] A subcommittee of the Conference Committee of National Labor Adjustment Agencies recommended a limitation of overtime to two hours, except in a great emergency and we have seen in a previous chapter that the "National Labor Policy" recommended by the Conference Committee for promulgation by the President called attention to the overtime evil and charged "all government authorities . . . to use every effort to put a stop to this abuse." But the proposed statement did not make any specific recommendations and it is very doubtful whether the general language which it employed would have had any practical effect.

[2] P. H. Douglas and F. E. Wolfe in *The Journal of Political Economy,* for May, 1919.

duce irregularity of attendance, made the rule that if an employee was to receive overtime he must work a minimum number of hours in a given week, but if more than two hours of overtime were served in any one day then he was entitled to overtime rates for that day, irrespective of the number of hours worked during the week. The general rule was, however, that men received pay for overtime without regard to the regularity of their attendance.[1]

When all is said and done, it seems to the writer that the lack of more effective curbing of overtime constituted the most serious failure of the Government's war-time labor administration. All the difficulties in the way of such action could have been brushed aside by the simple declaration, backed by proper authority, that more than a very limited amount of overtime was prohibited except under unusual circumstances, the determination of which would have rested with a board created for that purpose. To have made such a rule effective, it would have had to apply to all industry; yet in war-time, when the Federal Government possessed almost unlimited powers, it could easily have been accomplished, and an enormous amount of waste and confusion saved.

[1] In the case of the Sturtevant Company, Boston, Mass., Docket No. 393, the National War Labor Board decided that no men were to receive overtime payments unless they had worked 48 hours in the week during which the overtime was claimed, allowances being made for holidays, sickness or other just cause of absence. In a few other cases the War Labor Board required 48 hours of work in any week before the worker became entitled to overtime, but in these cases the employer guaranteed that an opportunity would be given the employees of 44 hours of work in the week. See Mason Machine Co., National War Labor Board, Docket No. 111.

CHAPTER XV

Wages

IN its immediate practical influence upon industry and upon the life and health of the workers the most important question is undoubtedly wages. This has always been true and was no less so during the war, when wage demands were by far the largest single cause of strikes.[1] Workers are always more or less dissatisfied with their pay, the opinion of employers to the contrary notwithstanding, and most strikes are either solely on account of wage disputes or have wage demands as one of their most important causes. During the war this was even more than usually the case, due to the constant and rapid increase in the cost of living.[2]

Because frequent readjustments in wages became imperative if continuous production was to be maintained, all Governments found it necessary to establish machinery by which wage demands could be considered and met. This was the case in the United States as well as in the other warring countries. Never before have the wages of so many millions of our workers been fixed by arbitral adjustment. Never before has so much ability and learning been applied to the task of finding principles by which judicially to determine the amount of pay which workers in a given industry should receive.

In the widespread attempts to fix wages, the truism was borne home to many adjusters that in the last analysis there are no standards by which scientifically to determine the amounts of compensation to which different members of the community are by right entitled.[3] Furthermore, not only are scientific standards for wage determination completely lacking, but the problems

---

[1] See Appendix No. 1.

[2] A fact equally true of Great Britain where the Commission on Causes of Unrest found that the rise in the cost of living was the greatest single source of labor trouble.

[3] Judge Alschuler in deciding the packing house case (referred to in Chapter V), says: "So far as I have been advised or know, there is no scientific method for accurate wage fixing. In my view of all the facts and conditions, I can only exercise my best judgment."

which the wage adjuster faces, especially during a time of emergency such as war, can seldom be solved in a purely judicial manner. This, because his primary task during war-time is less to do absolute justice than to keep production going. He is therefore forced to take into account—consciously or unconsciously—all of the surrounding circumstances—the temper, character and power of each side.[1] To as great an extent as possible his decision must satisfy both parties. This meant in practice that he had to compromise, almost inevitably giving a certain amount of advantage to the side which was most powerful or the most difficult to satisfy. The practical necessity for this attitude must be borne in mind in any discussion of wage adjustments especially during an emergency period.

A study of the work of the adjustment boards will show the following considerations to have been the most potent in influencing their decisions:

(a) A minimum living wage.

(b) Increases in the cost of living.

(c) Standardization, both within a given industry and over a given territory.

(d) Increase in productive efficiency.

(e) The effect of overtime in increasing weekly earnings.

Yet in spite of the fact that these principles were the determining ones in the work of practically all of the boards, nevertheless there was no common agreement as to the manner in which they should be applied or the emphasis that should be placed upon one rather than another. There was a large amount of confusion in wage fixing, which inevitably operated to increase unrest. This confusion was due in part to faulty organization and the desire of each department to push its own work even at the expense of some other department. It was also due to the fact that some of the agreements under which the adjustment boards were created prescribed different and inconsistent standards for wage fixing; [2] other wage boards were not hampered in their de-

---

[1] Perhaps it is a realization of this mental process on the part of most wage adjusters which frequently induces both sides to do so much "bluffing."

[2] We have seen in a previous chapter that the Conference Committee of Labor Adjustment Agencies recognized this weakness and had the war lasted longer it would doubtless have attempted to secure revisions of contracts to promote greater consistency and uniformity in wage awards.

cisions by any hard and fast standards. The consequence was that different boards fixed different scales of wages for workers in the same trade and locality. Some industries did not suffer from this difficulty because a single board had jurisdiction over all of the workers in the industry. Thus in the case of leather workers there was no conflict of jurisdiction within the trade because the National Harness and Saddlery Adjustment Commission fixed the wages of all the men in this industry.[1] But in the case of the building and metal trades, workers were employed by many different branches of the Government and wages were set by many different boards with a large amount of resulting confusion.

One of the important points gained by labor early in the war was the adoption in certain industries of *union* scales as standards for war-time adjustments. Thus the Baker-Gompers Agreement —creating the Cantonment Wage Adjustment Commission—provided that "union scales of wages, hours and conditions in force June 1, 1917, in the locality where such cantonment is situated" should be taken as basic standards and a similar provision is contained in the agreement creating the National Adjustment Commission. On the other hand the original contract creating the Shipbuilding Labor Adjustment Board does not make use of union scales but provides that wages shall be based upon the rates paid in each shipyard on July 15, 1917.[2] Other agreements between the unions and the Government creating wage boards, do not contain any express provision as to the standards to be used. But in practice, inasmuch as these boards were usually composed of representatives of the union and of employers, union scales did form the starting point from which wage adjustments were made. The same was true to a large extent in the case of the Industrial Service Sections, in whose creation the unions took no part and in whose membership neither they nor the employers were directly represented.[3]

---

[1] This was likewise the case for the coal mining industry and the railroad trainmen (except those employed by the small railroads which were not taken over by the Government).

[2] See Chapter III. This agreement was modified, however, in December, 1917, and the wage rates prevailing in the district, if established through agreement between employer and employee and if admitted to be equitable, were to be used as basic standards.

[3] In the adjustments made in localities where union organization was weakest this was naturally less true than in those places where the unions were strong.

As the war progressed, these original standards—that is to say, the rates used in the first adjustments made by the boards—became of less importance. Because of the unprecedented changes in the cost of living, the shortage of labor and the high wages voluntarily paid by many employers in their efforts to get workers, the original standards of early 1917 became obsolete and the determination of wages was more and more influenced by the considerations mentioned above.

THE MINIMUM WAGE

The one principle which stands out most prominently and on which, in theory at least, there was general agreement (though much difference in emphasis and practice) was the desirability of the payment to all workers of at least a minimum living wage.

One of the first statements of this principle is contained in General Order Number 13 of the Ordnance Department, to wit: "It is necessary that minimum wage rates bear a constant relation to increases in the cost of living." A much more definite statement was later enunciated in the principles of the National War Labor Board as follows: "The right of all workers, including common laborers, to a living wage is hereby declared. . . . In fixing wages, minimum rates of pay shall be established which will insure the subsistence of the worker and his family in health and reasonable comfort."

In order to fix a minimum wage standard, it was necessary first to ascertain what the cost of subsistence actually was. For this purpose, the National War Labor Board (whose efforts were more definitely directed toward this end than were those of other boards) created a Cost of Living Section associated with the Bureau of Labor Statistics of the Labor Department.[1] It was found in New York that in June, 1918, $1350 to $1400, and in December, 1918, $1500 a year was the lowest amount on which the average American family of five members could exist.[2] If every worker

[1] It was realized that a nation-wide survey of living costs was imperative. The Commissioner of Labor Statistics secured for this purpose an allotment of $300,000 from the President. A hundred different localities were studied, in collaboration with the War Labor Board. (See Report of the Secretary of the National War Labor Board for year ending May 31, 1919, page 28.)
[2] William F. Ogburn in *Proceedings of the Academy of Political Science,* February, 1919, page 108.

was to earn this amount, in an eight-hour day it would have been necessary to set the wages of unskilled labor at fifty-five cents an hour when the minimum cost of living was $1400, and at sixty cents an hour by the time the minimum had reached $1500. It was realized that these were impossible figures, and would, if put into operation, have entirely demoralized industry at a time when it was of the utmost importance that its smooth operation be maintained. It was also realized that the figures in question were theoretical, and that in practice—and especially during the war period—much overtime, usually at higher rates, would be worked.

For these reasons the minimum rates set by the National War Labor Board for unskilled labor were very much less than the minimum subsistence rates as theoretically determined. The first minimum fixed for unskilled labor was forty cents an hour and this amount was awarded in one case in which the men had demanded only thirty cents.[1] The War Labor Board subsequently increased its minimum to forty-two and one-half cents and then to forty-five cents.[2]

In addition to determining what constituted the minimum subsistence level the War Labor Board likewise fixed standards for a "minimum comfort level."[3] And although the Board could not fully meet these standards, yet there is no doubt that all of its decisions were very much influenced by a desire to approximate, as nearly as conditions would permit, the minimum subsistence level for the unskilled workers and the minimum comfort level for the semi-skilled.[4]

[1] The much discussed Waynesboro case in which the laborers were increased from 22 to 40 cents an hour, National War Labor Board, Docket No. 40.

[2] In a number of awards the War Labor Board provided that the minimum rate need not apply to workers who were handicapped by old age or physical disability.

[3] "Very little attention has been paid to this level in budget literature, but the standard is as much a reality as is that of any other budget. It is one level above that of the subsistence level and provides slightly more for comforts, insurance, clothing, and sundries, and is supposed to furnish a certain well-being above that of the physical level." Memorandum on the Minimum Wage and Increased Cost of Living, submitted to the National War Labor Board, by its Secretary, page 9.

[4] The influence on the National War Labor Board of a desire to conform to minimum standards is shown in its awards to street railway employees where minimum rates were set in different sections of the country and wages advanced to these standards although

Although no special reference is made to it in the agreements or orders under which they were constituted, the necessity for an approximation to a minimum wage rate was likewise appreciated by the other boards, and found its practical application in the practice of a number of them of giving to the lowest paid worker the largest relative increase (for instance, the graduated scale awarded by the Railroad Wage Commission [1]). There can be little question that the minimum wage, even if not strictly applied during the war, nevertheless received great publicity and wide acceptance through the activities of the National War Labor Board and other agencies. If we are to do justice to our industrial workers, the principles of the minimum wage will have to receive universal application—fortunately, during the war progress toward this goal was definitely made.

INCREASES IN THE COST OF LIVING

By far the most important question which was presented to every wage adjuster was the extent of the increase in the cost of living. It was generally felt by both employer and employee that although not necessarily the determining factor, yet the percentage by which living costs had increased had always to be given the fullest consideration before a wage award was made. And there were very few hearings at which evidence was not offered on this question.

The boards differed very much as to the extent to which they allowed the increased living costs to determine their awards. The Shipbuilding Labor Adjustment Board adopted the rule, in theory at least, of advancing wages in exactly the same proportion as the cost of living had increased. On the other hand the rule of the Emergency Construction Wage Adjustment Commission was to accept the scales agreed upon by local unions and employers ir-

this meant very much greater increases in some cases than in others. Thus men who in 1914 had been getting 21 cents an hour on the Lewiston, Augusta and Waterville Street Railroad were in Nov., 1918, awarded 43 cents an hour (an increase of 105%), Docket No. 448. The men of Charleston, S. C., who had received the same amount in 1914 were given 40 cents an hour, the rate for the Southern District (an increase of 91%), Docket No. 695; whereas the Street Railway men of Butte, Mont., who had been getting 45 cents an hour were awarded 65 cents (an increase of 45%), Docket No. 271.

[1] See Chapter VIII.

respective of whether or not such scales were commensurate with the increases in the cost of living, which, as a matter of fact in most cases in this particular industry, they were not.

Most boards did not adopt any deliberate policy but inasmuch as the men invariably pressed for increases which at least equalled the increased cost of living and inasmuch as this reason was always assigned as one of the main justifications for the new scale, the increased cost of living was almost invariably one of the principal factors in wage adjustments.[1]

It was soon realized by most boards that no decision could be regarded as permanent and after a while the principle was adopted of setting six months as the period for the duration of an award. At the expiration of this time the award was to be reopened if a change in conditions rendered it necessary.[2] The awards of many of the boards, however, did not specify the time for which the award was to remain effective.[3] Nevertheless there

---

[1] A number of boards, the Railroad Wage Commission, the Shipbuilding Labor Adjustment Board and the National War Labor Board, employed experts to study the increases in the cost of living. This work was usually done in coöperation with the U. S. Labor Department. The figures presented by the employees were usually exaggerated, due in part to the undue emphasis which they gave to the rise in food prices.

[2] This was the provision usually adopted by the National War Labor Board. Shortly before the armistice the suggestion was made in the Conference Committee of Labor Adjustment Agencies that readjustments in wages be made every six months, on April and October 1st, provided that the cost of living had increased at least 10% since the last award. This rule was adopted by the Shipbuilding Labor Adjustment Board in its decisions of Oct. 1, 1918. (The recommendation of the Conference Committee to the President was that revisions be made semi-annually. See Chapter XI.) Had the war lasted longer a uniform rule would doubtless have been adopted by all the boards.

[3] Thus General Order No. 27 of the Railway Administration fixed no time for the duration of the award, although a new Board was created for further adjustments, nor was there any time limit stated in most of the supplements to this order in which later adjustments were made. This is also true of the awards of the Harness and Saddlery Wage Adjustment Commission and of some of those of the National War Labor Board. In the award of the New York Harbor Board of June 1, 1918, a time limit of one year was set "unless in the judgment of the board conditions warrant a change prior to the date thus fixed for expiration." (*Monthly Labor Review*, September, 1918, page 26.) The awards of the Fuel Administration, for both bituminous and anthracite miners, were "to continue in force during the war, but not to exceed two years from April 1, 1918." (*Monthly Labor Review*, Nov., 1918, page 167.)

was a general willingness to reopen awards when changes in the cost of living made such a course desirable. Even in the case of wage agreements (usually made before the war) which still had considerable periods to run, it was realized that the unprecedented conditions made the continuance of these agreements unjust and employers were usually willing to revise them in the light of the new conditions.[1]

STANDARDIZATION

One of the most definitely marked economic phenomena of the war was the tendency manifested throughout all industry towards uniformity in wage rates. A leveling process was taking place, as a result of which wage differences, between skilled and un-skilled, union and non-union labor and between the workers in one part of the community and another, became very much re-duced as compared with what they had been before the war. This was both the natural result of general industrial conditions as well as the more or less artificial result of the action of the Government boards.

In normal times there existed very marked inequalities of wage payments, due not merely to differences in the skill of workers and to whether or not they were members of a union—these dif-ferences are easily enough understood. But in addition there were innumerable variations in the pay received by equally skilled men working in different localities in which the cost of living varied little. These differences existed even in the wages re-ceived by workers in the same industry and locality, sometimes indeed in the same shop. Variations of this kind have been pointed out by many writers, who have, however, found great difficulty in fully explaining them. A partial explanation of why labor does not automatically seek its highest wage level is to be found in the human failing of inertia. Inertia, together with a lack of knowledge of employment conditions elsewhere, attach-ment to a particular place or shop because of friendly association,

---

[1] This was not always the case; the Building Trades Employers' Association of New York, for example, refused to allow changes in existing agreements, and went so far as not to permit the employing electricians to revise their contract with their men (prior to its ex-piration), by readjusting wages. The reason for this attitude was undoubtedly the belief, which was then entertained, that the rise in the cost of living was merely a temporary phenomenon.

the cost of moving, the ownership of home, all of these play their part in normal times in preventing the worker from getting the highest wage.

On the other hand, in times of emergency and consequent abnormal labor demand, there arises a competition for men which disturbs to a marked degree the wage relationships of normal times. For normal times, as our economic system is constituted, have always meant times of labor surplus. And during such periods the labor unions have been able to modify the conventional action of the law of supply and demand and have prevented the competition of their members from resulting in the low wage levels which have frequently been caused by such competition, when unrestrained by union standards. Where a non-union man might reduce his wages to get a job, the members of a union would go without work in order to maintain the wage scale. In normal times the average wage of men in trade unions is considerably higher than that of unorganized men in the same industry. When, however, the demand for men far exceeds the supply employers compete among one another and are willing in many cases to pay wages even higher than union rates.[1] In open shop industries men were offered these increased rates irrespective of their union membership; consequently the differences between the union and the non-union scale of wages were largely wiped out.[2]

Moreover, a similar leveling process was taking place in the pay of the unskilled as compared with the skilled workers. This for the reason that unskilled workers were needed not only for the vastly increased work of the kind which would normally have been done by them, but also for those new tasks resulting from the dilution of the trades and the consequent use of the unskilled man or woman to do a very small portion of what had previously been the complete task of a highly skilled mechanic. Thus we see that unskilled and unorganized workers profit relatively to

[1] Normally union rates tend to become maximum rates, though according to the theory of the unions they set the minimum and not the maximum amount that should be paid.

[2] In many cases, indeed, the wages of union men had been fixed by previous agreement. And although, as we have seen, these agreements were sometimes modified before their expiration, in some cases the employers insisted that they be kept. This meant that the union workers received no increase in spite of wage advances in industry all about them.

a greater degree by the leveling process of abnormal times, than do the skilled and highly organized.[1]

A further consequence of the abnormal war conditions was an unprecedented mobility of labor. Every method, including patriotic appeals in the press and on public platforms, was used to bring home to the workers of other localities the need of men in places where war material was being produced. Influenced both by the patriotic motive and the desire for better wages, men and women left their homes and traveled to distant cities. This movement of the workers was accelerated by the action of employers who, not content with elaborate newspaper advertisements offering high rates of wages, even went as far as to send labor scouts all over the country.[2] In this manner some of the natural causes which made for previous wage inequalities were overcome by the extraordinary conditions produced by the war. Workers not only left their homes but they changed from one industry to another with a freedom never before known.[3] General wage levels were a matter of common knowledge. And the worker knew not only the pay of men in his own industry but also that of workers in many other trades. The inevitable result was a widespread leveling of wages and a flattening out of inequalities.[4]

[1] The most conspicuous illustration was furnished by the building industry. The wages of union men in the building trades increased very little during the war and although substantial advances were made in the post-armistice period, the wages of union men have barely kept pace with the cost of living. But the wage advance of unorganized men, especially before the armistice, was much more rapid. This was especially true in the South.

[2] Both of these practices had to be curtailed by the Government, when toward the end of the war the competition for men became fiercer than ever and the U. S. Employment Service was organized in an effort to control the situation. The Government itself then took charge of transferring workers to places where they were most needed.

[3] For example thousands of coal miners (especially in the anthracite fields) left the mines to work in other war industries. The difficulty of preventing the men under their jurisdiction from drifting into other industries was one of the reasons frequently assigned by wage boards for increased awards.

[4] The leveling effect of the action of the wage boards during the war period is well shown by a comparison in a number of typical war industries of wages in 1914 and 1919. Thus for deep water longshoremen the rates paid in July, 1914, varied from 20 cents in Charleston, S. C., and 25 cents in Baltimore, Savannah and Norfolk, all the way up to 55 cents in San Francisco and Portland, a difference of 175% between the high and the low rates. In July, 1919, 50 cents

These natural processes making for standardization were accelerated and deepened by the more or less artificial action of the various wage adjustment agencies. Since production was the primary concern of the Government, efficiency demanded that men be prevented from shifting from one place or industry to another where such change was unnecessary, and that such transfers be facilitated where they were imperative. Wage uniformity was needed to produce both of these results.[1] It also tended to remove the dissatisfaction which men of a particular trade or locality would naturally have felt because of higher wages paid to others. A further consideration was the conclusion reached by all of the boards that one of the reasons which had always been given for wage differentials—the difference in the cost of living in different localities—was no longer applicable to any appreciable degree. There was therefore an almost universal tendency on the part of adjustment boards to apply uniform wage scales over wider and wider areas. Thus the Shipping Board, whose first awards were for single yards and then for districts, ended by setting up practically uniform rates for the entire country.[2] The

was the lowest and 80 cents the highest. The difference instead of being 175% was 60%. On the other hand the Baltimore rates, which by decision of the National Adjustment Commission were made uniform with those of Newport and Boston increased 160%, whereas the rates at Portland and San Francisco advanced only 45%. For coastwise longshoremen the differences are even greater. Thus at Baltimore, the rate in July, 1914, was 20 cents an hour. It was increased to the same rates as Newport and Boston—to wit, 65 cents—a jump of 225%, whereas in Mobile these same men had been getting 30 cents per hour and received in July, 1919, only 45 cents an hour, an increase of only 50%.

[1] The writer does not mean to imply that uniformity was actually achieved. But only that a marked tendency toward uniformity existed.

[2] See Chapter III. In the decision of the Shipbuilding Labor Adjustment Board for October 1, 1918, for the Atlantic Coast, Gulf and Great Lake Shipyards, the "Reasons for a National Wage Scale" are stated as follows: "We have adopted these uniform national rates because experience has convinced us that by this means only can we put a stop to that shifting of employees from yard to yard and district to district, which continues to be a chief obstacle to efficient ship production. Added arguments for uniform national rates are that citizens working for a Government—and work on ships is now essentially Government work—feel that they should all be treated alike; that there are no longer any marked differences in the cost of living between different sections; and that the U. S. Employment

National Adjustment Commission adopted the same policy [1] as did to a lesser extent the War and Navy Departments in making adjustments in Arsenals and Navy Yards as well as in private ordnance plants. The awards of the Harness and Saddlery Adjustment Commission and of the Railroad Administration had always been countrywide in their application.

In the building trades, on the other hand, differentials were largely maintained and much confusion resulted. In the first place, as we have seen, the Emergency Construction Wage Adjustment adopted wage rates as fixed by local agreement of employers' associations and unions for each separate locality and for each separate trade. In the second place there were many different Government agencies which fixed wages for this industry. In theory these agencies acted in coöperation but in practice they often acted independently and two of them used widely different rules for wage adjustment.[2]

The policy of wage boards to standardize wages was almost everywhere resisted by the employers. They objected both to the removal of differentials as between localities and to the removal of differentials as between individuals in the same shop and craft.[3] Inasmuch as the process of wage leveling was always a leveling up, this hostility of the employers can be readily understood. With respect to differentials between different localities there was a certain amount of justice in the employers' position, especially in regard to the railroads, where the greatest variations

Service, rather than divergent wage rates with their unsettling tendencies, should be relied upon to effect whatever shifting of wage earners is necessary to the carrying out of the war program.

[1] See Chapter IV.

[2] The agencies above referred to were the Emergency Construction Wage Adjustment Commission, the Shipbuilding Labor Adjustment Board, whose jurisdiction extended over mechanics employed on building construction in the shipyards, and the housing departments of both the Emergency Fleet Corporation and the Labor Department which were independent of each other and of the other two. It should be mentioned, however, that the Emergency Construction Wage Commission had jurisdiction over many more workers than did the other boards. Its adjustments were therefore a dominant factor in the building industry and inasmuch as they were based purely on local rates, the result was illogical and unfortunate variations, whose effect was heightened by the mobility of labor previously referred to.

[3] See Chapter IV, where an exception is pointed out—to wit, the opposition of employers to the request of longshoremen for different rates of pay when handling different kinds of cargo.

exist both as to degree of service required and the conditions under which workers in widely scattered localities lived.[1] On the other hand the Government's needs, already referred to, were sufficient to justify it in overriding this opposition. But even if this had not been the case it would have been a physical impossibility for such boards as those of the railroads (dealing as they did with 2,000,000 employees) to have fixed wages in accordance with all of the minute variations which existed.

In considering the opposition of employers to the removal of differentials as between individuals we are brought face to face with a most difficult problem. Employers have found that their best means of obtaining both skill and industry has been by rewarding these qualities with higher wages. The unions, on the other hand, have realized that collective bargaining became more and more difficult as attempts were made to recognize individual variations in ability. There was also the danger of discrimination against labor organizations and the fact that the union derived a large part of its numerical strength by reason of the fact that it was a protection for the man of average ability, rather than the exceptionally skilled (who seldom needed help).[2]

All of these difficulties are well illustrated by the controversies in the machine industry in which the widest range of skill and productivity exists. The employers wished to be absolutely free to reward these variations of productive ability—a wish that was intensified by the fact that thousands of unskilled workers were inducted into the machine shops during the war and taken into the unions.[3]

[1] Both of these points are well illustrated by the railroad flagmen. Some are stationed in cities where hundreds of trains are constantly passing daily; others in remote country districts where there are perhaps only half a dozen trains a day and where the flagmen can easily own his own home, cultivate his own garden, etc. See Chapter VIII.

[2] Piece work met the difficulties of the employer and some of those of the union. But piece rates are applicable to only certain industries and do not safeguard the rights of the workers unless accompanied by well-organized collective bargaining. Even then many unions object to them because of the danger of "speeding up."

[3] At the hearing of the Bridgeport case before the National War Labor Board the attorney for the employers said: "We must preserve this right of the employer to assign and grade the men as he sees fit, without attempting to fix any inflexible name or any inflexible rate of pay. That it is only by maintaining this full freedom of the employer, that the employer is able to manage his establishment and secure that efficiency which ordinarily comes out of the

In localities where the union was strong it had made agreements with employers by which the men were classified according to their skill and a rate (considered by the union a minimum) set for the men of each group.[1] Thus there were toolmakers, first and second class machinists, helpers and others. The demands made by the machinists' union in the spring and summer of 1918, referred to in a previous chapter, were for minimum rates for certain definite classifications. And many of the employers were even more bitterly opposed to this arrangement than they were to the wage increases which the men demanded. The effort of the union was everywhere to establish minimum rates with broad classification, dividing the workers into as few groups as possible. The employers endeavored to defeat the establishment of minimum rates and where they were unable to do so, they sought to establish the largest possible number of wage groups.[2] It was in Bridgeport that the issue was most bitterly fought out and that the failure of the men to get the minimum rates for which they had been contending led to their final strike against the decision of the umpire of the National War Labor Board.

The tendency toward wage leveling which we have been examining was extended still further by the policy adopted by most of the Government Departments, especially toward the end of the war, of preventing employers from paying wages in excess of the

---

hourly rate, when the employer can reward each individual case. In other words, we have as many hourly rates as there are human beings."

[1] This had for some time been the practice of Arsenals and Navy Yards and was adopted by the Shipyards.

[2] In many industries in which the unions have long been powerful they have succeeded in establishing single wage rates for practically every man in the industry. Thus in the building trades, there is just one union rate for most trades. Whether a bricklayer is an expert, capable of doing the highest grade of work on the front of a building or a man who has just graduated from the ranks of the apprentice and possesses only a moderate amount of skill, he receives exactly the same amount of wages. This was not always the case but has been so for a number of years. An evolutionary process by which wage differentials have been gradually eliminated can be traced in other branches of the building trade. Thus the stonecutters of New York had three classifications with 50 cents a day difference in pay. In 1916 under pressure from the union the 3rd class was eliminated and in 1918 a single rate of pay was established. Very recently two different rates were abolished for mosaic workers and concrete laborers. Carpenters had a different rate for the shops and for outside men. In 1919 a single rate was established.

established rates.[1] The purpose was two-fold; to reduce the labor turnover which was caused by one employer hiring away the employees of another by the offer of larger wages, and to prevent excessive wage increases which would have resulted from this practice. Recognizing the necessity for this rule as a war measure the unions acquiesced in it.[2]

These standardizing processes are also illustrated by the fact that many classes of labor whose remuneration had always been the result of individual bargaining between employer and employee were during the war made the subject of collective bargaining. Thus the draughtsmen in the shipyards became organized and have had wage scales fixed by collective bargaining applied over large areas of the country.[3]

We have seen that natural causes tended to produce wage leveling and that Government boards intensified this natural movement by awarding wages standardized over increasingly wider areas. But a most disturbing factor in the general situation was the policy deliberately adopted by the Government of giving the shipyard workers a differential over mechanics employed in every other industry. It has already been pointed out that the need for ships and the unfavorable conditions surrounding their production led the Government to attempt to direct a flow of labor into the shipyards by giving to ship workers a higher wage than was paid to men in the same trade working in the same locality.[4] Each new award for the shipyards led to

[1] The fact that many contracts were "cost plus" facilitated the enforcement of this policy. See Chapter XI for efforts of War Labor Policies Board to establish standard wage rates for the entire country.

[2] After the signing of the armistice the determination of the Shipping Board to maintain this policy and not to allow shipyards to pay higher wages than the scale adopted by the Shipbuilding Labor Adjustment Board, was one of the causes of the general strike at Seattle. See Chapter III.

[3] The movement to organize architectural and mechanical draughtsmen has spread to architects' and engineers' offices and the draughtsmen's union hopes to compel the employment of its members by an alliance with the unions in the building trades under the terms of which it is expected that building mechanics will refuse to build from "non-union" plans.

[4] Inasmuch as the Shipbuilding Labor Adjustment Board, in its final awards, set practically uniform rates for the entire country (leveling up any inequalities that may have existed), the amount of this differential, substantial everywhere, became very great in those areas in which lower than average rates prevailed in other than shipbuilding plants.

demands in every other industry for wages equal to those paid to shipbuilders.[1] The workers in other industries could not see any justification for the differential and never became reconciled to it. The announcement of a new award for the shipyards inaugurated a struggle everywhere else to catch up with the pay of the ship workers and this pursuit was maintained during the entire period of the war. When, however, the Conference Committee of Labor Adjustment Agencies was formed and this shipyard differential was discussed, although condemned by many of the members of the conference, its maintenance was recommended by a majority.

INCREASE IN PRODUCTIVE EFFICIENCY

Inasmuch as production was the paramount object of war-time wage adjustments we might have expected that the effect of any wage increases on the efficiency of the workers would have received most careful consideration. To be sure the need for wage increases in order to allay unrest and to maintain the worker's efficiency was the reason frequently assigned for wage demands and the maintenance of the worker's strength is the reason often given for insisting that all employees shall receive at least enough to provide a minimum of subsistence. Except, however, in relation to the minimum wage, the principle of productive efficiency does not seem to have been given as much attention by the wage boards as were the other principles examined above.

A reason for this fact may have been the difficulty of determining just what was the effect of a wage increase upon efficiency and production. Another reason was the fact that the power of the men to enforce their demands made wage increases necessary irrespective of their effect upon the efficiency of the workers.

In fact, toward the end of the war the problem of promoting production involved not so much a question of giving the workers

---

[1] An illustration of the effect of shipyards awards is an occurrence toward the end of the war in Kings County. Concrete laborers, requiring both strength and skill, employed on Government work next door to a shipyard, had been receiving 43 cents per hour. Upon the announcement of the October award of the Shipbuilding Labor Adjustment Board, the shipyard laborers were raised to 54 cents an hour—25% more than the concrete laborers were getting. As a result the concrete men went out. The same thing occurred in many places all over the country.

more pay, but rather the fear that high earnings were lessening efficiency, And here we must distinguish between wage rates and earnings. The increase in wage rates was in most industries no greater than the increase in the cost of living. Earnings, however, and especially those of the entire family, did show a much greater increase. This was due in part to the elimination of unemployment, in part to overtime and in part also to the ease with which all members of a family could get work at high wages.[1] The large amounts which the men themselves were earning were in many cases much more than they had ever been accustomed to and these were often substantially increased by the unprecedented earning power of other members of the family.[2] Unfortunately this prosperity had one very bad effect. It led to inefficiency and to an attitude on the part of some of these workers of absolute indifference as to whether or not they kept their job. Modern industry has unfortunately been accompanied by a constant labor surplus. On the existence of this surplus we have to a large extent depended for the worker's incentive to maintain his efficiency. There have normally been more workers than jobs and this fact has produced the keenest competition for the positions that were available. Efficiency was maintained because of the worker's fear of losing his job. But the war period put an end to the over-supply of labor. There was no longer any difficulty to find work; on the contrary it was now the employers who competed with each other for men. The newspapers were filled

[1] The pay of boys and of women advanced even more rapidly than did that of men—especially of skilled men. Many young boys entered the shipyards and munition plants and after a few weeks earned very large amounts. Women, too, in aëroplane factories and other war work were frequently in receipt of large pay. Even in peace industries wages of women showed large increases. For contrast which this affords to the treatment of women during the Civil War, see quotation from E. D. Fite in note at p. 177.

[2] Evidence of high earnings was everywhere to be seen. Savings bank balances, one indication of the worker's financial condition are shown to have increased 8% in 1918 over 1916 and to have increased slightly in 1918 over 1917 in spite of large investments made by the workers in Liberty Bonds. Storekeepers in all industrial centers testified to the unusual buying power of working men and women; they mentioned silk shirts, pianos, phonographs and even automobiles. They said that the demand for these articles had changed. The people who had previously bought them were, in many cases, unable to do so, whereas hundreds of new customers for high priced articles of every kind had appeared from the ranks of the workers.

with advertisements offering high wages for men and women in every industry.[1]   If a worker lost his job he could go around the corner and get one equally good.   Furthermore, his earnings and those of other members of his family frequently exceeded the amount which he needed to maintain the standard of life to which he was accustomed.   The incentive to perform efficient and steady work was therefore weakened.[2]   To be sure, the economic motive was reinforced, during the war, by the patriotic motive, but this was not strong enough in large numbers of cases to induce the workers to do a good day's work and to prevent them from deliberately absenting themselves from the job.   The inefficiency of labor became a serious problem of war production, both because of abnormally large absenteeism [3] and because of more or less deliberate slacking on the job.[4]   Abundant evidence of these facts was presented to every wage board.   A committee was appointed by the Labor Policies Board to investigate and to suggest a remedy.   No means, however, was found to overcome the

[1] A new kind of competition among employers was begun.   Wages and, to a lesser extent, overtime having become standardized, it was to the employers' interest to improve shop conditions in order to attract workers.   Many of the advertisements during the war offered —as inducements—lunch and rest rooms, good light and ventilation, etc.

[2] Some of the shipbuilders deliberately attempted to raise the worker's standard of living in order to make him more willing to keep steadily at work.   Automobile salesmen (on the installment plan), and other purveyors of luxuries were given facilities for displaying their merchandise to shipyard workers.

[3] Definite facts in regard to absenteeism are difficult to obtain. We do not know what is the normal percentage of absences from work nor are such figures available for most war industries.   The Industrial Relations Division of the Emergency Fleet Corporation studied the attendance of over 320,000 employees of the shipyards and found that from January to September, 1918, the loss due to the absenteeism was 17.8% in steel shipyards and 13.2% in wooden shipyards.   See Paul H. Douglas in *Political Science Quarterly,* December, 1919, p. 596.   A similar condition undoubtedly prevailed in other war industries.   In fairness to the workers it should be pointed out that this excessive loss of time can be accounted for in part by the abnormal conditions surrounding the shipyards, and other war plants.   Bad housing, shockingly inadequate transportation facilities and large amounts of overtime were no doubt partly responsible for both inefficiency, lateness and absences from the job.

[4] The mine workers seem to have been an exception to this rule. Both employers and employees have testified that a larger quantity of coal was mined during the war than ever before although the force of miners was very much smaller.

inefficiency of the workers and this condition has gone over to peace time as one of our most serious problems of industry.[1]

OVERTIME

Attention has already been called to the disastrous extent to which overtime was practiced. It is desired at this place to indicate the influence of the excessive earnings due to overtime work upon the decisions of wage adjustment boards.

Two reasons are usually assigned to justify the payment of extra remuneration for overtime. In the first place it is pointed out that the higher rate of pay acts as a penalty to prevent employees from working more than the normal working day. In the second place the added remuneration is considered a bonus to the worker to compensate him for the extraordinary strain resulting from abnormally long hours. In peace times there would consequently be no justification for taking into account the extra pay accruing from overtime work and because of it awarding a lower wage than the men would otherwise have received. In war time the question is a more difficult one. Obviously the worker is still entitled to extra remuneration (unless the fatigue of overtime is to be regarded as a reasonable war sacrifice). The other reason for the payment of extra compensation—namely, to penalize the employer—would, however, seldom apply, inasmuch as the Government was usually the employer and in theory at least was not allowing overtime to be worked unless it was for the public good.

In normal times overtime is not worked except in emergencies. But during the war it became in most industries a regular prac-

---

[1] There was, to be sure, a short period immediately following the signing of the armistice, when with the removal of war-time pressure for production unemployment seemed to threaten and it was reported all over the country that efficiency had very much increased. But it quickly became apparent that the labor surplus which we then experienced was only a temporary condition. There were soon more jobs than men, and efficiency once more went down. Although accurate figures are difficult to obtain, the almost unanimous opinion of employers during 1919 was that the efficiency of their workers was no better than from 60 to 75% of what it was before the war. Toward the summer of 1920 the acute shortage of labor had abated. Indeed in some places there had come a labor surplus. With this change in employment conditions an increase in efficiency was also reported, though still below the pre-war standard.

tice. As a result weekly earnings were increased by amounts varying from 40 to 100 or more per cent. It was psychologically impossible to ignore a factor which so potently influenced the actual earnings of the men. Consciously or unconsciously these large amounts of pay due to overtime were taken into consideration and wages were fixed at rates lower than would otherwise have been the case.[1]

A further consideration with wage adjusters was the effect upon employers of a new wage scale. In many cases no difficulty was presented because employers were working on cost plus contracts and in these cases the extra cost resulting from wage increases was paid by the Government.[2] In some instances wage advances were deferred until employers' contracts for the disposal of their product at old prices had expired.[3] Where the burden of a wage increase fell directly upon the employer and could not be shifted to the Government or to a private consumer, this fact was undoubtedly taken into consideration.

Perhaps the most difficult cases from this standpoint were those of the street railway companies. Limited by law as to the amount of car fare they could charge, these companies were embarrassed by increases in all of their operating expenses. The wages which they were paying had always been abnormally low and increases in the cost of living made wage increases absolutely imperative. To make matters worse, the traction companies inherited from pre-war times both financial unsoundness and a lack

[1] It has already been pointed out that the War Labor Board took overtime earnings into consideration when it decided not to award as a minimum wage, an amount which seemed theoretically required for the worker's subsistence. Other wage boards have also expressly mentioned overtime as a reason for a smaller award than would otherwise have been made; for example, Judge Alschuler in his first Packing House decision.

[2] This was also true if work was being done under a contract containing the labor clause. In some cases indeed the employer profited by wage increases because his compensation was based on a percentage of cost.

[3] In the case of the coal dock operators of Duluth, National War Labor Board Docket No. 201, the selling price of the company's product had been fixed by the Fuel Administrator and the Board, in making a wage increase, did so on condition that the selling price be re-adjusted by the Fuel Administrator. The President's Mediation Commission granted an increase in wages to employees of a copper mining company in Arizona conditional upon an increase being allowed in the selling price of copper, if the increase in wages resulted in absorbing all the profit.

of public confidence and regard. If they were to be forced to pay materially higher wages and be denied an increased in fare, many, if not all of them, would face bankruptcy. This was the situation which confronted the National War Labor Board when the employees of the street railroads turned to it for wage relief. The War Labor Board, seeing clearly the utter inadequacy of the men's pay, established standards for different sections of the country and, irrespective of the financial condition of the street railway company, fixed wages in conformity with these standards.[1] At the same time the board always recommended that fares be increased to enable the companies to maintain their service.

After the signing of the armistice it was at first expected that the cost of living would immediately decline. It was thought that the transition of industry from a war to a peace basis would be facilitated by preventing further wage advances. The tendency to shift the burden of higher wages to the consumer in the shape of higher prices was realized and wage-earners were therefore asked not to press their demands for further increases but to

---

[1] In one case, that of the Kansas City Railways Co. National War Labor Board, Docket Nos. 265 and 266, the company's submission to the jurisdiction of the board was made "conditional upon the granting of an increase in the rate of fare to be charged . . . and subject to the financial ability of the company to meet the requirements of the award." The Board found the company's finances such as to require an increase in fare to enable it to put the award into effect, so that in this case the increase in wage was made conditional upon an increase in fare. The subsequent history of the case makes it a most remarkable one. The Company instead of applying to the State Commission for an increase in fare—where it was evident that an increase would immediately have been granted—applied instead to the Federal Court, "a most fantastic and unwarranted assumption in respect to the power of this (National War Labor) Board." Legal complications now ensued as a result of which the fare was not increased and the men were denied an increase in wages. A strike followed and the National War Labor Board was once more appealed to. The Board found that the Company had not used its best efforts, in good faith, to secure an increase in fare. It therefore declared the condition in which the wage increase had been predicated to be imperative and ordered the Company to immediately put the wage increase into effect. Space does not permit a full statement of the facts, but the reader is referred to the opinion of the War Labor Board, which is well worth careful study. The newspaper advertisements published by the company at the time of the second strike entitled "A Strike Against the Community," are excellent examples of the manner in which a public service corporation can trade upon the necessity of its service to the public, in order to fight a legitimate wage demand of its men.

give the Government a chance to reduce the cost of living. In some cases, for example the railroad workers, the men were willing to adopt this policy. But they were disappointed in their hopes that the cost of living would decline. The so-called "outlaw" strikes on the railroads, referred to in a previous chapter, followed. In spite of the efforts of their leaders, thousands of these men went on strike to secure wage increases which many months previously they had been induced to forego because it was claimed a reduction would be made in the cost of living.

BONUS AND PIECEWORK

Union demands were frequently made for the abolition of both bonus and piecework systems. Organized labor has been generally hostile to both on the ground that they tend to "speeding up" and that they are easily abused by unscrupulous employers. The unions maintained this position during the war and also objected to piecework and bonus systems for the same reasons which led them to prefer standardized union rates to the employer's method of rewarding individual merit by giving each employee a special rate of wages. The employers, on the other hand, insisted on the maintenance of both piece rates and bonuses on the ground that it was impossible to secure production without them.[1]

No mention of either piecework or bonus was made in the principles of the National War Labor Board nor in the agreements under which other wage boards were created. Nor was there any uniformity in the practice followed by the boards. In some places the bonus was abolished by the National War Labor Board and by the Administration for Labor Standards in Army Clothing; in others it was left undisturbed. The Conference Committee of Labor Adjustment Agencies recommended that bonuses "having the effect of interfering with established standards of compensation should be abolished" and the Fuel Administration, on the ground that such was the effect of bonuses in the coal mining industry, tried very hard to abolish them. In this, however, the Fuel Administration does not seem to have been successful. In general, the insistence of employers on the

[1] General Crozier, Chief of Ordnance, testified before the House Committee on Military Affairs, that arsenal workers who retapped 100—4.7 shells in ten hours, when paid on a premium system, required 22.95 hours for the same work when paid at an hourly rate.

maintenance of bonus and piecework prevailed and these systems were as a rule left undisturbed during the war.[1] There was, however, a very general agreement among wage boards that piece rates once established should not be reduced during the war and the Shipbuilding Labor Adjustment Boards required every shipyard to post a notice to this effect in a conspicuous place in the yard.[2]

[1] Perhaps the most important case in which the bonus was abolished was that of the Bethlehem Steel Company, National War Labor Board Docket No. 22. The Board found that "the main cause of dissatisfaction is a bonus system so complicated and difficult to understand that almost one-half of the time of the hearings was consumed in efforts to secure a clear idea of the system." The hearings did show very plainly that the company was using the bonus unfairly, especially in relation to overtime and that if both bonus and overtime had been earned only one of them would be paid.

[2] A number of strikes occurred in which the abolition of piece rates was one of the demands, but in no case with which the writer is familiar was this demand granted.

WAGE CHARTS

The following charts showing the course of money wages and real wages from December, 1914, to December, 1919, were prepared for this book by the Bureau of Applied Economics, Washington, D. C., and are based on data collected by the U. S. Bureau of Labor Statistics, Interstate Commerce Commission, U. S. Railroad Administration, Navy Department, Shipbuilding Labor Adjustment Board, and the U. S. Shipping Board, supplemented by material gathered from other sources. With the exception of marine and railroad employees, hourly rates rather than earnings are shown, as they are a better gauge of wage changes, not being affected by overtime or unemployment.

The cost of living figures used are those of the U. S. Bureau of Labor Statistics as published in the October, 1920, *Labor Review,* converted to a base of December, 1914.

Unweighted averages have been used except in the iron and steel industry and for marine employees. In the steel industry, because of the great variation in the rates and the number of employees, a weighting system seemed desirable, and each occupation was weighted by the number of employees in 1919. For marine employees, data were available for the Atlantic and Gulf coasts only and the averages were weighted. As the Atlantic and Gulf wage rate is intermediate between the Pacific and Trans-Atlantic it may be taken as fairly representative of the whole industry.

Since 1918 shipyard rates have been substantially uniform. Prior to 1918 the West Coast had considerably higher rates and obtained a lesser per cent of increase during the war. In preparing the chart for the shipyards an average has been taken of the wage rates on the East and West Coasts.

MONEY WAGES AND REAL WAGES, MONTHLY RATE, DECEMBER, 1914, TO DECEMBER, 1919—MARINE EMPLOYEES

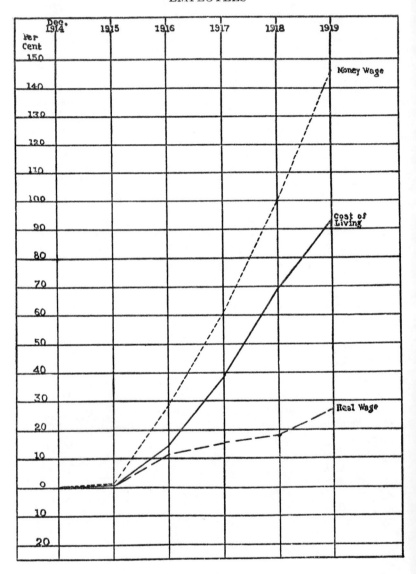

MONEY WAGES AND REAL WAGES, MONTHLY RATE, DECEMBER, 1914, TO DECEMBER, 1919—RAILROADS

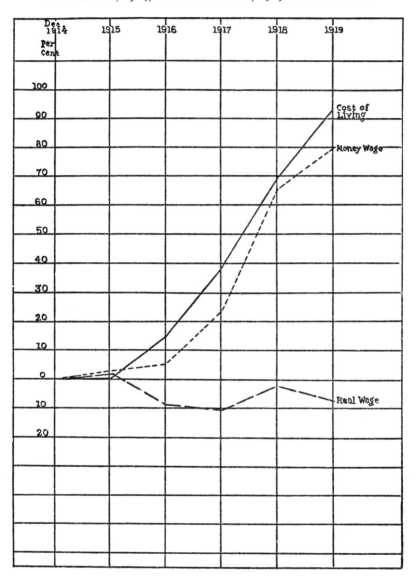

MONEY WAGES AND REAL WAGES, HOURLY RATE, DECEMBER, 1914, TO DECEMBER, 1919—IRON AND STEEL

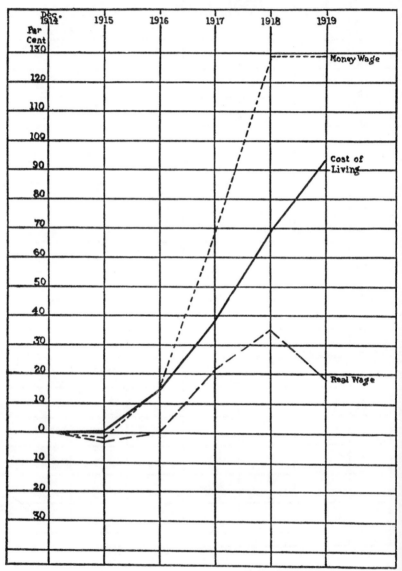

MONEY WAGES AND REAL WAGES, HOURLY RATE, DECEMBER, 1914, TO DECEMBER, 1919—SHIPYARDS

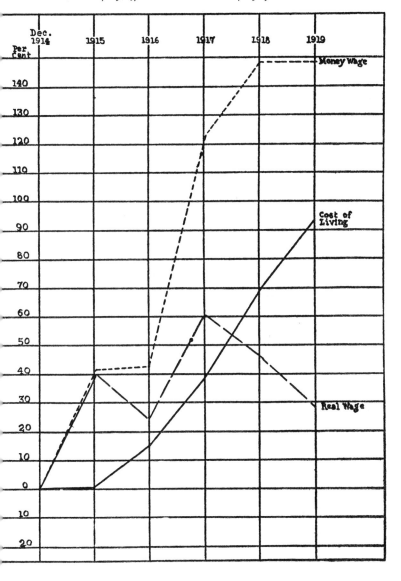

MONEY WAGES AND REAL WAGES, HOURLY RATE, DECEMBER, 1914, TO DECEMBER, 1919—NAVY YARDS

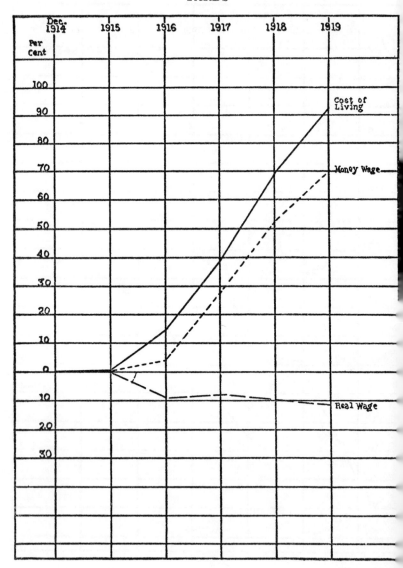

MONEY WAGES AND REAL WAGES, HOURLY RATE, DECEMBER, 1914, TO DECEMBER, 1919—METAL TRADES

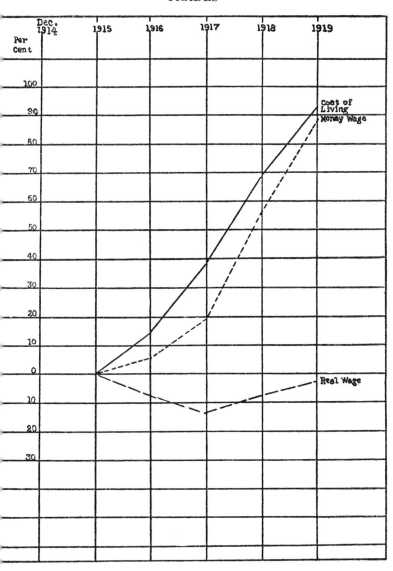

MONEY WAGES AND REAL WAGES, HOURLY RATE, DECEMBER, 1914, TO DECEMBER, 1919—BOOTS AND SHOES

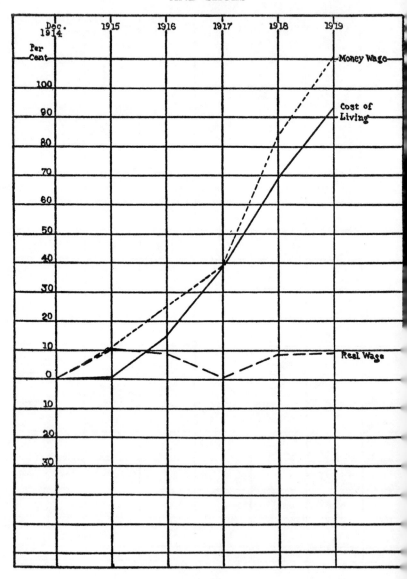

MONEY WAGES AND REAL WAGES, HOURLY RATE, DECEMBER, 1914, TO DECEMBER, 1919—BUILDING TRADES

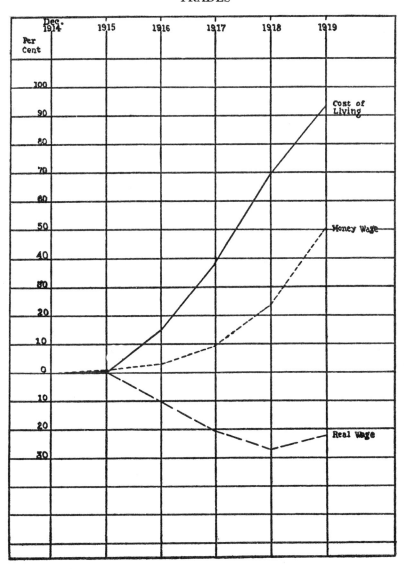

MONEY WAGES AND REAL WAGES, HOURLY RATE, DECEMBER, 1914, TO DECEMBER, 1919— LONGSHOREMEN

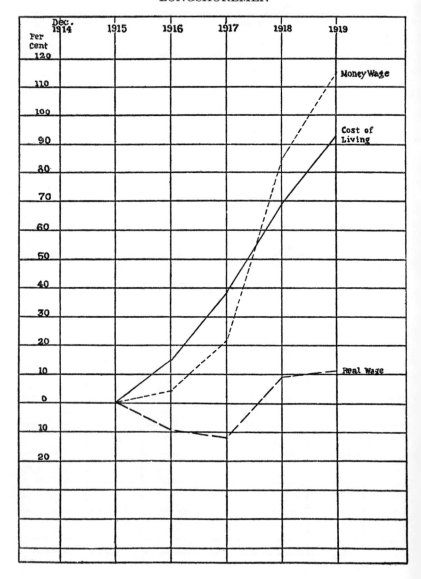

MONEY WAGES AND REAL WAGES, HOURLY RATE, DECEMBER, 1914, TO DECEMBER, 1919—PRINTING AND ELECTROTYPING

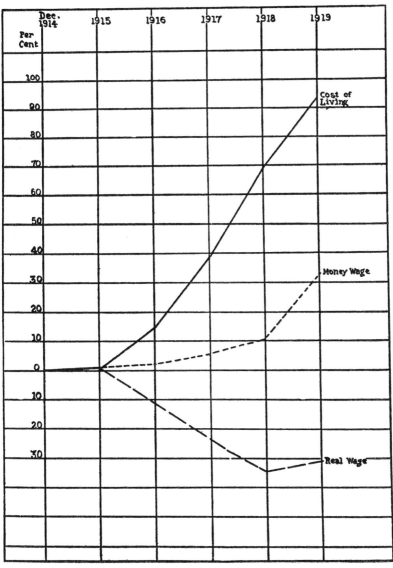

PART THREE

THE PSYCHOLOGICAL BACKGROUND OF INDUSTRIAL
UNREST

CHAPTER XVI

The Employer

WE have already referred to the position many employers took toward labor unions; the following chapters will be devoted to a more detailed examination of the attitudes of capital and labor toward each other and toward the Government, as well as the attitude of the public toward all three. Examples of extreme antagonism between capital and labor will be examined, not because they by any means represent the attitude of all or even of most employers or employees, but because they show the point of view of substantial numbers, and are so divergent and bitter that they should be carefully studied. If no way can be found to compose these antagonisms, the consequences may prove disastrous to the future prosperity of our country.

A strange contrast is afforded by the position taken by employers when acting collectively through their associations, and the position taken by many of their most prominent members when dealing individually with their own employees. As a rule, employers' associations took fairly liberal attitudes toward labor, and at their national meetings offered unstinted coöperation with the Government in its labor policy. Both the United States Chamber of Commerce and the National Industrial Conference Board, which between them represent a very large part of the financial and industrial resources of America, advocated Government arbitration of labor disputes, and the National Manufacturers' Association passed a resolution indorsing the principles of the Taft-Walsh Board.

In striking contrast to the position of these powerful associations was the attitude taken by many of their members, whose hostility to organized labor in their own plants, and whose unwillingness when dealing with their own employees to accede to the Government's suggestions, seriously hampered the administration in its war labor program.

Even with the war at its height the Lake Carriers' Association would not attend a meeting of the Shipping Board, at which employers from all over the country were present, because representatives of the Seamen's Union attended. The reason for this refusal was the claim that to sit in the same room with union representatives would constitute recognition. In New York the boat owners would not accept the Government's plan of local adjustment agencies because this involved a board on which a representative of the Longshoremen's Union would be a member; a special board had to be created with no representation of either employer or employee.[1] At San Francisco the same attitude prevented any Government arbitration of longshoremen's disputes.

The Western Union Telegraph Company preferred to have the Government take over the wires rather than tolerate union membership among its employees, and this same position was taken by the Smith & Wesson Company, of Springfield, Massachusetts. The President's Mediation Commission found opposition to unions the chief cause of unrest in the packing industry, and attributed the growth of the I. W. W. on the Pacific Coast, in great measure, to the same cause.

These are some of the most striking examples of employers' opposition to even conservative labor unions. They could be multiplied indefinitely. Toward the I. W. W., which in general estimation stands on quite another plane than the A. F. of L., the opposition was almost universal, and led to very much greater excesses. These will be dealt with separately in a later chapter.

Many employers were also much opposed to any form of collective bargaining. The Bridgeport manufacturers objected to the award of the National War Labor Board, claiming that they had submitted to the board the question of wages only and that the board had no right to compel them to bargain collectively with their employees. The Bethlehem Steel Company maintained its opposition to collective bargaining in spite of the efforts of Government mediators to induce them to accept it. After other Government agencies had failed to prevent strikes at the Bethlehem plant the National War Labor Board took up the case, held hearings and found the absence of collective bargaining to be one

---

[1] One of the New York employers at a conference with the Shipping Board said: "If we have a union harbor, God knows what will happen."

of the most potent causes for a condition of unrest that was seriously delaying the company's production of war material. After numerous attempts to evade putting the board's rulings into effect the company was finally induced to change its position and to introduce a system of collective bargaining satisfactory to the National War Labor Board.[1]

The Phelps-Dodge Company, replying to a letter of the President's Mediation Commission requiring the company to bargain collectively with its employees and not to discriminate against men for union membership, said that they considered such plans unnecessary and contrary to their best judgment. "But since we have no alternative in the matter, we shall endeavor to carry out your wishes in the spirit as well as the letter."

With respect to the attitude of employers toward the effort of workers to procure better wages and conditions, by strikes or by other means, we find repeated a number of peace-time assumptions, without any realization of how erroneous these assumptions often were in normal times, and how much more so in times of war.

In the first place, employers usually believed that "their men

---

[1] On December 6, 1918, the joint Chairman of the War Labor Board wrote to E. G. Grace, President of the Bethlehem Steel Company, in part as follows:

"Your letter, in our opinion, amounts to a refusal to apply the findings of the National War Labor Board or to respect its authority, on the ground that hostilities have ceased. . . .

"This action by your company presents a situation of grave importance to the nation. Last July when the outcome of the war was hanging in the balance, upon the representation of officials of the War Department that conditions in the Bethlehem Steel Company were gravely endangering the successful prosecution of the war and in order that our troops might not be left short of guns and amunition the War Labor Board exerted every resource to keep the employees of the Bethlehem Steel Company at work. . . .

"You personally agreed to the installation of a system of collective bargaining satisfactory to the board and under the supervision of the board's examiners. You now wish to repudiate that system of collective bargaining and ask that the board's examiners be withdrawn. . . .

"This is a question of the good faith of your company and of the Government itself. If the award of the board should now be repudiated, your workmen would have every right to feel that they had been deceived and grossly imposed upon by your company, by the War Labor Board and by the other officials of the Government who prevailed upon them to remain at work in the assurance that they would be justly dealt with."

were satisfied," that there was no danger of serious strikes, that any trouble with their workers would be the result of the actions of a few "agitators." Was there any labor adjuster in any part of the country who did not hear these statements repeated over and over again? The writer has gone from a meeting with employers where these statements were made, to a union meeting seething with bitterness and unrest, where the "agitators" most bitterly complained of were, as a matter of fact, the least radical of a large group of dissatisfied and protesting workers. He has left a factory where the management assured him there was not the least danger of a strike and before he could get back to his office one department of this very factory (unorganized at that) had struck; hundreds of men quickly followed suit.

In Arizona, the scene of some of the bitterest industrial warfare, the employers in the early days of the war assured the Council of National Defense (which was trying to arrange for arbitration in case of trouble) that there was no danger of strikes. Within a short time thousands of men had stopped work.

These cases are typical of hundreds of others. Moreover, when strikes occurred the employers not infrequently accused the men of profiteering and disloyalty. The strikers were "stealing cartridges from the boys on the other side." When the employers made these charges they frequently ignored well-founded grievances of the men, their own unwillingness to arbitrate and in certain cases their own provocative actions.

There were some strikes—many of them—that were unnecessary, that should not have occurred, and that are strongly to be condemned. But most strikes were the result of the failure of employers to advance wages in keeping with the increased cost of living, and to make other concessions which were demanded both by abstract justice and by the strategic strength of labor. The abuse and condemnation which greeted strikes that were justifiable simply added to the resentment of the workers. If the men, especially the better paid ones, asked for increases in wages larger than the increased cost of living they were roundly denounced as profiteers. And yet these demands were simply for wages commensurate with those already paid by aggressive employers, who, having profitable contracts, were bidding up wages to get men. In a word, the demands were for the equalization of the wage scale in a given industry; and often the requests of the men had already been granted by a Government board to other workers doing similar jobs in some other branch of the Government service.

In judging of the reasonableness of the employers' condemnatory attitude, when men asked for increases greater than just enough to cover increased living costs, the reader must bear in mind that it is impossible for a workman to improve his condition in slack times when labor is plentiful; at such times he is laid off with little thought of what idleness may mean to him and his family, and unless protected by a labor union he will, if he keeps his employment at all, almost invariably face a reduction in wages. The worker's opportunity comes when men are scarce and work is plentiful. Then he can strike successfully and improve his condition. If under these circumstances he asks for the eight-hour day in an industry which has lagged behind by not having established it, or if his demands for wage increases are somewhat more than the exact rise in the cost of living, the writer fails to see that such conduct is to be condemned. It takes two sides to make a strike; the men who make demands, and the employer who refuses them. The general attitude during the war was to hold the employee responsible for the occurrence of strikes, without taking into consideration the fact that the employer played an active part in causing them by refusing to grant the demands of the men. The apportionment of blame ought to have been determined by the reasonableness of the demands, and not by the mere fact of the occurrence of the strike. And the question of reasonableness frequently depended upon the justice of pre-war wages, hours, and conditions.

Employers would often ask, "What is going to be the attitude of the returning soldier, who has been facing death at the front for $30.00 a month and his keep, while his comrades at home have been out of danger and making big money? What is *he* going to say to you fellows when he gets back?" A labor leader answered this query in the writer's presence by asking the employer what the returning soldier would say about the employer's profits. If the employers had abandoned profits during the war—because of the sacrifice which was being made by the "boys at the front"—they might have been in a position to chide the workers for asking for higher wages. It seems incredible that men who were trying to make just as much money out of the war as they possibly could should not have realized the irony involved in their attitude of deprecating wage increases because of the feelings of the men at the front. The workers also gave the other obvious answer that the jobs awaiting the returning soldiers were going to be just that much better, because, through the insistence of those who stayed at home—either by means of strikes or other- wise—the eight-hour day was being extended, wages were keeping pace, more or less, with the rising living costs, and general con- ditions were improved. All this meant that the soldiers who had risked their lives at the front would return to conditions more nearly approximating those ideals of democracy for which they had fought.

Charges of corruption were also not uncommon—"enemy prop- aganda"; "enemy money"; "disloyalty." Many a labor adjust- ing board found that bitterness and antagonism were intensified by employers raising the "false issue of loyalty." Undoubtedly there were labor troubles induced by enemy influence, and also cases in which enemy propaganda was a factor. These, however, were probably very few in number; and yet hardly a strike oc- curred but the employer felt—and frequently said—that the strikers were disloyal and probably corrupt.[1]

In certain places where the I. W. W. was at all active there was likewise an attempt to connect any labor dispute with that organization and as such to brand it as revolutionary, "un-Ameri- can," and Socialistic. Many strikes were thus condemned, even though started by unorganized men or by members of unions af- filiated with the American Federation of Labor; and in some cases

[1] In the New York harbor strike hearing, before the National War Labor Board, January, 1919, the attorney for the shipowners called upon the unions to produce their books, "particularly those showing money from German sources." The opinion of Judge George W. Anderson as to the truth of most accusations of this kind is quoted in the *New Republic* for January 28, 1920, at page 251 as follows: "As United States Attorney from November, 1914, to October, 1917, I was charged with a large responsibility as to protecting the com- munity from pro-German plots. In October I went on the Inter- state Commerce Commission, and was until the armistice in intimate personal association with the Attorney General. . . . Now, I assert as my best judgment, grounded on the information that I can get, that more than ninety-nine per cent of the advertised and reported pro-German plots never existed. I think it is time that publicity be given to this view."

they were ruthlessly suppressed in the manner deemed fitting for "outlaw" organizations.

There was also a tendency to accuse strike leaders of selfishness, of thinking more of their own power, prestige, and salaries, than of the national welfare. These same accusations were made before the war, and have been made since. They may be successful in prejudicing the public, irrespective of their truth—they certainly increased bitterness among the men.[1]

Moreover, there was a disposition on the part of employers who indulged in any form of welfare work to lay stress upon such work in dealing with strike committees. In presenting their side of the case to labor adjusting agencies, group insurance, a sanitary factory, a fine lunch room, would be given prominence, when the workers were demanding that wages keep up with living costs, or that the eight-hour day be extended to their industry. The testimony of wage adjusting boards is full of examples of this kind, the only effect of which was to prejudice the workers against all forms of welfare work.

The one attitude of the employers with which the writer is in closer sympathy is the universal condemnation of the workers' inefficiency.[2] When all allowances are made, the impartial observer cannot escape the conclusion that in many cases there was an inexcusable slacking on the part of the men. While the nation was suffering for want of production, hundreds of thousands of workers lay down on their jobs and did just as little work as they could "get away with." This form of sabotage—not always deliberate perhaps—together with a considerable number of unjustifiable strikes, were the two things at which the employer's resentment was most legitimate.

What was the employer's attitude toward the Government labor administration?

There was quite a wide divergence of opinion, depending somewhat on the employer's previous relations with his workers, his attitude toward organized labor, and somewhat, too, upon his opinion as to his ability to defeat a strike.

Shortly before our entrance into the war, and much to the disgust of many employers, the Government had granted to the Railroad Brotherhoods the eight-hour day. In order to avoid a na-

---

[1] It goes without saying that in some cases these charges were true.
[2] See Chapter XV.

tion-wide railroad strike, Congress at the request of the President went so far as to enact into law the men's demands for a shorter day.[1] And as part of our war preparation the President of the American Federation of Labor had been appointed a member of the Council of National Defense and Chairman of its labor committee. It soon became evident that the Government intended to ask not only for the coöperation of big business in its prosecution of the war, but also for that of organized labor. When it was realized that the latter was to be given representation on wage boards, and that to a very great extent union standards were to be adopted, the natural distrust with which many business men looked upon the Government was very much increased.

In the pre-war period when labor was plentiful strikes were not very much feared, and there was little understanding by many employers of how different the conditions were during the war. Comparatively little systematic arbitration of industrial differences (except in a few industries) had been practiced in this country prior to our entry into the war. The employer, infinitely less wise in his dealings with labor than in the management of any other part of his business, was accustomed to handle labor disputes in his own way, without interference by the Government or other outside source.

Consequently the largest employers were sometimes bitterly opposed to any intervention by the Government in their disputes with their workers. Especially did they resent the Government's policy of forbidding discharges for union membership (a prohibition which, as we have seen elsewhere, was frequently violated). Indeed, there was a feeling that labor was actually being coddled and that the motive of the Government was in part at least political. One frequently heard it said that it was easy enough to deal with labor if you gave it all it wanted. There was apparently no general realization that the war had placed in the hands of the workers a new power and above all a realization of their new strength, and that the old method of fighting out industrial disputes was an impossible one during the war, entailing unthinkable

---

[1] It is interesting to note that many employers at the present time believe that this action on the part of Congress, which was and is described by them as cowardly yielding to the labor unions, is the most important factor in present extensive labor unrest.

delays, added bitterness, increased inefficiency, and in the end almost certain defeat for the employer.

When exasperated by inefficiency, by the heavy labor turnover, and by strikes, the final quarrel of the business man with the Government's labor policy was due to the administration's unwillingness to conscript labor. "If men can be conscripted for the army, if we can send them to the front to face privations and death, why cannot the Government conscript labor for war industry?" This question was asked thousands of times—publicly and privately, officially and unofficially.

The distinction between conscription for the army, where men were directly serving the Government, and conscription for private industry, where men would have been forced to work for private profit, was absolutely ignored. To be sure, workers in war industries were indirectly helping the Government, but they felt that primarily they were working for the profit of the employer. Time and again the men took the position, "Let the Government be our direct employer, and our attitude will be quite different; and if necessary, we will work for thirty dollars a month. We are perfectly willing that you conscript labor, if you will also conscript capital." It was lost sight of that the industrial conflicts which took place during the war were between the worker and the private employer. The public might suffer, but just as the employer blamed this upon the worker, so the worker in turn put the responsibility upon the employer.

Employers also felt that if men went on strike they should lose their draft exemption, and as a consequence the draft boards were used in many places for the purpose of intimidation and to break up strikes. This is a serious charge, but the writer does not see how an impartial observer can come to any other conclusion. The special district committees which had jurisdiction over questions of industrial exemption were composed largely of lawyers and business men. The rules provided that if a worker had been granted exemption from the draft on the ground of his industrial need to the community and thereafter left his job, it was the duty of the employer to notify the draft board of this fact. This was a perfectly proper rule as far as it related to the ordinary severance of employment. The trouble was that if there was talk of a strike, the employer would threaten the worker with the revocation of draft exemption, and immediately upon the occurrence of a strike would notify the draft board that the men had left his employment. Thereupon, the board would quickly put him back in class 1-A and the man would in a few days be taken to camp. In most cases the draft boards knew perfectly well that the man had not permanently left his employment, but that he was taking part in a strike. Both employer and draft board must have known that industrial draft exemption was given solely because the services of the worker were more valuable in industry than in the army, and yet they caused highly skilled men to be inducted into the service, who a short time before these very employers had stated were essential to a war industry.[1] This misuse of

[1] One of the grievances of the men, presented to the War Labor Board, in the Bridgeport case was coercion of the workers by means of the draft board. In support of this charge, the men produced the following order:

"American Can Company,
"Liberty Ordnance Plant,
"Union Avenue,

"Bridgeport, Conn., June 28, 1918.
"This plant employs a number of men who have received exemption or deferred classification on account of the value of their services in the production of munitions or guns. Any of these men who walk out in this crisis will automatically forfeit such classification and their local board will receive immediate advice to that effect. Every assurance has been given that these men will at once be placed in class 1-A of the draft and that further exemption at this or any other plant, will be refused.

"BY DIRECTION OF THE ACTING CHIEF OF ORDNANCE:
"C. F. Hepburn,
"Captain, O. R. C."

The above order was posted on the bulletin board of the American Can Company and it is claimed that the foreman stated, "If you fellows go out at 12 o'clock to-day, your draft exemption will be taken away and you will be in camp in a week." The workers also introduced in evidence an article in a Bridgeport paper, issued at the time of the strike, as follows: "Munition workers employed at the Remington Arms and other places, who have been placed in a deferred classification as registrants for the draft, by local boards, will be placed in Class 1-A if they go out on strike, according to a decision made yesterday by one of the city draft boards. It is probable that all of the other boards will take similar action."

"The decision to change the classification of munition workers who go out on strike thus violating their industrial value to the government, was made yesterday, upon the application of a machinist at the Remington Arms to determine his status if he went out in the strike which is threatening."

Complaints were made by the workers in many parts of the country that a position similar to the one outlined above was taken

the draft law was repeatedly called to the attention of the authorities in Washington and yet no definite orders seem to have been issued to correct this abuse.

by employers and draft boards in their districts. The International Seamen's Union claimed that the Lake Carriers' Association was using methods of intimidation to prevent the men from striking and quoted from a bulletin issued by the Association which, referring to seamen of draft age, stated: "The government's selective service regulations absolutely require that these men stuck (*sic*) to their job." The union points out to its members that this statement is false and goes on to say: "Your classification as seamen is for the purpose of enabling you to do your duty—your war duty—to the United States as seamen; it is not for the purpose of compelling you to submit to the Lake Carriers' Association or to any other private employer. . . . Why does the Lake Carriers' Association circulate false statements among seamen in these critical times?"

CHAPTER XVII

The Worker

It has already been pointed out that the worker's demands were generally confined to such conservative claims as improvement in working conditions, increases in wages, the eight-hour day, and the right of collective bargaining and of organization into trade unions. For the most part, demands for the closed shop, the forty-four-hour week, and for any radical industrial changes were during the period of the war waived by the workers, partly under Government pressure and partly under patriotic impulse.

The power of labor had been increasing even before the outbreak of the European war. A decided impetus was given to this growth of power by the labor shortage produced by the war, and by the dependence of the warring countries upon industrial forces, of which labor was the most important. Our American labor leaders had not failed to see the recognition which in European countries (especially the one closest to us, England) had increasingly been given to their industrial classes. It was therefore not strange that with the imminence of our entry into the war the feeling on the part of our labor leaders—that labor was entitled to play a new and most important part in our national affairs— should have become definitely crystallized. It found expression in the March 9, 1917, resolutions [1] of the American Federation of Labor wherein it was demanded that the workers be given representation on national boards "coequal with that given to any other part of the community."

This desire for adequate representation became all the more insistent because the men believed that the vigilance which was needed in ordinary times to protect their rights would have to be redoubled in war times in order to prevent standards from being lowered. Their new consciousness of power made them all the

[1] March 9, 1917, Conference of the American Federation of Labor, reported in the *American Federationist* for April, 1917.

more determined to protect their rights from the encroachments which in the past had accompanied times of violent disturbance of a national or an international kind. They believed that to "establish at home justice in the relation of men . . . " was a fundamental part of the preparedness of the nation. They asserted that "conditions of work and pay in Government employment and in all occupations should conform to principles of human welfare and justice." [1]

During the Civil War the workers fared bady.[2] There was a determination not only that this should not take place during this war,[3] but a desire in many quarters to better working conditions as much as was consistent with the war emergency.

This was exemplified by the fact that at all hearings before labor boards the workers demanded that wages keep pace with the increased living costs, and at many of them they not only made this demand but enlarged upon it, stating quite frankly that they realized that labor was scarce and that this was their opportunity substantially to improve their condition. When the war was over labor would once more be plentiful, employment would be difficult to find.[4] This, therefore, was their chance. Furthermore, the enormous increase in the earnings of large corporations was well known, and the men believed that there was a fortune in

[1] *Ibid.*: "Wage earners in war times must keep one eye on employers at home, the other on the enemy threatening the National Government."

[2] See E. D. Fite, Social and Industrial Conditions in the North During the Civil War.

[3] "All previous wars of magnitude have been accompanied by terrible financial suffering among the mass of the people. One of their most frequent results—a social injury enduring for a whole generation—has been the degradation of the standard of life among the wage earners. The last war waged by the United Kingdom on anything like the scale of the present Armaggeddon—the Napoleonic Conflict that lasted almost unceasingly from 1793 to 1815—reduced the British working class to a very general destitution, exhausted popular savings, filled the prisons, put 10% of the whole population on the pauper roll, brought down wages to the barest subsistence level, and destroyed for many years every vestige of either industrial or political power among the wage-earning classes." Sidney Webb in *The North American Review* for June, 1917, p. 877.

[4] This fear proved up to the summer of 1920 to have been unfounded. Owing partly to a cessation of immigration and to an enormous industrial activity caused by an abnormally large home demand, coupled with decreased production due to strikes and lessened efficiency of the individual workers, there did, in fact, develop a marked labor shortage.

every war contract. War prosperity was general and, as they expressed it, they wanted to get "theirs."[1]

A further example of the workers' determination not entirely to forego the opportunity for their improvement which the war afforded was illustrated by their desire to receive protection from many large employers with their policy of ruthless discharge solely on account of union membership. This desire was also the result of the feeling that if they were to give up demands for the closed shop, they should receive something in return. Nor did they hesitate, under the protection extended to them by the Government against discrimination, to do their utmost to increase trade union membership and to organize the men in establishments where the spread of the unions had been previously prevented by the aggressive opposition of the employers.

Furthermore, in addition to seeking the spread of trade unionism, they also, in sharp contrast to the English workers, insisted upon the maintenance of trade union customs. In England, shortly after the outbreak of the war, these customs were abandoned by the unions upon the promise of the Government to restore them upon the return of peace. This action of English trade union leaders was, however, the cause of much dissatisfaction and unrest among the men. Perhaps because of the realization of how unpopular this renunciation had been in that country no such general waiver of trade union practices took place in the United States. In fact, there were cases in which the men insisted most unreasonably upon the maintenance of customs that greatly retarded production. An example of this was the action of the ship caulkers on the Pacific Coast (already referred to), whose rules narrowly restricting the employment of apprentices prevented for many months the training of an adequate number of men. An exception to this policy was the ready acquiescence by the unions in the Government's inducting of women into industry to take the place of the men at the front.[2]

[1] As we have seen in a previous chapter, wages did not on the average increase to any greater extent than did the cost of living. However, in some industries, they did advance to a much greater extent. These extra large wage increases resulted from two causes —from the bidding up of wages by employers, and from the desire of the workers to share in war profits by taking advantage of the shortage of labor.

[2] They properly insisted, however, that in these cases the women receive equal pay for equal work, and they coöperated with the

Yet taken by and large, the attitude of the workers, and of the union leaders who represented many of them, was usually reasonable and coöperative. There were, however, cases in which their demands and their actions were unreasonable in the extreme. If men were unjustly discharged, they were of course entitled to reinstatement. Nevertheless, protests against discharge were not confined to cases of injustice, but were extended to cases where the justice of the discharge was beyond a reasonable doubt. Not infrequently reinstatement would be demanded on behalf of men who had acted in such a manner as to make their dismissal essential to the preservation of discipline. The indignation of employers against offenders of this kind was very much increased when the unions not only justified the offenses of the men but still sought in spite of them to have the men reinstated.

Thus in the case of the Savannah Electric Company, heard by the National War Labor Board, reinstatement was asked for men, some of whom the Board found to have been guilty of violence; others of cheating.[1] In another case, upon the occurrence of a strike, union leaders had ordered the men to remain at the benches but to do no work; the foreman demanded that the men either work or leave the factory. Upon the termination of the strike the representatives of the workers demanded the reinstatement of the men whose orders had been so subversive of all discipline. The employer was unwilling to take the men back, and in this position was sustained by the National War Labor Board.[2]

In most instances, it should in fairness be pointed out, the leaders of the unions did not intentionally ask for the reinstatement of men who they had any reason to believe were not entitled to it, and these requests, when made, were as a rule promptly withdrawn when it appeared that the employer had been justified in his actions.

Another respect in which the actions of labor leaders were not all that the Government desired was in the manner in which they represented the Government's attitude towards labor to the members of their unions and to workers whom they tried to persuade to join them. There was an earnest effort by all branches of the

Department of Labor to prevent women from being assigned to tasks beyond their strength.

[1] National War Labor Board Docket, No. 748.
[2] National War Labor Board Docket, No. 231. Case of the General Electric Company.

Government to treat both employer and worker with absolute impartiality, not favoring either one side or the other. It was extremely important that an attitude of industrial neutrality be maintained and that it be understood by both sides that each would be treated fairly. And yet some of the local leaders in their organizing campaigns persistently sought to give the impression that the United States Government favored workers who were organized as against those who were not. The fact that the various boards had asked the unions for assistance in securing additional labor was presented to the men in an exaggerated light, and it was stated that the Government had "turned over to union officers the task of mobilizing the workers." [1] Anti-union employers, who were themselves convinced that the Government was favoring organized labor, were irritated beyond measure by statements of this kind, making the work of conciliation all the more difficult.

There was also not infrequently a lack of candor on the part of local leaders in representing to their constituents the principles of the Taft-Walsh Board—the policy that there should be no strikes often being deliberately glossed over. The principles of the War Labor Board as enunciated by the President commence with the statement, "there should be no strikes." In reprinting these principles for circulation among the men there were cases in which this statement was intentionally omitted. It must be stated that this was done by local, not by national, leaders, and was undoubtedly contrary to the wishes of the latter.

In another chapter reference has been made to the resentment which the men felt at the frequent refusal of employers to meet the representatives of their unions. The Government insisted upon collective bargaining, that is to say, it compelled employers to meet committees of their own employees, as representatives of the men, and to discuss with them the adjustment of the difficulties in their individual plants. The reader must not confuse col-

---

[1] In an advertisement inserted by the machinists' union of Newark, New Jersey—in the Newark *Evening News* of May 20, 1918—the following sentence is used: "Uncle Sam has cast his lot with the wage-earner (the real American), and is playing the part of an organizer." There is also a cartoon, with the caption "Uncle Sam and His Boys—Find the Favorite Son," which depicts two men sleeping blissfully in bed, one of them, Uncle himself, the other, union labor—meanwhile another man, who in this case is labeled "unorganized labor," occupies an unhappy position on the floor.

lective bargaining with trade unionism, upon the first of which the Government insisted, but upon the second of which the rule was that no change would be forced during the war. Where an employer before the war had followed the practice of refusing to meet representatives of the union he would not be compelled to do so during the war. Many employers stood upon their rights in this matter, and continued to refuse to meet union representatives.

This persistent refusal, while within the employers' rights, was unquestionably the source of much dissatisfaction and resentment among the workers, and where it occurred the settlement of disputes was made much more difficult. It is a curious fact that in some cases these very union leaders, whom the employers refused to meet, were more conservative than the men themselves in the shops, and this refusal to meet the leaders removed a strong conciliating force.[1]

The adage that extremes provoke extremes is well illustrated by our labor experience. In places where the employers were most reactionary, the most aggressive and radical labor leadership was to be found. This was true of Arizona mines and Northwest lumber camps as well as of cities like Bridgeport, Newark, and Chicago, where an excessive conservatism on the part of the employers was, as is often the case, accompanied by labor leadership of the most fiery and extreme kind.

Now if, as we have seen, the relations between the workers and their employers were in many cases strained, it is important to point out that, broadly speaking, the feelings of the men toward the Government were cordial. To be sure, there was often a belief that the Government was catering to big business. This belief was in specific cases based upon dissatisfaction with wage

[1] In one strike with which the writer was acquainted, through being an adjuster, the employers at first refused to meet union representatives. They met a strike committee, consisting of their own employees and found it impossible to make any progress with them toward a settlement. After about a week of fruitless negotiations, they decided to meet with the representatives of the' union, and at the first conference terms were agreed upon which resulted in settling the strike. The explanation for this result was twofold—the employers by agreeing to meet the union representatives had by that one step removed one of the sources of dissatisfaction, and the union leaders, being in this case conservative and wanting to see production resumed, used their influence to induce the men to accept terms to which the more radical shop leaders had been opposed.

awards and upon the actions of individual Government officials, many of whom in peace times had been employers, in some cases employers of the reactionary type. A further feeling of resentment arose from the fact that many cost plus contracts were awarded to corporations which had always been more or less unfriendly to organized labor, the men claiming that these companies, in a desire to avoid employing members of unions, discriminated against them to the extent of using common laborers to do the work of skilled artisans—and paying them skilled artisans' wages. It was also felt that these discriminatory tactics, which the men believed resulted in reckless waste of the Government's money, had the approval of certain Government officials. In spite of these causes for friction, and in spite of the opinion that the Government was subservient to big business—an opinion almost as widespread as the opinion (on the employers' side) that the Government was coddling labor—yet on the whole there was a general belief that the Government was doing its best to treat labor fairly, and, in fact, that it was pursuing a broad and liberal policy.[1]

Perhaps because of this general confidence that they would receive fair treatment from Government labor boards, the men during the war period were more willing to submit to arbitration than were the employers. A further explanation lies in the fact that it is almost always the worker who has the grievance. The employer is quite satisfied with the *status quo;* the worker is seeking to better his condition or to prevent it from becoming worse by reason of adverse changes in the cost of living. He therefore makes demands for higher wages and for other improved

---

[1] Report of the officers of the Railway Employees Department of the A. F. of L. to the Fourth Biennial Convention, April, 1918 "We feel, however, that we are fortunate that Government control of railroads has been brought about under an administration which has been exceptionally fair to Labor, and ample assurance exists that dealing with our new employer will prove in many ways much more preferable to our former relations with many officials whose varying moods, idiosyncrasies and prejudices sometimes occasioned avoidable friction and loss to both parties.

At the 13th annual convention of the Building Trades Department of the A. F. of L. (page 101), a resolution was adopted in reference to the Government's adjustments under the Baker-Gompers agreement ". . . While in all cases we did not meet with success, we have reason to feel that in the aggregate we were treated very fairly."

conditions, which, if uncomplied with, must be either waived or enforced by Government intervention or by means of a strike. Consequently it is not unnatural that the initiative, when the intervention of Government mediation boards is sought, should come from the side which is looking for a change of conditions.[1]

While it is true that as a general rule labor was willing to arbitrate, there were cases in which there was a decided unwillingness to do so, because the men knew in advance from previous decisions of the boards that their demands would be refused. But these cases were exceptional. After all it must be realized that from the actual process of arbitration, labor derived a certain strength, for arbitration of itself inevitably implied a degree of recognition of trade unions—not recognition in the technical sense—but an acknowledgment of their existence and importance. The value of arbitration to the unions was augmented by the fact that the Government gave to organized labor representation on arbitration boards and it is therefore not unnatural that labor should have welcomed this opportunity for public service together with the prominence which such service implied.

[1] The records of both state and Federal labor boards substantiate this statement. See Monthly Bulletins for experience of the U. S. Labor Department, and also reports of the board of mediation for the railways (created by the Newlands Act), and finally, the records of the state labor boards.

CHAPTER XVIII

The Public

TURNING now to a consideration of the war-time attitude of the public toward both labor and capital, we are first of all impressed by the fact that at the outbreak of the war we did not possess any well-defined public policy toward labor.[1] In fact, there was so little comprehension of the problem that those in executive positions received practically no suggestions or intelligent comment from either the press or Congress. An examination of newspaper and magazine files, and of the Congressional Record for the entire period of the war will show how few helpful suggestions or fruitful ideas in relation to the organization of an adequate labor administration or the proper handling of industrial difficulties and disputes were forthcoming from these representatives of public opinion. The early declarations of the Council of National Defense, which, as we saw in a rather lengthy examination in Chapter XIII, contributed little to the creation of a sound labor policy, were greeted with a wealth of commendation out of all proportion to their usefulness or importance in the task of helping us to find a solution for the perplexities with which the nation's production problem was surrounded. Even among experts

---

[1] The break-up of the President's first Industrial Conference was a result of the absence of any common meeting ground for capital and labor. It would have been harder for either side to maintain a position of irreconcilability, if there had existed a clear-cut public opinion. This, however, was lacking, just as during the war there was no common assent to any definite labor policy. During the war, on the other hand, patriotism demanded production, and when the Government announced a policy which seemed to further this end, it received public endorsement. Both sides were thus compelled—in war-time—to accept the principles adopted by the Government. The war forced it to become a leader. But with the coming of peace the Government was unwilling or unable to take the lead. There was no unified opinion to take the place of the leadership which the Government had abandoned, and consequently nothing to clarify the resulting confusion.

there were few who recognized the necessity for the development of a broad, unified labor administration, and there was not a suspicion of this need in editorial sanctums or on the floor of Congress. A few liberal weeklies, however, made suggestions of some value.[1] But editorials in the daily papers were of no use whatever.

In Congress the debates displayed amazing ignorance of industrial conditions. During those early days, when it should have been apparent to the most inexperienced that the avoidance of industrial disputes was a vital part of any war program, appropriations for the conciliation work of the labor department were refused on the ground that the settlement of strikes was a *private* and not a Government affair.[2] The report of the President's Mediation Commission, one of the ablest labor documents produced during the war, was bitterly assailed in Congress. Throughout the discussions of measures for housing war workers, in the course of debates provoked by labor disputes, and in almost every case in which Congress attempted to discuss problems of labor or to provide remedies for industrial evils, there was a total lack of constructive statesmanship, and, in its place, prejudice and misunderstanding. Without any effort being made to determine whether or not the workers had just grievances, both in the press and in Congress there was a tendency to condemn them for the mere fact of striking. In numberless cases the men were blamed for stopping work, but in hardly a single case was fault found with the employer for his failure to grant reasonable demands. This was not so much because of prejudice against the workers, as because of a feeling that the men should have stayed at work irrespective of the existence of grievances. In most cases the jus-

[1] The *New Republic* of April 14, 1917: "With singular unanimity the press has magnified Gompers' recommendation that neither employers nor employees shall endeavor to take advantage of the country's necessities to change existing standards to a guarantee against all industrial unrest. Patriotic manifestos unsupported by definite administrative plans are no guarantee, since standards change daily as food costs mount . . . hence the Government should make them (wages) more flexible by creating joint conciliation committees to be provided with the power to make adjustments." Further suggestions are made as to how these committees should function.

[2] See V. E. Macy, Chairman Committee on Conciliation, Labor Committee of the Council of National Defense, and later of the Shipbuilding Labor Adjustment Board, in *Proceedings of the Academy of Political Science* for February, 1919, volume VIII, No. 2, page 92.

tice of a strike was not considered; its existence alone was enough to condemn it.

Senator Thomas of Colorado, in addressing the Senate on April 2, 1918, said: "I contend that the man who incites a strike at this time—I do not care what his motives are—is an enemy to the United States and should be treated as such. I declare, Mr. President, deliberately, that the fomenters of strikes in our labor ranks are traitors to the country whose protection they invoke."

Senator Calder of New York, in February, 1918, said: "I do not propose, Mr. President, that we shall kill men who stop work, but I propose that the men who stop work in Government plants during the war shall be denied the right of reëmployment while the war exists . . . and I would say to them that they shall be required to take their places side by side with the American soldiers in France who are struggling to uphold the honor and dignity of the nation."

Did the members of Congress think that the labor problems with which the country was confronted—which had their roots in our entire industrial history, and which were complicated by the constantly rising cost of living and all the other causes of industrial unrest—were going to be solved by indiscriminate and unthinking abuse of this kind? It is not too much to say that in the solution of the labor problems arising out of the war, the executive branch of the Government received practically no assistance from Congress. It was forced to create special technical boards, the members of which were drawn from the universities, the bar, and the ranks of business and labor—boards created without the sanction of Congress, and in most cases without its direct financial support. Not only did the executive branch in groping its way toward the formation of a definite policy fail to receive from Congress the assistance which it so much needed, but instead, the task of adjusting war-time difficulties and allaying industrial unrest was made all the harder by the lack of sympathy and perception in the utterances of our national legislators. It is a striking fact that this same lack of helpfulness in the solution of labor problems, which Congress displayed during the war, is still manifest to-day. This is especially unfortunate since the war mediating agencies, created by the executive, have been allowed to disappear without any effective effort having been made on the part of Congress to create substitutes, at a time when they have been so obviously needed, and at a time when permanent substitutes for these temporary boards might so readily have been created. Congress has been content to let labor affairs drift along unguided and uncontrolled.

This lack of discrimination also showed itself in the press, in the manner in which strikes were condemned, without even considering, in the apportionment of blame, so vital a factor as willingness to arbitrate. There were cases in which the men were willing to abide by the Government's decision as to the justice of their claims, but the employers were absolutely unwilling to do so, and the men did not go out until all reasonable efforts to secure arbitration had been exhausted. And yet even in these cases they were blamed for going out on strike.[1]

But much more serious than attitudes of prejudice against organized labor or than indiscriminate abuse of the workers for strikes were editorials in the press and speeches in Congress condoning and at times even advocating the use of violence against men who agitated for or indulged in strikes. At a time when feelings ran unusually high, when hysteria was sweeping over the world, when four years of war had unleashed the worst passions of men—at such a time as this it seems inexcusable that those to whom was entrusted the guidance of public opinion should have given utterances to expressions the only result of which must have been to augment passion and prejudice and to break down obedience to and respect for the law.

And yet many editorials appeared in the daily press in all parts of the country similar to the following: "Even if our shipyards were placed under martial law, we still have flabby public opinion which would wring its hands if we took the labor leader by the scruff of the neck, backed him up against the wall and filled him with lead. Countries which consider themselves every bit as civilized as our own do not hesitate about such a matter for a moment."

The I. W. W. publications and other radical organs made it a practice to republish and give wide publicity to these incitements to violence on the part of the conservative press, using this material for propaganda purposes. Thus *Solidarity* for July 17, 1917, quotes the Freeport,, Ill., *Bulletin* as saying that "any en-

---

[1] The strike of the machinists in Newark in July, 1918, is an excellent example. See Chapter VII.

deavor by the I. W. W. to prejudice the cause of the United States by fomenting strikes in the ore field should be met by hanging a few ringleaders to the nearest tree." From *Godwin's Weekly*, of Salt Lake City, the following is taken: "Unless the I. W. W. are branded as traitors and treated as such, the indignant citizen will take the situation in hand one of these days, and string up a few agitators of this contemptible cult without court procedure or any other form of ceremony." [1] The Tulsa *Daily World* for November 9, 1917, is quoted from as follows: "Any man who attempts to stop the supply for one-hundredth part of a second is a traitor and ought to be shot! . . . if the I. W. W. or its twin brother, the Oil Workers' Union, gets busy in your neighborhood, kindly take occasion to decrease the supply of hemp. A knowledge of how to tie a knot that will stick might come in handy in a few days. It is not time to dally with the enemies of the country. . . . We are either going to whip Germany or Germany is going to whip us. The first step in the whipping of Germany is to strangle the I. W. W.'s. Kill them, just as you would kill any other kind of a snake. Don't scotch 'em; kill 'em. And kill 'em dead. It is no time to waste money on trials and continuances and things like that. All that is necessary is the evidence and a firing squad. Probably the carpenters' union will contribute the timber for the coffins."

The I. W. W. Defense Bulletins quote a number of statements from the Sacramento *Bee* in which citizens are urged to take the law into their own hands if necessary. The newspapers of the West went so far as to justify the Arizona deportations and the tar and feathering of workers. For although many of our newspapers recognize the flagrant injustice of these acts of violence as well as their inexpediency, such newspapers were on the whole exceptional.[2] In Jerome, Arizona, was printed the following open defiance of the law: "There were two justifiable wholesale deportations in Arizona last summer. . . . The Jerome Wobblies were

---

[1] The present editor of the successor of *Godwin's Weekly* disclaims the sentiment expressed in the above quotation.

[2] Occasionally editorials of a different kind appeared (as is the case to-day). The following is well worth quoting, from the pen of Colonel Robertson, editor of the North Yakima *Republican:* "But the fact remains that there are half a hundred men in the Yakima jail who are being deprived of their liberty, indefinitely, arbitrarily, and without a shadow of legal authority or even a pretense that such authority exists in any officer or any court. I would be an

sent to Needles and then turned back on Arizona soil, where they dispersed. Bisbee shipped her undesirables over into New Mexico. . . . Let Hayden go ahead and get his anti-deportation bill passed, if he can. It won't make any difference to Jerome or Bisbee or any other place in Arizona, when conditions similar to those of last summer arise." And even so conservative a paper as the Boston *Transcript* said of the murder of Frank Little, which occurred in Butte, Montana, that it knew "of millions of people who, while sternly reprehending such proceedings as the lynching of members of that anti-patriotic society (the I. W. W.), will nevertheless be glad, in their hearts, that Montana did it in the case of Little," while the Helena *Independent* cynically remarked that Montana holds "that Butte disgraced itself like a gentleman." The natural result of all this advocacy of violence was to make irreconcilables of men and women who otherwise would have confined their efforts for betterment to moderate channels.

Even to-day we are still paying the penalty for this dangerous invitation to violence; the general use of force, together with the intolerance which always goes with it, and the suppression of all

I. W. W. myself, if I had to work for some of these employers on the terms they propose."

One of the clearest expressions of the indignation aroused by the Bisbee Deportations, appeared in the New York *Globe* in its issue of July 13, 1917, under an editorial captioned, Lynch Law in Arizona: "For some years as often as industrial trouble has arisen in the western mining regions, and the organizers of the skeleton and largely imaginary organization called the I. W. W. have appeared on the scene, the cry has arisen to suspend the law while the invaders are driven out . . . It also appears that the casualties are always greater among the strikers than among those who pretend to fear them, thus suggesting where the aggression began. Any one familiar with the published disclosures concerning what has been done in the name of law and order in Idaho, Montana, Colorado, and Michigan finds it difficult to resist the conclusion that the method of strike settlement followed is not only contrary to law, but is practically ineffective. What does a man think who is loaded in a bull-pen without warrant or charge against him, and then, with a pistol at his head, marched away and put on a train? Is he likely to have stimulated in him a law-abiding spirit and to believe that the great republic stands for law and equality of right? Grave have been the offenses against order that have been committed by those who pretend to want order. The Bisbee plan does not work. It is foolish and fatal and is planting the seeds of trouble. Lynch law is lynch law whether committed by a gang of white-cappers, or Ku Klux or by citizens in frock coats. The I. W. W. is a most objectionable organization. It exists because it is able plausibly to say a square deal is denied and our Government is in the hands of a selfish class."

unpopular ideas on one side, with the inevitable accompaniment of extreme radicalism on the other, have become all too tragically widespread. This disregard for the law and the impulse to achieve results by violent means, which might reasonably have been expected to follow five years of world war, have been augmented by these inflammatory utterances. They have found expression, among other places, in widespread race riots, acts of violence by the American Legion, and the arrest and brutal treatment of strikers (as for example in Wyoming during the coal strike and throughout Pennsylvania during the steel strike).[1]

One of the most flagrant of recent examples was the full page advertisement in the Seattle *Post-Intelligencer* of November 18, 1919: "There is just one chance left—and by the Eternal God, we must take it or we are lost. . . . Real Americans must rise as one man in the righteous wrath of outraged patriotism. First invoke such legal machinery as we have; and if that is not sufficient, then hastily construct something fool-proof. We must smash every un-American and anti-American organization in the land. We must put to death the leaders of this gigantic conspiracy of murder, pillage and revolution. We must imprison for life all its aiders and abettors of native birth. We must deport all aliens. . . . The I. W. W., the Non-partisan League, the so-called Triple Alliance in the State of Washington, the pro-German Socialists, the Closed Shop labor unions, the agitators, malcontents, anarchists, syndicalists, seditionists, traitors—the whole motley crew of Bolshevists and near-Bolshevists—must be outlawed by public opinion and hunted down and hounded until driven beyond the horizon of civic decency."[2]

Similar utterances, which undoubtedly had the same unfortunate results, were made in the United States Senate, and public

[1] These incidents of the steel and coal strikes are made all the worse because many of them were committed by representatives of the Government.

[2] This, like similar utterances on the part of the reactionaries during the war, was spread far and wide by the radical press. (The New York *Call,* for example, devoted a series of articles to it.) Yet perhaps the most significant reaction was that of the labor men connected with the newspaper in which it appeared. Immediately after it was printed, the employees of the paper met and refused to continue work until the advertisement was removed. The Government also stepped in and declared the issue non-mailable. The men adopted a resolution of protest which is so remarkable that the following sections are reproduced: "We have been patient under mis-

opinion does not seem to have been shocked when doctrines so subversive of all democratic Government were promulgated in the highest legislative body in the land.

Senator King, of Utah, said: "There has been too much maudlin sympathy lavished upon them by silly cranks and foolish uplifters. Recently a large number of I. W. W.'s gathered in one of these mining towns of Arizona; they called strikes, defied the law, and committed many crimes; took possession of property; prevented honest men from working, and created a condition of anarchy and terror. Finally the residents of the town organized and drove the I. W. W.'s from their midst. It was a drastic step. It was perhaps without legal sanction. But the frightful conditions brought about by the reign of the organization which knows no law became intolerable to those who had homes and property and who desired peace and opportunity to labor." [1]

Senator McCumber, after describing how several hundred I. W. W.'s congregated, goes on to say, "They were ordered to leave. They were arrested. They refused to work. There were too many of them to put into jail, so the farmers organized

representation, faithful in the face of slander, long suffering under insult; we have upheld our agreements and produced your paper, even though in so doing we were braiding the rope with which you propose to hang us; day after day we have put in type, stereotyped, printed and mailed calumny after calumny, lie after lie, insult after insult . . . So long as these things appeared to be a part of your unfair fight against organization—our organization and others—we have been able to endure them in the hope that at last truth must prevail. But there must be a limit to all things. In the page advertisement, purporting to have been written and paid for by one Selvin, but which had as well have occupied the position in your paper usually taken up by your editorial page, your utter depravity as a newspaper, your shameless disregard of the laws of the land, your hatred of opposition, your reckless policy of appeal to the passions of citizenry, reached depths of malice and malignancy hitherto unbelievable. It is nothing less than excitation to violence, stark and naked invitation to anarchy. If your business management cannot demonstrate its capacity and sagacity, if your editorial directing heads must remain blind to the things they are bringing us to; if, together, you cannot see the abyss to which you are leading us—all of us; if you have no more love for our common country than is manifested in your efforts to plunge it into anarchy, then as loyal American citizens—many of us ex-service men who very clearly proved our faith in America and its institutions—we must—not because we are unionists, but because we are Americans—find means to protect ourselves from the stigma of having aided and abetted your campaign of destruction."

[1] Congressional Record, LVI, pp. 6565; May 6, 1918.

and came to town with their shotguns and they gave them orders to leave. They got out, and they did not come back, and if they had, there would have been a great many funerals in that part of the state."[1]

As to the attitude of the press toward the Government's labor policies, it can be stated, speaking generally, that most newspapers during the war supported these policies. Although the passage of the Adamson law in the fall of 1916 had met with a good deal of adverse criticism, nevertheless after we entered the war, there was comparatively little opposition to the administration's treatment of industrial difficulties.

In some places, however, the opinion of employers that the Government was coddling labor was echoed in the press, and some of the more partisan and reactionary publications indulged in attacks of a most bitter character upon the administration. It will doubtless seem surprising that the insistence of the Government that union men be not dismissed solely for membership in unions, and that collective bargaining between the firm and committees of its own employees be installed, should have resulted in any very violent protest; and yet the taking over of the plant of Smith & Wesson by the War Department—because of its refusal to submit to the ruling of the Taft-Walsh board that the firm reinstate the men whom it had discharged because they belonged to labor unions, and that it deal with committees of its men (not of the union, but of its own employees)—called forth the following from the *North American Review's War Weekly*, for September 7, 1918: "Is our Pacifist-Socialist Secretary of War strongly for efficiency in war industries or for the imposition of Socialistic fads upon this country? . . . We can conceive no possible ground of justification for this astounding action of the War Labor Board. We know of no legislation authorizing the executives thus to require private business concerns to revolutionize their business methods. We cannot see that the War Labor Board or the War Department has any more right to prescribe collective bargaining instead of individual bargaining than it has to prescribe red ink instead of black ink in the firm's letterheads."

Another example of this unreasonable hostility appeared in the *American Lumberman*, which, when speaking of the lumber

[1] Congressional Record, March 21, 1918, Vol. 56, Pl. 4, page 3821.

strikes in the Northwest—the principal cause for which was the demand for the eight-hour day—said: "When we consider the situation without prejudice or passion it is really pitiable to see the Government groveling in the dust, truckling to a lot of treasonable labor agitators and showing a willingness to practically paralyze a great industry simply to placate these agitators who are playing into the hands of our enemies."

The same sort of thing was echoed in Congress. Senator Sherman, for example, and others attacked the President's Mediation Commission. Senator McCumber, of North Dakota, criticizing a speech made by James O'Connell at the Boilermakers' Convention, said: "The only excuse I can find for this is that they have been misled by the doctrines promulgated by their leaders—the doctrine of more and more and always more, and feel that they are justified in taking advantage of their Government even to the extent of fatally crippling its war endeavors. Nor is the Government at all blameless in this matter; it has surrendered soul and conscience to unionized labor. I am informed that on the West Coast the Government itself stepped in, forced yards either to close business or to recognize labor unions with all their disastrous rules."

Other branches of the Government, in their desire to help along production, sometimes took similarly unreasonable and unthinking positions. Patriotic speakers occasionally urged workers not to join unions and not to listen to agitators. Agents of the Department of Justice and representatives of the Intelligence Bureau, of the Army and Navy, many of whom were doubtless hurriedly recruited and untrained for their duties, were ludicrously ignorant of the fact that their superiors in Washington were coöperating with labor unions and entrusting them with a large measure of responsibility. Unlike the more important officials they looked with suspicion and frequently ill-concealed hostility upon any demands of these organizations for better working conditions. In most cases their motives were patriotic, but their actions resulted in increased irritation among the workers and in further labor unrest.

Turning from a consideration of the attitude of the press and Congress to an examination of the positions taken by the men themselves who were on Government boards, we find that most of them did their best to be fair to both sides. In this they did not always succeed, because they took with them to public life those prejudices which were the result of their private occupations and previous environment. Many of the most important Government representatives in the Ordnance Department and elsewhere were, not unnaturally, recruited from the ranks of big manufacturers who in their own business were hostile to organized labor, and they inevitably carried over to their new positions some of their former bias. Indeed, in a few cases the officials were absolutely unfair to organized labor.[1] On the other hand, there were also a few cases, it has been reliably stated, where individuals took positions in war adjustment labor boards with the deliberate intention of using these strategic positions more to further the cause of organized labor than to find equitable solutions of the labor disputes with which they came in contact. These extreme cases were, however, very rare. By and large, Government officials performed their duties of production management, adjustment, and investigation, with creditable fairness to both sides. It can be said especially of the men who occupied important positions on the Boards of Adjustment that their very arduous tasks were performed with the utmost conscientiousness and an earnest desire to do justice to both sides. The Government was fortunate in having secured for these positions men of integrity and in almost all cases of great ability.

[1] A Government mediator said to the writer that when he was called upon to grant a wage increase in a particular locality, he would endeavor to delay matters and to "jolly the men along" as far as possible. If, however, it appeared that the men would actually go out, he would speedily make an adjustment. In fairness, it ought to be stated that this was a very exceptional case.

CHAPTER XIX

The I. W. W. and the Loyal Legion of Loggers and Lumbermen

THE I. W. W.

In its philosophy the Industrial Workers of the World is uncompromisingly revolutionary, desiring to see the immediate and complete overthrow of the capitalistic system, and at the same time justifying practically any means to accomplish this end. With these revolutionary theories and with the I. W. W.'s justification of sabotage the writer has absolutely no sympathy—on the contrary, he dissents most strongly from both of these points of view. However, in its actual work as a labor organization attempting to improve the condition of the lowest workers in the social scale, the I. W. W. has been the victim of such outrageous treatment during the war that it is desirable that the facts should be set forth as accurately as possible. This, not in justification or defense of I. W. W. theories,—the writer is as far as he possibly can be from any desire to defend or justify them—but because no good can be accomplished by prejudice, injustice, or violence, from all three of which the I. W. W. has suffered.

Judging it only by the doctrines contained in the preamble to its constitution, and by the utterances of many of its leaders before and during the war, it is not strange that a society organized as is the one under which we live should look upon the I. W. W. with hostility, and that in war-time this feeling should have developed into active hatred and persecution. But an impartial study of the things it actually did during the war, not of its theoretical philosophy, but of its work in the field, and an impartial study of the nature and conduct of the rank and file will show:

(1) That the large majority of its members were and are ignorant of its subversive doctrines.[1]

[1] Report of the President's Mediation Commission, page 14. This opinion is not shared by many persons whose occupations have brought

(2) That during the war its functions were those of the ordinary trade union,[1] even though its leaders expressed extremely radical and frequently revolutionary opinions.

(3) That in time of war the natural test of patriotism is the support given by the individual to the government in its prosecution of the war. Judged by this standard, the leaders of the I. W. W. were unpatriotic. They believed that this war was no different from previous wars; that its basis was capitalistic exploitation,[2] and that the laboring classes had no interest in participating in it. During the early months of the war *Solidarity*, the official I. W. W. organ, opposed the draft, as did many leaders of the organization.[3] Later the I. W. W. does not seem to have taken any official position toward the war, neither supporting it nor opposing it.[4] They became indifferent to the success or fail-

them into conflict with the I. W. W. But it is the belief of the best qualified neutral observers.

[1] Carleton H. Parker in an article on the I. W. W. in the *Atlantic Monthly* for November, 1917, says: "The I. W. W. movement can be described with complete accuracy as an extension of the American labor strike into the zone of casual migratory labor. All the superficial features, such as its syndicalist philosophy, its sabotage, threats of burnings and destruction, are the natural and normal accompaniments of organized labor disturbance in this field."

[2] *Solidarity*, July 7, 1917: "Capitalism is a Hydra with many heads. War is but one of them; government repression is but one of them and the prostituted press is one of them. If the working class had the power to cut off one of these heads it would have the power to kill the monster outright. It is the historic mission of the working class to do away with the Beast, for there is no room on the earth for both Capitalism and the producing class." On August 18, 1917, in the very midst of the war, *Solidarity* said: "The time for talk is past; the time for action is here—ACT. If each of us will do his bit, Capitalism will be at our mercy within a month. Stir up the smoldery flames of discontent until the conflagration can be seen around the world."

[3] There were also leaders of the more radical branches of the A. F. of L. and of other labor organizations who at the beginning of the war were opposed to our participation in it and to the draft. The report of the President's Mediation Commission at page 6 says: "The labor difficulties (in Arizona) were further complicated by factors created by the war. This was particularly true of the situation in the Globe district. Doctrines of internationalism, which before the war had permeated the minds of labor the world over, strongly marked the labor leadership in the Globe district. It led to resolutions of opposition to the war by the miners' local at the outbreak of the war."

[4] *The Literary Digest* of July 28, 1917, quotes from an interview with Wm. D. Haywood of a Chicago correspondent of the N. Y.

ure of either side, feeling that in any case the industrial battle would have to be fought out under the same capitalistic conditions. The activities of the organization were thereafter confined to industrial matters and efforts to improve the condition of the working classes. It ought to be pointed out that this early hostility and later indifference to the war were not shared by the rank and file, whose feelings were much like those of most other workmen—in most cases the war had their enthusiastic support, in others they were indifferent to it.

(4) That officers and members of the I. W. W. were in many places treated as outlaws, no effort being made to distinguish in the case of particular individuals, between their theoretical principles and their practical activities.

(5) That employers made the existence and the doctrines of the I. W. W. excuse for illegal and violent conduct toward any organized effort to improve wages, hours, or working conditions, whether by members of the I. W. W., the A. F. of L., or otherwise.

(6) That in practically all cases the workers had legitimate causes for complaint and that in many cases men who became identified with the I. W. W. worked under conditions of great hardship for which the employers were directly to blame; [1] and that, in spite of these genuine grievances, the workers had ordinarily no means of securing redress except the strike.

(7) That during the war, with the exception of certain conspicuous cases, the I. W. W. was the frequent victim of brutal violence on the part of employers and the public, and of illegal action by Government officials who in some cases went so far as to participate in and even to lead in the commission of acts of extreme brutality. And that these actions were treated with

Tribune: "We are not thinking of the war at all in these strikes. In that respect we don't know there is a war. What we are doing is trying to improve the conditions of our boys—their living and working condition."

[1] The report of the President's Mediation Commission, at page 13, speaking of conditions in the lumber industry of the Pacific Northwest says: . . . "but the rigors of nature have been reinforced by the neglects of men. Social conditions have been allowed to grow up full of danger to the country. . . . The living conditions of many of the camps have long demanded attention." At page 6 speaking of conditions in the Arizona copper mines the Report says: "But neither sinister influences (of the enemy) nor the I. W. W. can account for these strikes. The explanation is to be found in unremedied and unremediable industrial disorders."

approval by large sections of the press, Congress, and speakers on public platforms.

The I. W. W. has succeeded best among common laborers, who have been largely neglected by other unions, among foreigners, among scattered and migratory workers whom the American Federation of Labor has been unable—or indisposed—to organize, and also among those men who were prevented by the opposition of employers from joining the conservative type of craft union, thus leaving the field open to aggressive organizations. We hear of it during the war as operating chiefly in the States west of the Mississippi and in three occupations, lumber, mining, and agriculture, in each one of which the above elements were largely present.

In almost every case which a search of available material discloses, the demands during the war of the workers in these three industries (whether of I. W. W. or other origin) were precisely the demands made by labor everywhere else in the United States, with very significant emphasis in many cases on improvement in sanitary conditions, which in other sections of the country and in other industries is heard of less frequently and less insistently. They were demands which were sanctioned by the principles of the Taft-Walsh and of every other war labor board, and most of them would in large part have been granted to the workers by any of these war labor adjusting agencies.

These demands [1] were almost entirely confined to the right to organize, increases in wages, the eight-hour day, and better sanitary conditions. Occasionally there is the orthodox union demand for the abolition of piecework and the bonus system. The "rustling card" which in its application to longshoremen had been abolished by the National Adjustment Commission was also a frequent cause of complaint.

The leaders of the I. W. W. in their stump speeches and in their literature preached the socialistic doctrines of class war and ad-

---

[1] The demands of the lumber-jacks, whose strike crippled the lumber industry of the Northwest during a large part of 1917 were:
Better sanitary and working conditions.
The eight hour day.
A minimum wage of $60 a month.
The right to organize.
Men to be hired on the job or at the union hall, but not through "rustling cards." Charles Merz; *New Republic,* September 29, 1917.

vocated the complete abolition of the wage system. This was part of their radical propaganda, but did not enter into any particular controversy except incidentally through the fact that this kind of agitation was from the psychological point of view particularly obnoxious to the employer, and, indeed, to many of the workers themselves. In some cases there were demands that the Government take over the industries in which strikes were occurring. These were, however, infrequent, and seemed to have been based on the theory of the temporary exercise of the Government's war-time powers, in orders to restore production, rather than on any desire to bring about State ownership as such. This demand was made by the conservative unions in other places, and as we have seen, the Government did take over a number of industries because of industrial disturbances, and threatened to do the same in many other cases.

Inasmuch as members of the I. W. W. were frequently workers in isolated and inaccessible communities, the employer in many cases furnished board and lodging. This added another element of possible trouble, and any one who has seen labor camps in or near settled communities will not find it difficult to believe that sanitary conditions in the lumber belt of the Northwest and in similar isolated places were very bad indeed. That this was the case is the judgment of many official investigators, and there can be no doubt whatever that the demand of the men for improved working and living conditions was amply justified.[1]

Nor do we find in the wages asked for by the I. W. W. any justification for the resentment with which these demands were met. Judged by the increases in the cost of living and the wage advances which took place in other industries in the United States,

[1] In many of the lumber camps, bunk houses were dangerously overcrowded, constructed in an insanitary manner, with double tiers of continuous bunks, and in some cases provided with no means of ventilation except the door. In many of the camps no place was provided for the men's damp and steaming clothes, all the vapor and foulness being confined to the already overcrowded bunk houses. The condition of toilets can be judged from the following quotation from the *Camp Sanitation Survey,* made by the Loyal Legion of Loggers and Lumbermen, and published at Portland, Oregon, in June, 1918, page 48.

"One of the Sanitary Officers reports that at a certain camp which he visited, and in which the toilets were unusually bad even for a logging camp, he was informed by the camp foreman that he had not seen the inside of the men's toilet for at least two years. The

the demands of the I. W. W. were not excessive and were often in fact moderate.

As to hours, the demands were largely confined to the eight-hour day, which the President of the United States had spoken of in a message to Congress in 1916 as demanded "by the whole spirit of the times and the preponderance of evidence in recent economic experience." When we consider how steadily the eight-hour day has been spreading from one industry to another, and that many recent strikes have not been for the eight-hour day as asked for by the I. W. W. but for the forty-four-hour week, and, finally, that the shorter week is now rapidly being adopted, it is difficult to believe that only two short years ago one of the most serious strikes of the war—the lumber strike of the Northwest—should have been caused by the demand for the reduction of working hours from ten to eight daily. And yet this was undoubtedly the chief cause of one of the hardest fought strikes with which the I. W. W. was connected—the tie-up during the greater part of 1917 of the lumber industry of the Northwest. Strikes in the wooden shipyards, of the Pacific Coast, lasting for several months, also resulted from this strike, the shipbuilders refusing to handle "ten-hour lumber." Neither the existence of the war, with the resulting dire need for spruce, nor the appeal of the Secretary of War and the Governor of the State of Washington, were sufficient to induce the lumber owners to grant a working day which so many other industries in the country had adopted.

The demands of the I. W. W. almost always included the right to organize and protection against discrimination. Inasmuch as this was one of the fundamental war labor principles guaranteed by the President's Proclamation in creating the National War Labor Board, and insisted upon by every other adjusting agency, we could quickly pass to the next grievance, were it not for the fact that because of the revolutionary doctrines of the I. W. W.

officer invited him to inspect it at once, which he did, and was so impressed by what he found that he immediately set fire to the shack and ordered a new latrine built at once."

These were some of the sanitary conditions which were undoubtedly responsible for the growth of the I. W. W. in the Northwest. The success of that organization, when it tied up the production of lumber, was unquestionably one of the principal factors which focussed attention upon these insanitary conditions, and led to very great improvements, which took place during the war period.

it might be argued that this organization was not entitled to the protection which was accorded to so-called "legitimate unions." Employers frequently took this position: that the purposes of the I. W. W. leaders were revolutionary; that their demands had as their ultimate object the taking over of industry by the workers; that they were led by the most radical element who were unwilling to make agreements with employers, and who openly preached the doctrine that there can be no peace between employer and employee until the workers have taken over all industry.

If any clear-cut distinction had been made between the I. W. W. and more conservative unions—that is to say, if the employers had conceded to the ordinary trade union the right to organize (or where the men were not organized at all, had allowed them to form a union), but had at the same time taken the position that they were unwilling to have their men join the I. W. W. because it preached revolution and sabotage and was opposed to any time agreements with employers—the question would be a very much easier one to deal with. Amid the confusion with which the entire subject is surrounded there can be no doubt, however, that in most cases no such distinction was made. In many places where the I. W. W. was active, the employers followed the practice of hitting a union head if they saw one, without examining very carefully to see whether the body to which the head was attached carried a card issued by a branch of the I. W. W. or by the American Federation of Labor. The revolutionary doctrines of the I. W. W. were in many cases exploited to inflame the public mind against every form of unionism. These doctrines were used as an excuse for ruthless violence against persons who made demands for improvements, wherever and by whomsoever these demands were made.[1]

As a matter of fact the war furnished us with a number of conspicuous cases in which those responsible for production coöperated with the I. W. W. The United States Forest Reserve, a bureau of the Department of the Interior, charged among other things with the duty of fighting forest fires in the great Pacific Northwest, the Loyal Legion of Loggers and Lumbermen organized by Colonel (later General) Disque of the War Department Spruce-Production Board, the National Adjustment Com-

[1] As in the Bisbee deportation case where only one-third of the men belonged to the I. W. W.

mission in the Port of Philadelphia, all worked with the I. W. W., going as far as to coöperate with its representatives when new men were to be hired. The testimony of those in authority is unanimous that the men responded to good treatment and worked loyally. As a practical question, therefore, production having been all-important during the war, the policy of repression and violence pursued in most places seems to the writer to have been a serious blunder. It did not succeed in ending strikes, but only served to embitter the workers and to increase the "strikes on the job."

On its merits as a question of war labor jurisprudence or equity, the writer also believes that the I. W. W. was entitled to immunity from discharge or other interference solely because of membership in that organization. There was almost unanimity of opinion among those charged with the duty of war labor administration that the war period should be one of truce as to certain controversial industrial questions. This principle of an industrial truce was in some cases tactitly and in others openly agreed to. Thus demands for the closed shop were barred by our war labor policy, and demands for radical social changes were likewise out of the question for the war period.[1]

The workers could, had they seen fit to do so, have taken advantage of the scarcity of labor and the enormous need for commodities, which the war produced, and have demanded radical changes in industry, and it is very difficult to see how such demands could have been successfully resisted. As a rule, however, the workers, radicals as well as conservative, observed the truce and did not make any serious attempts to press those claims which were, for the time being, barred out. During this period it seems very clear to the writer that a sound and liberal labor policy required the extension to all labor organizations, including the I. W. W., of the right to organize. No matter how objectionable to a particular employer or community the industrial activity of this organization may have been, as long as it confined its actions to legitimate efforts to improve working conditions, it should, during the war period, have been fairly and decently treated.

---

[1] It is true that this truce was not always respected by the I. W. W. leaders; neither was it always respected by the employers. But the breaches of the truce do not seem to have been of sufficient importance to affect the present discussion.

The war demands made by the I. W. W. are thus seen to have been, for the most part, no different than those made by the more conservative labor unions, and they were generally reasonable and even moderate. And yet the I. W. W. was throughout this period treated as an outlaw organization. The entire community (with a few exceptions) acted on the theory that it possessed no rights whatever of privacy, liberty, or even life itself, which deserved respect.

Here the question naturally arises why, if these statements are correct, was the treatment accorded to the I. W. W. so drastic? Why were the I. W. W. leaders outlawed when making their demands, whereas the A. F. of L. was listened to, its demands granted, and its leaders given positions of great responsibility? Perhaps the most important reason was that, in the public mind, the unpatriotic and revolutionary opinions of the leaders were attributed to all the members of the organization, and the entire movement was identified with revolutionary doctrines and a failure to support the Government. This feeling was natural and to certain extent justified (especially against the leaders), but it was irrelevant as far as disputes about wages, hours, and sanitary conditions were concerned. Nor were the employers slow to take advantage of this popular resentment to discredit perfectly legitimate demands; they focused attention in the press and elsewhere upon the subversive doctrines, using them as a smoke screen to hide from the public—and perhaps from themselves— the real grievances.

If an organizer appeared in an agricultural section to demand increases in wages, he was immediately thrown into jail.[1] In the midst of strikes in the mines and lumber camps, in some cases for the redress of intolerable conditions, the offices of the striking

---

[1] The following from the New York *Times,* appearing at as late a date as June 13, 1919, illustrates the complacency with which arrests were reported for apparently no greater offense than an effort to organize the workers:

"Seize I. W. W.'s in Kansas.

"Quick Action Follows Attempt to Start Trouble in Wheat Belt.

"Kansas City, Mo., June 12.—Five men are under arrest to-day at Hutchinson, Kas., on a charge of fomenting revolution, and it is believed by the Federal authorities that they are members of the Industrial Workers of the World.

"'These arrests,' said Fred Robertson, United States District Attorney for Kansas, 'followed the first reports of the appearance of I. W. W. agitators in the Kansas wheat belt, and their efforts to or-

unions were raided, their members were thrown into jails (frequently to be released weeks or months later without trial), hundreds of strikers were deported without the slightest semblance of lawful action, and, in at least one case, a deliberate and cold-blooded murder was committed.[1]

The deportation at Bisbee, Arizona,[2] is probably the most deplorable act of industrial violence which has occurred in the history of our country. It consisted of the forcible deportation of 1,186 strikers in the Warren District of Arizona, who were put on board trains and dumped out at the town of Hermanas, New Mexico, and for months deprived of their right to return to their homes at Bisbee. Under the leadership of the Sheriff of the county, many of its leading citizens were part of a mob of 2,000 armed men responsible for this outrage. They took possession of the telegraph and telephone, rounded up the strikers in a ball field, and placed those unwilling to return to work in box cars, sending them out of the state. They set up a "Kangaroo Court," which sat for several months, summoned men before it for alleged disloyalty—the test of which seems to have been their willingness to return to work—and if they were unwilling to do so, offered these men, without the slightest pretense of legality, the alternative of imprisonment or deportation.[3] The 1,186 deported men were, after great hardship, taken care of it by the United States Army, whose investigation disclosed the fact that only about one-third of the men were members of the I. W. W. One-third were members of the American Federation of Labor, and the other one-third were unorganized.

In partial explanation of this unprecedented example of defiance of all natural rights and legal guarantees, it should be pointed out that copper, the production of which was being so seriously

---

ganize the harvesters. We are not going to waste a minute with these troublemakers.'

"Other arrests are expected as the Federal authorities believe many organizers of the I. W. W. are at work in the grain belt of Kansas."

[1] Many of these events have been set forth in official reports, but it seemed proper to include in this volume a list of such of the more important of these acts of violence and oppression as were clearly connected with industrial disputes. Other cases are not relevant to the subject of this inquiry.

[2] See Report on Bisbee Deportation made by the President's Mediation Commission, November 6, 1917.

[3] Robert Bruere in the *Nation* (New York), February 28, 1918.

interfered with in this strike, was an essential for the prosecution of the war. Patriotic resentment was therefore particularly strong and was fanned into frenzy by the revolutionary and unpatriotic teachings of the leaders of the strike. Another factor arose from the fact that Bisbee is located on the Mexican border, and fear of raids is never wholly absent. It was reported that members of the I. W. W. were pouring into town and a serious uprising was feared. An appeal was made for Federal troops, but the Army officers sent on two occasions, June 30 and July 2, to investigate reported that everything was peaceable and that the troops were not needed, and they were therefore refused. Their absence undoubtedly increased the hysterical condition of the residents.

The Federal and State Governments have each proceeded criminally against the men responsible for this wrong but, so far, both prosecutions have failed. In the Federal Court a demurrer to the indictment was sustained on the ground that the jurisdiction was in the State rather than the Federal Courts [1] and an appeal to the Supreme Court has been taken but is not yet decided. In the courts of Arizona one of the defendants was recently brought to trial on the charge of kidnapping. The jury brought in a verdict of acquittal apparently on the ground that the act of deportation was one of "necessity," justified by the circumstances surrounding it—in much the same way that an individual would be justified if he committed homicide in self-defense. The trial of the case lasted three months and was remarkable in many ways. One cannot help wondering how a minority —especially one which entertains unpopular beliefs—would have any rights which the majority would be bound to respect, and any acts of violence even if committed on so reckless a scale as the Bisbee deportations would go unpunished, if the decision of the Court in this case is a correct one.[2]

[1] Federal Reporter, Volume 254, p. 611.
[2] The Court ruled as follows: "The offer of proof as to conditions existing in the Warren district at the time of the so-called deportations, the purpose and intent of the persons deported, the contemplated destruction of lives and property within that district, the preparations to carry out that intent and the acts and conduct as well as the statements of the persons deported, present a situation where it cannot be said as a matter of law that the rule of necessity cannot be applicable but rather leaves the question of the existence of such necessity to be determined by the jury as a question of a fact under proper instructions if such were the conditions and the citizens

Civil suits are also pending on behalf of the deported men against the mining companies and their officials. A settlement of these claims by which each of the men would have received a substantial sum was almost consummated in the month of October, 1919, but fell through, and the suits are still awaiting trial.

Other deportations occurred at Jerome, Arizona, where sixty-five I. W. W. were sent to Needles, Cal., but, not being allowed to detrain, they were sent on to Kingman, Arizona. At Gallup, New Mexico, during a strike of the United Mine Workers (A. F. of L.) deportations took place under charges of disloyalty. At Tulsa, Oklahoma, on November 7, 1917, seventeen members of the I. W. W. were taken from the custody of the police and whipped and tarred and feathered. It seems that shortly after the murder of Frank Little a bomb was exploded at the home of a prominent oil man, who narrowly escaped death. A fire of apparent incendiary origin also broke out in the refineries. Both of these occurrences were attributed to the I. W. W. by the local newspapers

of Bisbee had called in vain upon state and federal authorities for protection against a threatened calamity such as is set forth in the offer of proof, it cannot be said as a matter of law that they must sit by and await the destruction of their lives and property, without having the right to take steps to protect themselves." *Douglas Dispatch*, March 25, 1920. And in his charge to the jury the Court said: "There is no presumption that one who forcibly seizes and carries a person into another state acts under the law of necessity and when such a claim is made the burden is upon the one asserting it, but such burden only goes to this extent, that he must produce such evidence as will raise in the minds of the jury a reasonable doubt whether he did not act, under all the circumstances, in accordance with the rule of necessity. If the jury, after the consideration of all the evidence, entertains a reasonable doubt whether the defendant and those acting with him were not justified in acting as they did under the law of necessity their duty is always to give the defendant the benefit of such doubt and acquit him, but if they have no reasonable doubt they should return a verdict of guilty." *Bisbee Review*, April 29, 1920. The *Douglas International* for May 5, 1920, reprints an editorial from the *El Paso Times*, which after commending the action of the jury and the general principles upon which its verdict was based, gives an account of the strike and the resulting deportations and says: "The community took steps to protect itself. It went about the matter in an orderly and effective manner. There was no resort to mob violence. The sheriff of the county swore in hundreds of deputies. The undesirables and agitators and their sympathizers merely were rounded up and shipped out of town. That was all there was to it. *Only in its magnitude was the proceeding very different from the practice common enough all over the country of running undesirables out of town.*" (Italics the writer's.)

and violence against this organization was openly advocated. Although there was apparently no evidence connecting the I. W. W. with these outrages, yet the following took place: Seventeen I. W. W. were arrested for vagrancy.   They were taken from jail in automobiles which after going a short distance were stopped by armed and masked men, who told the police to "beat it"— which the police did.   The seventeen men were made to strip to the waist, whipped and tarred and feathered.   After this their clothes were burned and they were ordered to leave Tulsa and never to return.

At Jackson, Michigan, in November, 1918, a machinist was tarred and feathered.

At Aberdeen, S. D., an I. W. W. organizer was taken to the outskirts of the town and beaten with clubs.

At Franklin, N. J., another I. W. W. organizer was hung to a tree—it is alleged, by the chief of police and a mob, and cut down only when unconscious.

Similar cases of violence are reported from Yakima and Aberdeen, Washington, and Yerrington, Nevada.

In Montana, seventy-five striking Finns, in the coal mines, were crowded into jail by the "Liberty Committee," for failure to register under the draft.   The men could not speak or understand English and were released by Federal officers on the ground that there was no intent to disobey the law.   Shortly thereafter, some of the leaders of the men were seized by the "Liberty Committee" and thrown into jail on the charge of being members of the I. W. W. (criminal Syndicalism) and several Finns were tortured in efforts by the Liberty Committee to find out the leaders of the I. W. W.

Most degrading of all, perhaps, was the murder of Frank Little, an I. W. W. organizer who had come to Butte, Montana, a cripple suffering from a broken leg, to organize the workers.   He was seized in the middle of the night by armed citizens, taken a distance out of town and, in cold blood, hung up from railroad ties.   This incident occurred shortly after the Bisbee deportation and no one was ever punished for it.

These acts of physical violence which we have recorded, although inexcusable, were still not the first incidents of this kind which have marred the industrial history of our country.   The war period served only to multiply these occurrences and to intensify their bitterness. But the war period did witness the introduction of a new era of *legal*—that is to say, *criminal*—condemnation of certain radical industrial and political organizations. Laws were passed by a number of states as well as by the Federal Government which were so worded as to be susceptible of an interpretation broad enough to include many kinds of labor agitation, innocent as well as dangerous.

Now the writer wishes to make it clear that he has no desire to question these measures so far as they were used by the Government to protect itself against enemy propaganda and violence, or sedition and disloyalty by our own citizens. But unfortunately these laws were frequently used, not for their legitimate purpose, but for the illegitimate one of curbing any agitation for industrial betterment, and steps were taken and procedure adopted in the enforcement of these laws which made the attainment of justice impossible.

In looking back over the record of legal prosecutions during the war, there can be no doubt that war hysteria placed in the hands of Government officials and unscrupulous employers the power of criminal prosecutions of strikers and the suppression of attempts —not to interfere with the successful waging of the war—but to secure improvement in industrial conditions. Many persons regarded strikes, at this critical time, as in themselves necessarily disloyal, on the ground that they interfered with production— hampering our Government and aiding the enemy. We have already pointed out that frequently this was not the case; that on the contrary many strikes resulted in better working conditions and in making the men better satisfied. And therefore, in the long run, a strike which had this effect stimulated rather than retarded production.[1]

The facts were, however, that in certain parts of the country, especially those in which the I. W. W. was active, organizers were thrown into jail immediately upon their appearance among the workers. This was noticeably the case in the wheat and oil fields, the timber belt, and the mines, where men were often im-

---

[1] Even if it were always true that strikes retarded production, it must still be borne in mind, as has been pointed out elsewhere, that workers were not always to blame for their occurrence. Frequently the responsibility rested on employers, the strike having been the only method by which the workers could secure redress of very real grievances.

prisoned, seemingly for no greater offense than attempting to secure for the workers higher wages and better working conditions.
Not only were they arrested, but they were kept in jails for
months and months without trial, in some cases dying or becoming
insane as a result, it is alleged, of bad prison conditions and ill-
treatment. Sometimes these men were released after long periods
of incarceration without any effort to bring them to trial; sometimes they were tried under laws enacted after their original arrest. "Mass" trials took place, in one case as many as sixty-five
men being placed on trial at the same time—as a result of which
many of these men received prison terms equivalent to life sen-
tences. These trials have been condemned by responsible lawyers;
in fact, the utter impossibility of any fair judgment being reached
as to the guilt or innocence of all these sixty-five men will be
realized by any one familiar with the jury system.

The intolerance with which the I. W. W. was treated during
the war seemed at the time to be the result purely of war hysteria.
But the ending of the war nevertheless brought no abatement;
on the contrary the feeling became intensified and at the present
writing the spirit of intolerance seems to be as strong as ever. [1]

[1] The statement recently issued by twelve prominent attorneys including Dean Roscoe Pound of Harvard Law School, Ernst Freund
of the University of Chicago, Felix Frankfurter, Francis Fisher Kane
and Frank P. Walsh sets forth illegal practices committed by the
U. S. Department of Justice since the signing of the armistice similar
to those referred to above. "Wholesale arrests both of aliens and
citizens have been made without warrant or any process of law; men
and women have been jailed and held *incommunicado* without access
of friends or counsel; homes have been entered without search warrant and property seized and removed; other property has been
wantonly destroyed; workingmen and workingwomen suspected of
radical views have been shamefully abused and maltreated. . . .
Punishment of the utmost cruelty, and heretofore unthinkable in
America, have become usual. Great numbers of persons arrested,
both aliens and citizens, have been threatened, beaten with black-
jacks, struck with fists, jailed under abominable conditions, or actually tortured." Following the statement, exhibits are presented containing affidavits and other proof of the charges. Exhibit 8 refers
to evidence taken by a commission sent by the Interchurch World
Movement to investigate the Steel Strike which is stated to show
that "the steel and coal companies use the local and Federal Governments to harass and get rid of troublesome workers." Exhibit 15
contains the decision of Judge Bourquin of the U. S. District Court
of Montana in proceedings for a writ of *habeas corpus* on behalf of
an alien held for deportation. The record shows, says the Court
that: "from August, 1918, to February, 1919, the Butte union of the

LOYAL LEGION OF LOGGERS AND LUMBERMEN

In a previous chapter we have seen that in the summer of 1917 the entire lumber industry of the Northwest was crippled by strikes in which the principal demand of the men—for the eight-hour day—was bitterly resisted by the lumber operators.[1] The President's Mediation Commission, which in the early fall of 1917, had visited the scene of the trouble, did not succeed in harmonizing the difficulties. The strike had been a failure to the extent that the employers had not granted the demands of the strikers and that lumbering had been partially resumed. Many of the workers, however, who under the best conditions did not remain very long in one place, or even in one occupation, had drifted into fields where hours and conditions of employment were better than in the lumber camps. Among those who remained "strikes on the job" were to an alarming extent increasing the inefficiency of the workers.

In order to meet this situation, the Spruce Division of the War Department[2] sent Colonel (later General) Brice P. Disque into the fields, charged with the difficult mission of restoring production. To accomplish this end two steps were taken: First, a considerable number of enlisted men were sent into the woods to get out the timber; second, an organization was created, known as the Loyal Legion of Loggers and Lumbermen, which endeavored to establish harmony between the operators and their employees, to fix wages, improve conditions, and thus to obtain the desired production.

The 4 L's, as it came to be known, consisted of both employer

Industrial Workers of the World was dissatisfied with working places, conditions and wages in the mining industry, and to remedy them were discussing ways and means, including a strike if necessary. In consequence its hall and orderly meetings were several times raided by employers' agents, federal agents and soldiers duly officered, acting by Federal authority and without warrant . . . broke and destroyed property . . . cursed, insulted, beat, dispersed and bayoneted members by order of the captain commanding . . . perpetrated an orgy of terror, violence and crime against citizens and aliens in public assemblage, etc.

[1] The data gathered by the Labor Department and published in *Monthly Review*, Bureau of Labor Statistics, June, 1919, see Appendix No. 1, shows that as against 44 strikes in the lumber industry in 1916, the number rose to 295 in 1917. In 1918 it dropped to 74.

[2] Aircraft Production Board.

and employee. In order to become a member, the applicant was required to sign a pledge of loyalty, but during the war no dues were expected to be paid. The Loyal Legion was organized into locals which elected representatives for the various districts into which the entire territory was divided. Conventions were held in which representatives of both employers and employees for the district met with Colonel Disque or his assistants.

On March 1, 1918, the employers established the eight-hour day without reduction of wages; [1] a sanitary survey of camps and mills was undertaken, which resulted in the publication by the Loyal Legion of an excellent pamphlet describing minimum sanitary requirements. A Sanitation Division was established under the direction of which sanitary conditions in the camps were very much improved. Other welfare features were also provided, such as the installation of reading rooms, libraries, recreation and movie halls.

The Loyal Legion operated largely in Oregon, Washington and Idaho, and its organizers claim a remarkable record of successful achievement. Before the armistice was signed it is said that nearly 100,000 workers were enrolled as members; [2] a monthly magazine, published by the Legion, had a circulation of over 90,000 copies. It is claimed that the labor turnover, which had previously been over a thousand per cent per annum, was substantially reduced, and that the lumber output was increased five hundred per cent. [3]

When the Loyal Legion was first organized, it met with bitter opposition from both operators and to a lesser degree from the unions. [4] As the war progressed, the operators seem to have be-

---

[1] There is a good deal of dispute as to whom credit should be given for the establishment of the 8-hour day—whether to Gen. Disque, the Loyal Legion or the unions; Robert S. Gill, Editor of the Four L Bulletin, in *The Survey*, May 1, 1920, after speaking of the new spirit of coöperation which the Four L's inaugurated, puts it in this way: "In March, 1918, the eight-hour day was conceded by the operators, on request of the government and owing to the new feel."

[2] *American Lumberman*, September 14, 1918.

[3] Eighth Biennial Report, Bureau of Labor Statistics, State of Oregon, p. 30, and Bulletins of Loyal Legion.

[4] A curious incident connected with this opposition was due to an error in the office of the War Department. An inquiry was directed to the Department as to whether or not the Loyal Legion had official sanction. Although the organization had the direct approval of the Secretary of War, this inquiry came into the hands of an officer who

come reconciled to the existence of the organization and to have become its enthusiastic supporters; the unions, however—the International Association of Timber Workers (affiliated with the American Federation of Labor) and the I. W. W.—became more and more antagonistic.[1]

There does not seem to be much doubt that General Disque's Department, when employing men, did not discriminate against union members and even went so far as to ask the coöperation of the unions. There is considerable conflict of opinion, however, as to whether or not the Department allowed men, after they had joined the Legion, to become members of labor unions, and some of the younger officers on General Disque's staff, in patriotic zeal, undoubtedly exceeded their authority, and interfered in an unwarranted manner with meetings to organize the lumber workers into labor organizations. General Disque issued a bulletin, stating that the civil rights of members of the Loyal Legion could not be interfered with and in the main this policy seems to have been carried out. After the signing of the armistice, the Government support was withdrawn. A number of men, who had been officers of the Loyal Legion as members of General Disque's staff, retained such positions in a civil capacity, and the Loyal Legion has continued as a peace body. As such it seems to be receiving the support of the operators, but the determined opposition of organized labor, being regarded by the latter with feelings similar to those aroused by the so-called "household" unions.

As an instrument for procuring war production, it was certainly a most successful one. What its record will be in time of peace is a more difficult question to determine.

was not informed on the subject and who, without proper investigation, wrote a letter stating the the Loyal Legion did not have the sanction of the War Department. This letter was given wide publicity by the opponents of the Legion. It was contradicted, however, by the publication of a telegram from the Secretary of War.

[1] The continuance of the Loyal Legion as a peace-time organization was submitted to a vote of the membership and 85% favored it. Robert S. Gill, *The Survey*, May 1, 1920.

CHAPTER XX

Conclusions

A STUDY of the conditions set forth in the preceding chapters emphasizes the conclusion that the difficulties which industry experienced in meeting the needs of the war and of the post-armistice period were the result of pre-war difficulties rather than new ones created by the war emergency. Irritations, caused by war conditions, were added to previous bad industrial relations. As a result former difficulties were intensified, a large number of strikes occurred and the Government was forced to step in to overcome the impediments to production.

At the beginning the Government seemed indifferent, then it took steps gropingly without the formulation of any clearly defined policy. The means at first adopted were the result of the suggestions of the particular individuals who represented the Government at the points of disturbance. Gradually a recognition of the need for greater uniformity and a more coherent policy was forced upon all parts of the community and there was evolved a body of war labor principles which represented the most enlightened attitude toward labor which the nation has ever attained or has yet been prepared to accept.

The liberal and progressive attitude taken at this period by the administration brought down upon it the bitter reproaches of the employers, who felt that the Government was catering to the labor vote. Nor was labor on its side satisfied, but was convinced that the Government was favoring capital.

In judging of the wisdom and fairness of the Government's conduct it must be borne in mind that the nation faced a grave emergency and that as a result of war conditions an unprecedented power was placed in the hands of labor. The men were in a position to force large concessions from the employers. How far they could have gone by the sheer exercise of the power of the moment is difficult to say. But an examination of what actually was awarded them will make it apparent that they did not take undue advantage of the situation and that the actions of the Government were amply justified both by justice and expediency.

There is a widespread belief that the workers were greatly over-paid and that they profiteered at the expense of the nation. It is most important to determine the justice of this charge.

The cost of living at the time of the armistice had increased about 70% and by the summer of 1920 had about doubled. But this rise in the cost of living started before any increase took place in wages and there can be no doubt that living costs would have gone up irrespective of wage advances. From statistics compiled in many occupations it appears that the wages of unorganized common labor have more than doubled; in some industries they have even tripled. It is, however, not open to argument that pre-war wage levels for common labor were insufficient to support decent American standards. These increases were furthermore the result of economic conditions rather than of the action of Government boards. The unprecedented shortage of common labor made it only natural that the wages of these very poorly paid men should have risen sharply as competition increased among employers for their services. In some cases, it is true, the wage boards made more or less arbitrary increases in order to standardize wages and thus to prevent the men of one industry or locality from being attracted to a wage elsewhere which more nearly conformed to the general wage standard. But on the whole the wage increases of the unskilled worker were the result of the law of supply and demand and not of the actions of Government Boards.

The wages of skilled mechanics are somewhat more difficult to analyze. Some crafts did not during the war period receive anything like as great an advance as the cost of living. This, for instance, was true generally of the building trades. On the other hand shipbuilders received a considerably greater increase. By 1920 there were still great variations but certain trades in which wages had lagged rose sharply. Others, including some of those in which wages advanced most during the war, stood still or advanced very little. The schedules of different trades indicate that the increase in the wages of skilled workers was on an average about equal to the increased cost of living and by the summer of 1920 this was still approximately true.[1] Nevertheless the workers were undoubtedly better off during the war and up to the summer of 1920 than they had ever been. Weekly earnings of the individual, and especially the aggregate earnings of the entire family showed a higher percentage of increase than hourly rates indicated, due to the large amounts of overtime and the elimination of unemployment.

Although the Government's wage awards were on the whole equitable, where it failed most conspicuously was in handling overtime. Here an almost total lack of control resulted in glaring and disruptive abuses, leading to extravagant costs for Government work and giving to the men the hope of a continuance of weekly earnings far in excess of the productive power of industry.

That part of the Government's war labor policy which related to the treatment of labor unions has been even more sharply criticised than has its wage awards. Employers have the very definite opinion that the attitude of the Government toward the unions resulted not only in the large growth of union membership but also in increasing union aggressiveness and self-assertion. This judgment does not take into account the economic strength of labor nor that concessions were insisted upon from labor as well as from capital. The Government on the one hand prevented the employer from discharging an employee solely for union membership, on the other hand it insisted that labor abandon demands for the extension of the closed shop and union recognition. Labor's waiver was a sacrifice at least equal to that of the employer.

Whereas in previous wars labor had suffered great hardship by the reduction in the purchasing power of wages, during this war labor at least held its own. Though it was accorded greater recognition by the Government, yet taking into consideration all of the facts, it cannot be said that labor was unduly favored. Had the Government adopted a less liberal policy it is extremely doubtful if labor's coöperation could have been secured.

During the post-armistice period, when the extreme emergency

[1] See: How Wages Kept Pace with the Cost of Living, Erville B. Woods; *The Annals* of the American Academy of Political and Social Science, May, 1920. Wages in Various Industries, Bureau of Applied Economics, Washington, D. C., 1919 and 1920. Wartime Changes in Wages, Research Report No. 20, National Industrial Conference Board. Profits, Wages, and Prices, David Friday.

was over, the Government's attitude radically changed. War boards of all kinds were disbanded. Forms of compulsion, which in the midst of the emergency had not been attempted, were used to prevent strikes. Instead of planning for the transition of the nation from a state of war to one of peace the difficult adjustments which were necessary were left to the haphazard and self-regarding actions of the business and laboring community. The supports which had been placed under the industrial structure while the changes due to the war were taking place were suddenly withdrawn. Both employer and labor, to be sure, welcomed this withdrawal. But the public by its failure to insist on the continuance of the war boards deprived itself of protection against a condition of disorganization for which it has had to pay the largest part of the bill.

To many of the workers it seemed that during the emergency of war they had been, as they expressed it, "jollied along" and that with the emergency over the Government and the employers deliberately broke their promises. There can be no doubt that the men's charges were justified in a number of cases. This changed attitude was the cause of widespread unrest and men insisted on striking even though their leaders opposed this action. Scores of unauthorized strikes occurred, the result of the disillusionments that followed the war.

Among the many hopes raised by the war was the hope that never again would we go back to the old days of unregulated industry. The practicability of arbitration seemed so conclusively demonstrated that it was widely believed that industry would never again exist without adequate provision for the avoidance of industrial disputes. But this hope proved illusory.

Nor is it difficult to see why arbitration in a great emergency was more successful than in normal times. War psychology gave to all members of the community the impulse to make sacrifices for the common good. Capital and labor both consented to waive certain controversial demands for which representatives of each side fight bitterly in times of peace. Some of the chief sources of present day conflict were thus removed. What remained was the difficult, although comparatively simple, task of applying the rules that had been agreed upon.

But the moment the war was over each side was eager to reassert the rights which it had temporarily waived. Labor immediately returned to an aggressive policy of extending union influence, forcing to the front its insistence that employers deal with union officials. This was the cause of many important strikes, notably the steel strike. The demand for the closed shop was renewed. The forty-eight-hour week, which had almost crystallized into a fixed principle of Government boards, was no longer satisfactory to workers in many trades who demanded the forty-four-hour week or a shorter one. There was an unwillingness to leave the settlement of these questions to the decision of adjustment boards.

The desire once more to resort to force rather than to submit to the uncertainties of judicial process was not confined to the men. The employers also had been chafing under the constraint which the power of the Government had placed upon them. They wanted to be free to fix wages and to control their men. Feeling intensely that the spread of unionism was due to Government protection, they wanted most of all to resume the practice of discharging workers for union activity. Some corporations seemed, indeed, to welcome strikes as a means of checking the spread of unionism. Whatever the motive, there can be no doubt that the practice of union discrimination was resumed and that a determination to maintain this practice was one of the factors which made impossible the continued success of arbitration.

More important even than war psychology in forcing the acceptance of decisions of labor boards had been the industrial power of the Government in war-time. It became the employers' largest customer. It controlled the supplies of raw materials and of credit; it operated the railroads; it had the right to commandeer any plant needed for 'war production. In some occupations it became practically the only employer. It was thus in a position to force the directors of industry if they wished to continue in business—and to a lesser extent to force the workers—to accept its labor policies and to arbitrate labor difficulties rather than to fight them out.

The success of arbitration under these conditions made us too sanguine. The implications of a continuous use of arbitral processes were not generally realized. We overlooked the very important fact that the submission of industrial controversies to judicial settlement meant the relinquishment of an attempt by one or both sides to achieve its own way by force; that it meant the substitution of the judgment of the arbitrator for the will of the parties to the dispute. But the same factors which, through the centuries, have kept nations from settling their disputes in a peaceful manner are at work to destroy industrial peace—the unwillingness of the individual or the group to substitute arbitration for force.

Another difficulty is the absence of any agreement upon a set of principles as a basis for the adjustment of disputes. A code may be improvised in an emergency and imposed on each side by the power of a Government, but the acceptance of Government-made standards can be procured only for the period of the emergency. Just as soon as it has passed, neither side will continue to accept compromises. This was well illustrated by the President's first Industrial Conference where it was impossible to reach an agreement in spite of the difficulties confronting the nation. The President's second Conference, in order to agree unanimously upon a report, was forced to eliminate most controversial matter, and produced a document unacceptable to labor and not particularly welcome to capital.

Nor has either side faith in the impartiality or the wisdom of the judges who must be called upon to decide industrial controversies. The questions at issue are often of so controversial a nature and involve so many technical problems of industry that it is almost impossible to obtain judges who possess the necessary knowledge and impartiality.

The greatest obstacle to the continuous use of arbitration boards lies, perhaps, in a weakness inherent in any attempt to settle disputes by judicial process. By its very nature, arbitration, a semi-legal procedure, tends to produce fixation, tends to the uniform application of hard and fast rules. A board of judges will almost inevitably seek precedents for its guidance. Even during so short a period as that which elapsed from the creation of the National War Labor Board in April, 1918, to the signing of the armistice, the tendency toward rigidity was already manifest. But progress in industry must come from continuous growth and change. If we are to avoid the danger of revolution we must find the means for constant evolution, bringing about modifications which are neither too rapid to be assimilated nor too slow to be effective. There is far too wide a difference of opinion on industrial questions—the present structure of society falls far too short of the ideals of every thinking person—to make advisable the creation of any arbitral machinery which is likely to impede a continuous process of industrial growth.

All this was not realized at the conclusion of the war. The extreme need for production in order to reduce the cost of living made the use of arbitration seem essential. And when, in spite of the war-time success of arbitration, the men went out on innumerable strikes in 1919, the general feeling of resentment was not unnatural. This resentment was very much increased because many of the strikes were led by foreigners and many of them were started without the sanction of the national officers of organized labor—"outlaw," the press seemed to delight in calling them.

All this led, not to an effort to remove legitimate grievances, but to an increase in the intolerance and the repression which accompanied the war and to the advocacy of new and quick remedies to cure difficulties which had been accumulating since the advent of the factory system. Ill-considered laws were advocated for the suppression of freedom of speech, for interference with academic freedom. There has been much agitation for the introduction of compulsory arbitration, especially in connection with public utilities. The adoption by Congress of such a plan for the railways was prevented by only a narrow margin and in many jurisdictions attempts were made to set up tribunals similar to the Kansas Industrial Court.

But experience has shown that you cannot, for any length of time, successfully deprive workers of the right to strike. In England where the heads of the unions agreed that there should be no strikes for the period of the war, the unwillingness of the men to abide by this renunciation led to the assumption of power by the shop stewards, who called the men out on strikes which the leaders had promised would not take place. In Australia, where compulsory arbitration has received its most extensive trial, the verdict of impartial investigators is that the system is not the solution of the industrial conflict. Men cannot be forced to abide by decisions which do not appeal to their sense of fairness. Dangerous as the occurrence of strikes may be, nothing seems plainer than that compulsory arbitration or any attempt to forbid strikes by law is certain to fail.

But it does not therefore follow that the Government ought not to use every means to facilitate the peaceful adjustment of industrial disputes. Although machinery created by agreement between employers' associations and strongly organized unions is the best means which can to-day be devised to prevent the occurrence of strikes, yet in most industries such agreements have not been possible. Even where they exist, there often comes a time when the industry may require outside assistance to prevent a rupture. To keep the peace in such emergencies as well as in the vast realm of industry in which no such agreements have been made, the creation of adequate arbitral machinery seems highly desirable. And the war experience has shown, not that it is possible to entirely prevent strikes, but that the existence of proper facilities for arbitration is a tremendous help in accomplishing this task.

To what extent then has all of this experience enabled us to state what the requisites are for any successfully constituted system of arbitration? The greatest obstacle to the creation of such a system is the antagonism between many of the large employers and the labor unions. On its side, labor is unalterably opposed to the creation of any boards of arbitration on which it is not represented and it is therefore a matter of serious doubt whether the successful creation of any arbitral machinery is possible if the employer maintains his opposition to organized labor. During the war the Government used its economic power to compel employers to abide by the decisions of boards of adjustment on which organized labor was represented. But when the war was over and the continuance of the boards as peace-time agencies was being considered, it was the presence of union men which was particularly unacceptable to the employers. That an impasse had been reached was evident from the experience of the two Industrial Conferences called by the President.

No matter how unpalatable to employers their existence may be, an impartial reading of industrial history will show that the many improvements that have taken place in the condition of the workers have been largely the result of the efforts of the labor unions and of the economic and political power they have been able to exert. And this was no less true during the war. The most potent influence in preventing a lowering of the workers' economic status, such as took place during the Civil War, was the existence in many industries of labor unions and the fear in others that low wages would invite their spread. In many places where unions did not exist and there was little or no fear of the strike, employees fared badly. Let any one compare the treatment given by the Government to its teachers or clerks with the treatment accorded to organized mechanics. The same comparison can be made between the organized and the unorganized groups of employees of any industry.

The natural representatives of the workers are the labor unions —organizations which they themselves have voluntarily formed. Unfortunately these organizations, like so many other groups in the community, are sometimes badly and even corruptly managed. The difficulty with the average employer is that he sees the faults of the other side so much more clearly than he sees the weaknesses of his own and he fails to recognize very real grievances of the workers. The same lack of vision can be imputed to the employees who see the employer's shortcomings without understanding his difficulties. Most of the things which each side says about the other are true, or largely true, but in neither case are they the whole truth. When an employer criticizes the management of a union and charges it with making for inefficiency and limiting production, the charge is in many cases true. But the employer does not see that in a competitive system the existence of the union is essential to the protection of the workers and that he himself limits production when he thinks it to his interest to do so. He fails to realize that the faults of union management are the faults of most democratically controlled bodies. No one can defend corruption and mismanagement in labor unions, but one of the best ways of helping to eliminate these evils is to allow the unions to concentrate their attention upon them and not compel the unions to dissipate their energies in a struggle for existence against the attacks of powerful employers.

Unless the industrial development of America is to be greatly different from that of every other industrial country the unions will continue to grow in numbers and in power. An attitude of irreconcilable hostility by big business interests runs contrary to the processes of social evolution. It creates an impossible situation, delaying the successful organization of industry and the peaceful adjustment of disputes.

As to the technique of arbitration, the size of boards, the manner of their organization, their constituency and like questions, our experience during the war was very broad indeed and embraced many differently constituted agencies, and yet this experience does not point as clearly and unmistakably to definite conclusions as one might have wished. Boards of all sizes were created during the war. Thus disputes in the clothing trade were settled by one man; so were some of those in munition plants. Many boards contained three members, some five and six, some eight and one even twelve. All of them were, in the main, successful and the war experience therefore fails to indicate that any particular importance attaches to size. It is interesting to note that when Congress, upon the relinquishment of public control, was called upon to create a permanent board of adjustment for the railroads it did not model this upon any of those created during the war but decided upon a board of nine members—a much larger one than those previously created.

The representative character of the members is a more important question. Should the public be represented? Should employer and employee? Boards created during the war contained examples of all kinds. Usually all three were given places. But on some boards the public only was represented; in others the public was not represented at all. Unquestionably the war emergency emphasized the public character of industry. The old idea of the employer that "this is my business" is being modified by the recognition of the workers' share. But we are gradually realizing that the employer and employee are not the only ones who have a stake in industry—the public too has its share. The boards which were created in the early days of the war contained representatives of the public in whom was vested the power of decision if the spokesmen of labor and capital disagreed. Those organized in the second year of the war usually contained employee and employer members only. The National War Labor Board was a distinct variation in that it had an equal number of representatives of labor and of capital, with each group electing a chairman who was in theory to represent the public. But the fact that the chairmen were chosen by the groups made them at least in part representative of the group rather than of the public and there were not infrequent deadlocks caused by each chairman voting with his group. The joint chairmen were not, however, merely representatives of employer and employee. Deadlocks would have been of much more frequent occurrence had not ex-President Taft, the joint chairman elected by the employers, voted in many important matters with the employees. The conspicuous failures of the board, however, were cases which were decided by umpires— exclusively the representatives of the public.

The railroad boards created in the second year of the war consisted of even numbers of representatives of each side, with no public representation (except that in theory these boards were only advisory to the Director General of Railways). They were eminently successful and in every case reached an agreement. On the other hand the Board of Appeals of the Shipbuilding Labor Adjustment Board, which was also composed of an equal number of representatives of capital and of labor with no public representation, was deadlocked shortly after the armistice, with disastrous consequences—the Seattle general strike.

It will thus be seen that, although the war period witnessed heretofore unusual recognition of the public interest in the composition of most of the boards, yet it cannot be said, as a result of that experience, that public representation will necessarily insure the success of the board. Most unions and most employers prefer arbitration conducted exclusively by representatives of the two sides. In their opinion the representative of the public is apt to become the deciding member of the board with the probability that his decision will be unsatisfactory to at least one side and perhaps to both. They believe that boards on which employer and employee are equally represented usually manage to agree and that there will then be a feeling that the settlement, even if unsatisfactory, is self-imposed. Undoubtedly there is much sound psychology in this view, and yet it cannot be the solution of the future. The public has a real interest which must be recognized and which both sides are apt to forget. The boards which lack public representation are liable to deadlock and more important still, their decisions can too easily ignore the public. They may, indeed, by joint agreement go so far as to create a monopoly of the business, labor upon payment of high wages consenting to what amounts to a conspiracy among employers to extort unfair profits from the public. It seems clear that a properly constituted board of arbitration will include representatives of all three of the parties interested in the outcome of the dispute, although a new form of representation of the public may prove desirable. Perhaps experiments with industrial parliaments and trade guilds, now being made, will develop a finer organization of industry and more harmonious industrial relations.

The area of jurisdiction is also important. Should a system of arbitration be national or are disputes better adjusted by a board with only local authority? Should machinery be created within each industry like the Industrial Councils of England or should the boards have general authority to adjust any disputes within definite geographic areas? Whenever it is possible to create an adjustment board with jurisdiction confined to a particular industry such a course would seem best. To the fact that the jurisdiction of most of the war boards was confined to one industry was due a large part of their success. The "public" member of the board was thus able to become thoroughly familiar with the details of the industry, to acquire expert knowledge of the industrial processes in connection with which labor adjustments were to be made. Even the National War Labor Board subdivided its work so that disputes in certain industries were in the first instance handled by particular members of the board.

If an industry is national in scope, with nation-wide competition such as the shipbuilding, clothing or steel industries, it would seem that a national agency, able to standardize working conditions for the entire country, would be desirable, with local examiners or deputies. For an industry like building in which competition is limited to the immediate locality in which the work is done, it is not so important—although still highly desirable—that wages and working conditions be standardized on a national scale. In industries of this kind purely local boards would probably function best, for in many ways a local tribunal being closer to the situation is better able to reach a decision satisfactory to both sides. It is easier for purely local boards to make differentiations in wages and working conditions and to render prompt decisions. Our entire emergency experience has shown that delay leads to endless complications. Many a controversy, if promptly decided, can be amicably settled, but when delayed passions are aroused, the subtle forces underlying industrial relations are disturbed and irretrievable harm is done. Strikes have often been due solely to the delay of the boards in taking jurisdiction. Nothing could be more wasteful than such a strike. And yet the boards are often not to blame as they are usually overburdened with work. A local board is less likely to have a crowded calendar;

and being on the spot it can get to work more promptly and decide more expeditiously. It seems wiser, therefore, to confine arbitration to local bodies in cases where the creation of national boards is not imperative.

The difficulties of arbitration were not the only ones illuminated by our war experience. At every point it threw light upon general industrial problems. Immigration, for instance, was shown as one of the controlling factors in determining the conditions of the workers. It was the cessation of immigration during the war that more than anything else gave labor its economic power. From 1914 to the summer of 1920 immigration practically stopped and it has been estimated that there are in this country one million less workers for each year of that period. Before 1914 our industries could count on the yearly arrival of vast hordes of men and women accustomed to low standards of living, difficult to organize and glad to work for the then prevailing wages of from fifteen to twenty cents an hour. If the large industries of the country continue to have at their disposal an unlimited supply of ignorant immigrants, eager to work long hours for amounts of pay less than enough properly to support American standards of life, then the wages of common labor will once more decline and the wage standards of the entire industrial population will be in danger of debasement.

One of the disappointments of the workers was the small benefit which because of the increased cost of living they derived from high wages. It is partly on this account the post-armistice period witnessed demands on a scale heretofore unknown for more sweeping changes in our industrial structure. Thus, in two of the most powerful labor organizations in the country, the miners and railroad men, demands have been put forward not only for government control, but for participation therein by the workers. In many other trades, this same spirit has become increasingly evident, sometimes taking the form of a desire to establish a kind of Guild Socialism. It cannot be said to affect the majority of American workers. But there can be no doubt that the number of men and women is daily increasing who desire a thoroughgoing change in industry rather than merely the betterment which would result from an increase in wages, or a shortening of hours. And the widespread growth of sentiment of this kind is distinctly a result of the war.

As the answer of many conservative men and women to this war-engendered radicalism has come the intense reaction and repression of the post-armistice period. This has been accompanied by a willingness to use violence and suppression, to permit our constitutional liberties to be abused and abridged. Intolerance with any differences of opinion has frequently supplanted that broad and generous hospitality to new ideas with which we have liked to associate the name of America. It is quite probable that this willingness to use force and repression against an unpopular minority is merely a passing phase. With the return to more normal economic conditions, a large mass of our people will probably realize that the best methods of promoting evolutionary changes are by the extension of American civil liberties and by efforts to correct abuses rather than to imprison those who point them out. Reaction breeds radicalism and radicalism in turn makes for reaction. We are thus in a vicious circle which constitutes a real danger. It is to be hoped that as the excitement and hysteria bred by the war die down, this vicious circle will be broken and we will return to a state of mind in which the liberty of the citizen is respected even when it leads him to differ radically in his economic views from the opinion of the majority.

The state of industrial unpreparedness in which the country found itself at the outbreak of the war was in a measure overcome and on the whole a fairly creditable showing made. But the condition of our industrial relations was such that we might have faced serious consequences had not the emergency forced a temporary truce between capital and labor. It cannot be said that we are better off to-day. On the contrary, the occurrences of the post-armistice period have tended to increase the bitterness with which many of the workers and employers have always regarded each other.

During the war itself, progress was made toward securing a broader spirit of coöperation. But to-day we are more than ever in need of a better understanding between employer and employee. It is imperative that present feelings of hostility be replaced by a mutual desire to coöperate. This cannot come unless the very real improvement which has already been made in the conditions of many wage-earners be further extended and unless the workers be gradually given a substantial share of the control of industry.

Just how far it will be possible to go and just how quickly are questions about which reasonable men differ. What is needed is a disposition to welcome a change and a willingness to help bring it about as rapidly as conditions warrant. There must also come a keener realization that in the struggles between employer and employee their positions are not equal. The stake, on the one side, is frequently a little more or a little less money to a group which already has much. On the other, it is frequently more or less food and shelter for the man and his family when he has not enough of either to live. Many employers can shut down their plants for years without even inconvenience, but to the workers enforced idleness means at best the exhaustion of hard-earned savings; at worst want and perhaps starvation.

The essential need is the development by both employer and employee of a new conception of efficiency and a new ideal of service. The efficiency of the worker has been secured largely through the fear of losing his job. Society has not supplied him with any other motive. Without the fear of enforced idleness efficiency has slumped and indifference has taken its place. Industry, in the past, has been conducted by both sides without sentiment and to a great extent without ideals. Almost any business man will probably say, quite frankly, that his object in conducting his business is to make profits and nothing else. In the stress of competition and dominated by his limited conception of business an employer will not hesitate to cut wages and to discontinue the employment of his workers irrespective of the hardship which such a course may entail. The idea of service either to the public or to those employed in industry is seldom present. And the worker, who is just about the same sort of human as the employer, will give just as little return for his wages as he can without any belief in the dignity of his occupation or any realization of society's need that he gives the best that is in him.

Fortunately both employer and employee are here and there showing the workings of a new spirit. The idea of service is beginning to take its place in the new conception of industry. Some employers are endeavoring to give their workers a larger share of control. They are groping their way toward organization on the basis of coöperation and service. Some of the workers also see that if they are to share in this control they too must develop a new conception of coöperative efficiency. Among the churches, as well, there has come the desire to translate theology and ethics into terms of industrial policy and practice. A number of our most important religious bodies have given utterance to programs for better industrial relations which show how widespread is the conviction that industry must be reshaped to conform to our traditional ideals of democracy and to express our newer ideals of service.

APPENDICES

APPENDIX I

STRIKE DATA, 1914 TO 1919

STATISTICAL information is perhaps of less value in regard to strikes than to other sociological phenomena. This partly because there are many important factors concerning industrial conflicts which cannot be set forth in terms of statistics; partly also because available information is very incomplete. Prior to 1880 no reliable data are to be had as to the number of strikes or their size and other characteristics. But because of the importance which industrial controversies were beginning to assume, the Tenth Census (1880) contained a special report dealing with them. And for the next twenty-five years, that is to say, from 1881 to 1905, the United States Bureau of Labor Statistics undertook a study of the strikes which occurred during these years, publishing its results in four annual reports of the Bureau, in 1887, 1894, 1901 and 1906. The *Monthly Review* of the Department said of them: "The data for these reports were secured by thorough investigations by trained field agents, and it is probable that few strikes and lockouts were omitted. Because of the time and expense involved the Bureau has not considered it possible to continue this method, although it is probably the only one likely to secure complete returns." [1]

Between the years 1905 and 1914 the Bureau of Labor Statistics did not publish any information as to the number of strikes which took place although data were issued by the American Federation of Labor as to disputes which affected that organization. In 1914 the Bureau of Statistics of the newly organized Labor Department compiled "a record of strikes and lockouts entirely from printed sources—newspapers, labor journals, trade union periodicals, and manufactures', trade, and other papers. In 1915 the same method was continued, and in connection with about

[1] *Monthly Review,* U. S. Bureau of Labor Statistics, April, 1916, p. 13.

1,400 strikes an attempt was made to supplement the information thus obtained by sending a schedule of inquiry to persons thought to have detailed knowledge concerning them." [1] This method has been continued to this date and the *Monthly Labor Review* has published annually the material thus obtained. In June, 1919, a more extended study was made of the data for the years 1916, 1917 and 1918, which was published in the *Monthly Review* for that month, and a year later the figures for 1919 were added. [2] Attention is called by the Labor Department to the fact that the information gathered by it since 1914 is less complete than that obtained by the more careful methods employed from 1881 to 1905 and that no comparisons can therefore be made between these two periods. [3]

In the period from 1881 to 1905 there occurred a total of 38,303 strikes and lockouts, or an average of 1,532 a year. In 1881 the number was only 477. For the twelve years following 1889 it fluctuated from 1,111 in that year to 1,839 in 1900. In 1901 the number rose to 3,012 and in 1903 there occurred the largest number of strikes and lockouts of the period—3,648. (A useful series of tables and charts is given in Groat—An Introduction to the Study of Organized Labor in America, pp. 168 et seq.)

The largest number of strikes and lockouts beginning in a single month was 617 in May, 1916. In May, 1917, there was 463; 391 in May, 1918, and 413 in May, 1919. The largest annual number of strikes and lockouts in a single city occurred in New York, where, in 1916, there were 363; in 1917, 484; in 1918, 484; in 1919, 360. See *Monthly Labor Review*, June, 1920. (The figures vary slightly from those given in *Monthly Labor Review*, June, 1919.)

It will be seen from Table No. 1 that the largest number of strikes in the country's history occurred in 1917, the first year of the war. There were about the same number of workers involved in the strikes of 1917 and 1918 and many more in those of 1916. In 1919 the number of strikes was nearly one thousand less than in 1917, whereas the number of workers involved far

---

[1] *Monthly Review*, U. S. Bureau of Labor Statistics, April, 1916, p. 13.

[2] *Monthly Labor Review*, U. S. Bureau of Labor Statistics, June, 1920, p. 20.

[3] *Ibid.*, April, 1916.

exceeded that of any previous year and was over three times the number in 1917.

TABLE NO. I

	Number of Strikes	Lock-outs	Total	Number of Employees Involved		
				Strikes	Lock-outs	Total
1914.........	979	101	1080	**	**	** (1)
1915.........	1246	159	1405	468,983	35,292	504,275 (2)
1916.........	3678	108	3786	1,546,428	53,182	1,599,610 (3)
1917.........	4233	126	4359	1,193,867	19,133	1,213,000 (4)
1918.........	3181	104	3285	1,192,418	43,041	1,235,459 (5)
1919.........	3253	121	3374	3,950,411	162,096	4,112,507 (6)

(1) ** Information not given.
(2) Information as to number of employees available in 873 cases.
(3) Information as to number of employees available in 2664 cases.
(4) Information as to number of employees available in 2220 cases.
(5) Information as to number of employees available in 2097 cases.
(6) Information as to number of employees available in 2493 cases.

It will be seen from Table No. II that by far the largest single cause of strikes has been wages and that there was a

TABLE NO. II

Principal Causes of Strikes and Lockouts from 1914 to 1919.*

Causes	1914		1915		1916		1917		1918		1919	
	No.	% of to-tal	No.	% of to-tal	No.	% of to-tal	No.	% of to-tal	No.	% of to-tal	No.	% of to-tal
Wages alone.............	294	36.3	409	29.1	1349	42.7	1578	44.2	1433	50.8	1115	35.3
Wages with or without other demands............	387	47.6	623	44.3	2110	66.8	2260	63.3	1906	67.6	2087	66.0
Hours alone.............	48	5.9	81	5.7	120	3.8	521	14.6	85	3.	122	3.9
Hours with or without other demands........	96	10.1	251	17.8	725	22.9	649	18.1	427	15.5	932	29.5
General conditions.......	72	8.9	39	2.7	59	1.8	99	2.7	56	1.9	65	2.0
Conditions and other demands................	110	13.6	86	6.1	145	4.2	227	6.3	125	4.4	176	5.6
Recognition of the union..	63	7.7	52	3.7	366	11.6	314	8.8	221	7.8	397	12.6
Recognition and other demands................	96	11.8	96	6.6	586	18.5	564	15.8	406	14.4	748	23.7
Discharge of employees ...	47	5.8	73	5.1	127	4.	206	5.7	137	4.8	141	4.5
Total for which information was furnished....	808		1405		3155		3567		2819		3161	

* Percentages given in Tables II and III are based on the number of strikes for which information is available as to the subject matter of each table.

marked increase from 1916 to 1918 in the proportionate number of strikes for this cause. Nor is this to be wondered at when we consider the rise in the cost of living during the period in question. In 1918 one-half of all the strikes were solely for higher wages and two-thirds of the entire number had wage advances as one of their demands. In 1919 the number of strikes solely on account of wages declined but the number in which wage demands figured was still two-thirds.

Other periods show a like preponderance in strikes for this cause. Carroll Wright in "Battles of Labor" gives estimates of the number of strikes from 1741 to 1880 and says that out of 1,491 strikes and lockouts during this period 1,089 were for wages. In 1881 over 70% of the stoppages of work were for wage demands alone. But in the period from 1881 to 1905 the general tendency was toward fewer strikes solely on account of wages and more of them for recognition of the union or the enforcement of union rules, the number of strikes for the latter cause rising in 1905 to almost 35%. On the other hand, during the war period there was an increasingly large number of strikes for wages and a fluctuating percentage for union recognition—as low as 3.7% in 1915, 8.8% in 1917 and 7.8 in 1918. When the war-time waiver of labor's demand for recognition of the union came to an end in 1919, the percentage of strikes for recognition alone rose sharply to 12.6% and to 23.7% when the strikes in which this demand was combined with others are included.

The number of strikes solely for the shortening of hours was unusually large in 1917—14.6%; it dropped to 3% in 1918. Combined with other demands the percentage rose, in 1919, to the highest percentage of the war period.

Table No. III shows that strikes which occurred during the war years of 1917 and 1918 were of substantially shorter duration than those of the preceding years. Almost half of the strikes of 1917 and 1918 did not last more than six days. In 1919 the duration of strikes once more increased; less than one-quarter lasted six days or less, whereas over half lasted from fifteen days to several months. During 1917 and 1918 the largest number of strikes were for the short periods; but in 1919 the largest number were for the longer periods, the highest percentage lasting from one to three months.

TABLE NO. III
Duration of Strikes *

Time	1915		1916		1917		1918		1919	
	No.	% of total	No.	% of total	No.	% of total	No.	% of total	No.	% of total
2 days or less........	84	14.4	364	17.2	389	28.7	393	24.	163	9.4
3 to 6 days..........	124	21.3	514	24.3	257	18.9	357	21.8	252	14.2
7 to 14 days.........	130	22.4	510	24.	290	21.4	376	23.	328	18.8
15 to 31 days........	96	16.5	384	18.1	198	14.6	282	17.2	378	21.7
32 to 91 days........	100	17.2	219	10.3	157	11.6	172	10.5	455	26.2
92 to 200 days.......	29	5.	99	4.6	53	3.9	30	1.8	144	8.3
Over 200 days........	17	2.9	23	1.0	9	.7	21	1.2	21	1.2
Total (for which information was given)	580		2113		1353		1633		1741	

* Percentages given in Tables II and III are based on the number of strikes for which information is available as to the subject matter of each table.

For purposes of comparison it would have been desirable to include a table showing the number of individuals engaged in the industries enumerated above. But the classification in the census reports do not correspond with the classifications of Table IV.

TABLE NO. IV
Strikes and Lockouts in the Leading Industrial Groups *

Industry	1914		1915		1916		1917		1918		1919	
	No.	% of total	No.	% of total	No.	% of total	No.	% of total	No.	% of total	No.	% of total
Building trades..........	275	25.4	231	16.4	394	10.4	460	10.5	427	12.9	442	13.1
Clothing...............	78	7.2	139	9.8	227	5.2	487	11.1	428	13.0	308	9.1
Iron and steel...........	14	1.2	30	2.1	72	1.9	56	1.2	73	2.2	75	2.2
Lumber................	40	3.7	14	.9	44	1.1	299	6.8	75	2.2	41	1.2
Leather................	....	....	....	....	34	.8	19	.4	16	.4	32	1.0
Meat Cutting...........	....	....	....	....	70	1.8	37	.8	39	1.1	69	2.0
Metal trades............	129	11.9	321	22.	561	14.8	535	12.1	458	13.9	556	16.5
Mining................	51	4.7	67	4.7	402	10.6	407	9.3	182	5.5	172	5.1
Shipbuilding............	....	....	....	....	27	.7	101	2.3	138	4.2	102	3.0
Textiles................	54	5.	84	5.9	261	6.8	238	5.4	205	6.2	267	7.9
Transportation..........	52	4.8	18	1.2	228	6.	331	7.5	186	5.6	234	7.0
Total................	1080		1405		3786		4359		3285		3374	

* Percentages are figured on the entire number of strikes and lockouts as given in Table No. I.

In a general way, however, the census shows that by far the largest number of employees in any one industry was engaged in transportation, in which comparatively few strikes occurred. The five industries in which the largest number of strikes took place —the metal trades, building, clothing, textiles and mining—employed the largest number of workers except transportation. In other words, with that exception, the number of strikes correspond roughly with the number of workers. It must be borne in mind that these figures relate to the number of strikes and do not take into consideration the number of employees involved.

It should be noted that the data published by the National Conference Board, which relate, however, to strikes occurring only during the first six months of the war, do not agree with the figures given above for the year 1917 and show the following percentages—demands refused, 35%; demands granted, 27%; compromised, 38%.

Perhaps the most significant fact shown by Table V is the small number of cases in which the men returned to work pend-

TABLE NO. V

Results of Strikes

	1915		1916		1917		1918		1919	
	No.	%	No.	%	No.	%	No.	%	No.	%
In favor of employer..	128	19	724	31	366	21	417	23	624	32
In favor of employee..	193	29	733	32	581	33	591	32	533	28
Compromised........	322	47	766	34	679	39	659	35	729	38
Employee returned pending arbitration .	31	5	70	3	131	7	198	10	42	2
Not reported.........	69	....	99	....	142	....	212	....	33	....
(Have not been included in figuring percentages.)										

ing arbitration. In 1916 this was only 3%. In 1917 it rose to 7% and in 1918 to 10%—a substantial increase, but not very impressive, considering the development of arbitral machinery and the large number of strikes which nevertheless took place. In 1919, however, when the wage boards were abolished, the percentage dropped to 2.2%.

TABLE NO. VI

Year	Number and percentage of strikes and lockouts in which employees were members of a union		Number and percentage of strikes and lockouts in which employees were not members of a union		Number and percentage of strikes and lockouts in which employees were not members of a union when strike began but became organized		Unreported (not included in figuring percentages)
1914..	no data						
1915..	929	82	176	15.5	29	2.5	459
1916..	2455	82.7	446	15	71	2.3	814
1917..	2372	90	204	8	55	2	1728
1918..	1884	83	360	16	26	1	1015
1919..	1913	92	136	6.6	29	1.4	1296

APPENDIX NO. II

EMERGENCY CONSTRUCTION WAGE COMMISSION

The first members of the Board were:

General E. A. Garlington, representing the War Department.

John R. Alpine, representing labor.

Walter Lippmann, representing the public.

General Garlington was succeeded by Colonel S. K. Ansell, who in turn was succeeded by Colonel J. H. Alexander. Colonel Alexander, after his appointment in April, 1918, was chairman of the board and its most active member.

Walter Lippman was succeeded by Stanley King, who was followed by Dr. E. M. Hopkins.

The Board was constituted under the following agreement:

June 19, 1917.

For the adjustment and control of wages, hours and conditions of labor in the construction of cantonments, there shall be created an adjustment commission of three persons, appointed by the Secretary of War; one to represent the Army, one the public, and one labor; the last to be nominated by Samuel Gompers, member of the Advisory Commission of the Council of National Defense, and President of the American Federation of Labor.

As basic standards with reference to each cantonment, such commission shall use the union scales of wages, hours and conditions in force on June 1, 1917, in the locality where such cantonment is situated. Consideration shall be given to special circumstances, if any, arising after said date which may require particular advances in wages or changes in other standards. Adjustments of wages, hours or conditions made by such board are to be treated as binding by all parties.

(Signed) NEWTON D. BAKER.
(Signed) SAMUEL GOMPERS.

Explanatory letters and telegrams followed between Louis B. Wehle, representing the War Department, and Samuel Gompers and Frank Morrison, representing the American Federation of Labor, in which Mr. Wehle explained that the "Government cannot commit itself in any way to the closed shop and that the conditions in force on June 1, 1917, which are to serve as part of the basic standards, do not include any provisions which have reference to the employment of non-union labor. . . . The word 'conditions' is of course clearly understood to refer only to the union arrangements in the event of overtime, holiday work, and matters of that kind." Mr. Gompers telegraphed, "Your understanding of the memorandum signed by Secretary Baker and me is right. It had reference to union hours and wages. The question of union shop was not included."

APPENDIX NO. III

SHIPBUILDING LABOR ADJUSTMENT BOARD

The original members of the Board were:

V. Everitt Macy, chairman, appointed by the President.

E. F. Carry, appointed by the Shipping Board.

A. J. Berres, representing the American Federation of Labor.

Mr. Carry was, after a very short time, succeeded by Louis B. Coolidge, and Mr. Coolidge, toward the end of the war, by Dr. L. C. Marshall.

Henry R. Seager was secretary of the Board and was, some time after the signing of the armistice, succeeded by W. E. Hotchkiss.

The country was divided into nine districts, co-terminus with the districts of the Emergency Fleet Corporation, viz.—New England, North Atlantic, Delaware River, Middle Atlantic, South Atlantic, Gulf, Great Lakes, South Pacific and North Pacific.

The original agreement provided for a board of three members —one representing the public, one the Shipping Board and one appointed by the President of the American Federation of Labor. The Navy was entitled to separate representation when matters affecting it were under consideration; two representatives of labor were also provided for, one to act when matters concerning the metal trades were to be decided, the other to represent the carpenters and joiners. Local representation of both sides was another feature of the original contract and the board before which the Seattle hearings, in the fall of 1917, were held, contained such local representation. The agreement, as amended on December 8, 1917, abolished all of these forms of special representation and provided for a simplified board of three members, one representing the public, the second representing the Shipping Board and Navy Department jointly, and the third representing the workers.

The Board had jurisdiction over the following types of work: [1]

(a) The construction and repair of Shipbuilding plants paid for by the Emergency Fleet Corporation or the Navy.

(b) The construction or repair of ships in yards either directly under the Emergency Fleet Corporation and Shipping Board or under direct contract with them.

(c) The construction or repair of ships in private plants doing work for the Navy.

(d) The outfitting of vessels after launching.

APPENDIX NO. IV

NATIONAL ADJUSTMENT COMMISSION

As originally constituted consisted of:

Raymond B. Stevens, chairman, representing the United States Shipping Board.

Walter Lippmann, representing the War Department.

---

[1] P. H. Douglas and F. S. Wolfe, *The Journal of Political Economy*, March, 1919, page 154.

T. V. O'Connor, representing the International Longshoremen's Association.

P. A. S. Franklin and H. H. Raymond nominated by the Committee on Shipping of the Council of National Defense, representing Deep-Sea and Coastwise Shipping interests, respectively. Each served separately when either deep-sea or coastwise shipping matters was being considered.

Raymond B. Stevens was succeeded by Robert P. Bass (John G. Palfrey was acting chairman in August, 1918). On January 1, 1919, Mr. Bass was succeeded by William Z. Ripley.

Walter Lippmann was succeeded by Stanley King, who was followed by E. M. Hopkins (John R. McLane, alternate). On January 1, 1919, Samuel J. Rosensohn succeeded E. M. Hopkins.

In the spring of 1918 it was decided to have the Shipping interests represented by a number of men, rather than one permanent member of the board. The following were appointed to represent Coastwise Shipping: W. P. Coria, John Crowley, E. A. Kelly, E. E. Palen, J. H. W. Steele, William M. Tupper; the following to represent Deep-Sea Shipping: E. J. Barber, H. C. Blackiston, R. K. Freeman, J. H. Rossiter, M. J. Sanders.

APPENDIX NO. V

NEW YORK HARBOR WAGE ADJUSTMENT BOARD

Organized October 20, 1917; for text of original and supplementary agreements see B. M. Squires in *Monthly Labor Review*, September, 1918, pages 4 and 12.

As first constituted the personnel of the board was as follows:

Lieutenant Colonel W. B. Baker, representing the War Department and Shipping Board.

George P. Putnam, representing the Department of Commerce.

Ethelbert Stewart, representing the Department of Labor.

T. V. O'Connor and T. L. Delahunty were added to the Board to represent labor and William Simmons and W. B. Pollack to represent the employers and the railroads.

Lieutenant Colonel Baker was succeeded by Keyes Winter as member of the Board but not as chairman.

Ethelbert Stewart was succeeded by B. M. Squires, who was elected chairman of the Board.

William Simmons was succeeded by F. A. Bishop.

APPENDIX NO. VI

RAILROAD WAGE BOARDS

The Eight-Hour Commission (appointed by the President):

Geo. W. Goethels, Chairman; Edgar E. Clark, George Rublee, and M. O. Lorenz, Secretary.

The Committee appointed by the Council of National Defense:

Franklin K. Lane, Secretary of Interior; W. B. Wilson, Secretary of Labor; Daniel Willard, President Baltimore & Ohio Railroad, and Samuel Gompers, President American Federation of Labor.

The Commission of Eight:

Elisha Lee; J. W. Higgins, Secretary, Western Managers Bureau; Chas. P. Neill, Chairman, ex-Commissioner, Bureau of Labor Statistics; John G. Walber, Secretary, Eastern Managers Bureau; W. S. Stone, Grand Chief Engineer, Brotherhood of Locomotive Engineers; Timothy Shea, Acting President, Brotherhood of Locomotive Firemen and Enginemen; G. H. Sines, Vice-President, Brotherhood Railroad Trainmen, and L. E. Sheppard, Acting President, Order of Railroad Conductors.

Railroad Wage Commission (known as the Lane Commission):

Franklin K. Lane, Chairman, Secretary of Interior; Charles C. McChord, Lawyer; J. H. Covington, Chief Justice, D. C. Supreme Court, and Wm. R. Wilcox, Lawyer.

Board of Railroad Wages and Working Conditions, established under Article VII of General Order No. 27, May 25, 1918:

G. H. Sines, Chairman, Vice-President, Brotherhood of Railroad Trainmen; F. F. Gaines, Vice-Chairman, Superintendent of Motive Power of Central Railroad of Georgia; J. J. Dermody,

Vice-President, Order of Railroad Telegraphy; C. E. Lindsay, Division Engineer, Maintenance of Pay Department, New York Central Lines; W. E. Morse, Vice-President and General Manager, Denver & Salt Lake Railroad Company, and A. O. Wharton, President, Railway Employees' Department, A. F. of L.

Railroad Board of Adjustment No. 1, established by Article IX of General Order No. 13, March 29, 1918:

Charles P. Neill, Chairman, ex-Commissioner, Bureau of Labor Statistics; L. E. Sheppard, Vice-Chairman; F. A. Burgess, Assistant Grand Chief Engineer, Brotherhood of Locomotive Engineers; W. N. Doak, Vice-President, Brotherhood of Railroad Trainmen; J. W. Higgins, Secretary, Western Managers Bureau; Albert Phillips, Vice-President, Brotherhood of Locomotive Firemen and Engineers; John G. Walber, Secretary of Eastern Managers Bureau, and E. T. Whiter, Assistant General Manager, Pennsylvania Lines West.

Railroad Board of Adjustment No. 2, established by General Order No. 29, May 31, 1918:

E. F. Potter, Chairman, Assistant General Manager of the Soo Lines; F. J. McNulty, Vice-Chairman; A. C. Adams, Superintendent of Shops, New York, New Haven & Hartford Railroad; H. J. Carr, Member Executive Board, International Association of Machinists; Otto E. Hoard, Vice-President, Amalgamated Sheet Metal Workers International Alliance; F. H. Knight, Assistant to President, Brotherhood Railroad Carmen; W. S. Murrian, Superintendent of Motive Power of Southern Railway; W. H. Penrith, Assistant to General Manager of Chicago & Alton Railway; Geo. W. Pring, Vice-President, Railway Employees' Department, A. F. of L.; E. A. Sweeley, Master Car Builder, Seaboard Air Line; R. J. Turnbull, Inspector of Transportation, Atlantic Coastline Railroad, and G. C. Van Dornes, Vice-President, International Brotherhood of Blacksmiths.

Railroad Board of Adjustment No. 3, established by General Order No. 53:

H. A. Kennedy, Chairman; T. H. Gerrey, Vice-Chairman; Richard P. Dee, E. A. Gould, S. N. Harrison, F. Hartenstein, G. E. Kipp, and W. A. Titus.

Division of Labor, created February, 1918:

W. S. Carter, President, Brotherhood Locomotive Firemen and Enginemen, assisted by G. W. Hanger, formerly member of Board of Mediation and Conciliation, and J. A. Franklin, formerly President, Brotherhood of Boiler Makers and Iron Ship Builders.

Women's Service Section: Miss Pauline Goldmark, Manager.

APPENDIX NO. VII

NATIONAL WAR LABOR BOARD

The membership of the National War Labor Board as constituted at the time of its appointment was as follows: [1]

William Howard Taft, joint chairman and public representative of the employers.

Frank P. Walsh, of Kansas City, Mo., joint chairman and public representative of employees.

For employers:

L. F. Loree, of the Delaware & Hudson Railroad Company.

W. H. Van Dervoort, of the Root and Van Dervoort Engineering Company, of East Moline, Ill.

C. Edwin Michael, of the Virginia Bridge and Iron Company, Roanoke, Va.

Loyall A. Osborne, of the Westinghouse Electric and Manufacturing Company.

B. L. Worden, of the Submarine Boat Corporation, Newark, N. J.

For employees:

Frank J. Hayes, of the United Mine Workers of America.

Wm. L. Hutcheson, of the United Brotherhood of Carpenters and Joiners.

Wm. H. Johnston, of the International Association of Machinists.

[1] Report Secretary of National War Labor to the Secretary of Labor.

Victor Olander, of the International Seamen's Union of America.
Thomas A. Rickert, of the United Garment Workers.

These appointments of the Secretary of Labor were approved and affirmed by the President of the United States by a proclamation issued April 8, 1918.

The following appointments and changes in personnel took place:

W. Jett Lauck, economist, of Chevy Chase, Md., to be permanent secretary, May 9, 1918.

Thomas J. Savage, of the International Association of Machinists, alternate for Mr. Johnston.

T. M. Guerin, of the United Brotherhood of Carpenters and Joiners, alternate for Mr. Hutcheson, May 13, 1918.

F. C. Hood, of the Hood Rubber Company, Watertown, Mass., alternate for Mr. Loree, May 17, 1918.

C. A. Crocker, of the Crocker-McElwain Company, Holyoke, Mass., alternate for Mr. Worden, June 1, 1918.

F. C. Hood, alternate for Mr. Loree, to become principal on the the resignation of Mr. Loree, June 1, 1918.

John F. Perkins, of the Calumet-Hecla Copper Company, alternate for Mr. Osborne, June 1, 1918.

Frederick N. Judson, lawyer, of St. Louis, Mo., vice-chairman and alternate for Mr. Taft, June 18, 1918.

John F. Perkins, alternate for Mr. Osborne, alternate for Mr. Hood, June 27, 1918.

H. H. Rice, of the General Motors Corporation, Detroit, Mich., alternate for Mr. Van Dervoort, July 1, 1918.

Wm. Harman Black, lawyer, of New York City, vice-chairman and alternate for Mr. Walsh, July 20, 1918.

Matthew Woll, of the International Photo-Engravers' Union, alternate for Mr. Olander, July 24, 1918.

John J. Manning, of the United Garment Workers, alternate for Mr. Rickert, July 24, 1918.

J. W. Marsh, of the Westinghouse Electric and Manufacturing Company, alternate for Mr. Michael, September 1, 1918.

On October 9, 1918, the board was notified of the death of Thomas J. Savage, and Fred Hewitt, of the International Association of Machinists, was designated alternate for Mr. Johnston, October 22, 1918.

F. C. Hood resigned as member of the board on November 19, 1918.

P. F. Sullivan, of the Bay State Street Railway Company, of Massachusetts, alternate for Mr. Osborne, December 3, 1918.

Frank P. Walsh, joint chairman, resigned as a member of the board on December 3, 1918.

Wm. Harman Black, vice-chairman and alternate for Mr. Walsh, resigned as a member of the board on December 3, 1918.

Basil M. Manly, journalist, of Washington, D. C., joint chairman, to fill the vacancy caused by the resignation of Mr. Walsh, December 4, 1918.

Wm. Harman Black, vice-chairman and alternate for Mr. Manly, December 4, 1918.

John F. Perkins, alternate for Mr. Hood, to fill the vacancy caused by the resignation of Mr. Hood, December 4, 1918.

B. L. Worden resigned as a member of the board on December 9, 1918.

C. A. Crocker, alternate for Mr. Worden, to fill the vacancy caused by the resignation of Mr. Worden, December 11, 1918.

Harold O. Smith, of the J. and D. Tire Company, Charlotte, N. C., alternate for Mr. Crocker, January 17, 1919.

Granville E. Foss, of the Brightwood Manufacturing Company, of North Andover, Mass., alternate for Mr. Perkins, February 11, 1919.

C. A. Crocker resigned as a member of the board on February 24, 1919.

Principal members and alternates appointed subsequent to the creation of the board were nominated and appointed in the same manner as were the original members, the date given above being the date of appointment or of entering upon duty.

Proclamation by the President of the United States Establishing National War Labor Board

Whereas in January, 1918, the Secretary of Labor, upon the nomination of the president of the American Federation of Labor, and the president of the National Industrial Conference Board, appointed a War Labor Conference Board for the purpose of devising for the period of the war a method of labor adjustment which would be acceptable to employers and employees; and

Whereas said board has made a report recommending the creation for the period of the war of a National War Labor Board with the same number of members as, and to be selected by the same agencies that created, the War Labor Conference Board, whose duty it shall be to adjust labor disputes in the manner specified and in accordance with certain conditions set forth in the said report; and

Whereas the Secretary of Labor has, in accordance with the recommendation contained in the report of said War Labor Conference Board dated March 29, 1918, appointed as members of the National War Labor Board Hon. William Howard Taft and Hon. Frank P. Walsh, representatives of the general public of the United States; Messrs. Loyall A. Osborne, L. F. Loree, W. H. Van Dervoort, C. E. Michael, and B. L. Worden, representatives of the employers of the United States; and Messrs. Frank J. Hayes, William L. Hutcheson, William H. Johnston, Victor A. Olander, and T. A. Rickert, representatives of the employees of the United States:.

Now, therefore, I, WOODROW WILSON, President of the United States of America, do hereby approve and affirm the said appointments, and make due proclamation thereof and of the following for the information and guidance of all concerned:

The powers, functions, and duties of the National War Labor Board shall be to settle by mediation and conciliation controversies arising between employers and workers in fields of production necessary for the effective conduct of the war, or in other fields of national activity, delays and obstructions in which might, in the opinion of the National Board, affect detrimentally such production; to provide, by indirect appointment, or otherwise, for committees or boards to sit in various parts of the country where controversies arise and secure settlement by local mediation and conciliation; and to summon the parties to controversies for hearing and action by the National Board in event of failure to secure settlement by mediation and conciliation.

The principles to be observed and the methods to be followed by the National Board in exercising such powers and functions and performing such duties shall be those specified in the said report of the War Labor Conference Board dated March 29, 1918, a complete copy of which is hereunto appended.

The National Board shall refuse to take cognizance of a controversy between employer and workers in any field of industrial or other activity where there is by agreement or Federal law a means of settlement which has been invoked.

And I do hereby urge upon all employers and employees within the United States the necessity of utilizing the means and methods thus provided for the adjustment of all industrial disputes, and request that during the pendency of mediation or arbitration through the said means and methods, there shall be no discontinuance of industrial operations which would result in curtailment of the production of war necessities.

In witness whereof, I have hereunto set my hand and caused the seal of the United States to be affixed.

Done in the District of Columbia, this eighth day of April, in the year of our Lord one thousand nine hundred and eighteen, and of the independence of the United States the one hundred and forty-second.

(Seal)   WOODROW WILSON.

By the President:

Robert Lansing,
    Secretary of State.

FUNCTIONS, POWERS, AND DUTIES OF THE BOARD

The functions and powers of the National War Labor Board are as follows:

To bring about a settlement, by mediation and conciliation, of every controversy arising between employers and workers in the field of production necessary for the effective conduct of the war.

To do the same thing in similar controversies in other fields of national activity, delays and obstructions in which may, in the opinion of the National Board, affect detrimentally such production.

To provide such machinery, by direct appointment or otherwise, for the selection of committees or boards to sit in various parts of the country where controversies arise, to secure settlement by local mediation and conciliation.

To summon the parties to the controversy for hearing and action by the National Board in case of failure to secure settlement by local mediation and conciliation.

If the sincere and determined effort of the National Board

shall fail to bring about a voluntary settlement and the members of the board shall be unable unanimously to agree upon a decision, then and in that case and only as a last resort an umpire appointed in the manner provided in the next paragraph shall hear and finally decide the controversy under simple rules of procedure prescribed by the National Board.

The members of the National Board shall choose the umpire by unanimous vote. Failing such choice, the name of the umpire shall be drawn by lot from a list of ten suitable and disinterested persons to be nominated for the purpose by the President of the United States.

The National Board shall hold its regular meetings in the city of Washington, with power to meet at any other place convenient for the board and the occasion.

The National Board may alter its methods and practice in settlement of controversies hereunder from time to time as experience may suggest.

The National Board shall refuse to take cognizance of a controversy between employer and workers in any field of industrial or other activity where there is by agreement or Federal law a means of settlement which has not been invoked.

The place of each member of the National Board unavoidably detained from attending one or more of its sessions may be filled by a substitute to be named by such member as his regular substitute. The substitute shall have the same representative character as his principal.

The National Board shall have power to appoint a secretary and to create such other clerical organization under it as may be in its judgment necessary for the discharge of its duties.

The National Board may apply to the Secretary of Labor for authority to use the machinery of the Department in its work of conciliation and mediation.

The action of the National Board may be invoked, in respect to controversies within its jurisdiction, by the Secretary of Labor or by either side in a controversy or its duly authorized representative. The board, after summary consideration, may refuse further hearing if the case is not of such character or importance as to justify it.

In the appointment of committees of its own members to act for the board in general or local matters, and in the creation of local committees, the employers and the workers shall be equally represented.

The representatives of the public in the board shall preside alternately at successive sessions of the board or as agreed upon.

The board in its mediating and conciliatory action, and the umpire in his consideration of a controversy, shall be governed by the following principles:

Principles and Policies to Govern Relations Between Workers and Employers in War Industries for the Duration of the War

There should be no strikes or lockouts during the war.

RIGHT TO ORGANIZE

The right of workers to organize in trade-unions and to bargain collectively through chosen representatives is recognized and affirmed. This right shall not be denied, abridged, or interfered with by the employers in any manner whatsoever.

The right of employers to organize in associations or groups and to bargain collectively through chosen representatives is recognized and affirmed. This right shall not be denied, abridged, or interfered with by the workers in any manner whatsoever.

Employers should not discharge workers for membership in trade-unions, nor for legitimate trade-union activities.

The workers, in the exercise of their right to organize, should not use coercive measures of any kind to induce persons to join their organizations nor to induce employers to bargain or deal therewith.

EXISTING CONDITIONS

In establishments where the union shop exists the same shall continue, and the union standards as to wages, hours of labor, and other conditions of employment shall be maintained.

In establishments where union and non-union men and women now work together and the employer meets only with employees or representatives engaged in said establishments, the continuance of such conditions shall not be deemed a grievance. This declaration, however, is not intended in any manner to deny the right or discourage the practice of the formation of labor unions or the joining of the same by the workers in said establishments, as guaranteed in the preceding section, nor to prevent the War Labor Board from urging or any umpire from granting, under the machinery herein provided, improvements of their situation in the matter of wages, hours of labor, or other conditions as shall be found desirable from time to time.

Established safeguards and regulations for the protection of the health and safety of workers shall not be relaxed.

WOMEN IN INDUSTRY

If it shall become necessary to employ women on work ordinarily performed by men, they must be allowed equal pay for equal work and must not be allotted tasks disproportionate to their strength.

HOURS OF LABOR

The basic eight-hour day is recognized as applying in all cases in which existing law requires it. In all other cases the question of hours of labor shall be settled with due regard to governmental necessities and the welfare, health, and proper comfort of the workers.

MAXIMUM PRODUCTION

The maximum production of all war industries should be maintained and methods of work and operation on the part of employers or workers, which operate to delay or limit production, or which have a tendency to artificially increase the cost thereof, should be discouraged.

MOBILIZATION OF LABOR

For the purpose of mobilizing the labor supply with a view to its rapid and effective distribution, a permanent list of the numbers of skilled and other workers available in different parts of the country shall be kept on file by the Department of Labor, the information to be constantly furnished—

1. By the trade unions.

2. By State employment bureaus and Federal agencies of like character.

3. By the managers and operators of industrial establishments throughout the country.

These agencies shall be given opportunity to aid in the distribution of labor as necessity demands.

CUSTOM OF LOCALITIES

In fixing wages, hours, and conditions of labor, regard should always be had to the labor standards, wage scales, and other conditions prevailing in the localities affected.

THE LIVING WAGE

1. The right of all workers, including common laborers, to a living wage is hereby declared.

2. In fixing wages, minimum rates of pay shall be established which will insure the subsistence of the worker and his family in health and reasonable comfort.

APPENDIX NO. VIII

WAR LABOR POLICIES BOARD

Department of Labor—Felix Frankfurter, professor of law, Harvard University, chairman; Max Lowenthal, assistant to chairman; Miss Mary Van Kleeck, director of Women in Industry Service.

War Department—Dr. E. M. Hopkins, assistant to the Secretary of War.

Navy Department—F. D. Roosevelt, Assistant Secretary of the Navy.

Department of Agriculture—G. I. Christie, assistant to the Secretary of Agriculture, in charge of farm labor activities.

War Industries Board—Hugh Frayne, general organizer, American Federation of Labor, New York City.

Fuel Administration—John P. White, ex-president of the United Mine Workers of America.

Shipping Board—Robt. P. Bass, ex-governor of New Hampshire.

Emergency Fleet Corporation—Charles Piez, general manager.

Food Administration—M. B. Hammond, professor of economics and sociology, Ohio State University.

Railroad Administration—W. I. Tyler, assistant director, Division of Operations.

Committee on Public Information—W. L. Chenery, Chicago.

Executive secretary—George L. Bell, San Francisco.

Industrial adviser—Herbert F. Perkins, Chicago.

Labor Adviser—John R. Alpine, vice-president, American Federation of Labor.

Economic adviser—L. C. Marshall, dean, University of Chicago.

The purposes and proposed operation of the War Labor Policies Board, as stated by Mr. Frankfurter, are in part as follows:

The War Labor Policies Board and the board representing the various bureaus of the Labor Department will constitute a dovetailing process linking up every agency of the Government whose activies in any way involve the employment or the direction of labor. The policies board will be representative of the War Department, the Navy Department, the Department of Agriculture, the Shipping Board, the Fuel Administration, the Food Administration, the Emergency Fleet Corporation, the Railroad Administration, and the War Industries Board. Its functions, while in a sense technical, will be thoroughly administrative, inasmuch as its decisions will be carried out by the departments and agencies represented in its membership.

In the matter of wages it will not attempt to set a flat rate for any one craft or trade in the country as a whole; but it will fix standards to be determined for all industries in a given section of the country after investigations disclosing the conditions of life, including the cost of living and the services rendered. The facts will be ascertained justly and comprehensively from information to be sought from the workers' own organization, private employers and their organizations, Government bureaus, and wherever else exact knowledge may be secured.

We must husband our labor supply, so as to satisfy the war needs of the country to the fullest possible practical extent. It is necessary, therefore, that the sources of supply be wisely directed and employed. With respect to this phase of the industrial problem it will be the function of the war policies board to allocate the supply according to the productive needs of the country. Under decisions of the board on this score it will be impossible for one industry to draw the labor supply from another unless it has been regularly determined that the first industry has a higher claim upon the supply on the basis of a more pressing Government need than the industry from which it would draw the workers. This question will, of course, be determined by the war policies board. But by the establishment of standardized wage conditions the incentive for workers to leave one industry and go to another will have been removed anyhow.

In addition to controlling the labor supply by the methods just reviewed the policies board will also regulate hours of labor in the various industries and determine the needs of industry with regard to housing and transportation facilities, etc.

The need of the hour is production, the fullest munitioning, equipment, and feeding of the forces at the front. Labor, industrial managers, and Government officials are all heartily united to bring about this end. There will be the utmost pooling, not only of the industrial resources but of the resources of goodwill and intelligence, and in this spirit the work will proceed efficiently. There is much to be done, but it will be done because it must be done.

The following resolution was passed by the policies board pertaining to standardization of wages:

Whereas the recent uncoördinated activities of Government contractors in the matter of hiring labor for war industry have resulted in competitive bidding by one contractor against another for the available labor at any scale deemed expedient for the occasion, which has resulted in producing restlessness and wasteful movement of labor from one industry to another, and whereas it is absolutely essential to the stabilization of industry throughout the United States that all wages for both skilled and unskilled labor engaged in war work be standardized: Therefore be it resolved, That wages paid by Government departments and contractors engaged in war work should, after conference with representatives of labor and by industrial management, be stabilized by this board; that the committee on standardization is hereby instructed to proceed with its work with all possible expedition, and that as soon as such standardized scales are established the full influence and authority of all departments of the

Government represented on this board will be exercised to maintain them.

APPENDIX NO. IX

CONFERENCE COMMITTEE OF LABOR ADJUSTMENT AGENCIES

Felix Frankfurter, Chairman.

Labor Department—Felix Frankfurter and J. B. Lennon.

Railroad Administration—G. H. Sines and C. E. Lindsay.

National War Labor Board—Wm. H. Taft and Frank P. Walsh.

Fuel Administration—Rembrandt Peale and W. J. Diamond.

National Adjustment Commission—Robert P. Bass and T. V. O'Connor.

Emergency Construction Wage Commission—Col. J. H. Alexander and John R. Alpine.

National Harness and Saddlery Adjustment Commission—Major Samuel J. Rosensohn.

Navy Department—Franklin D. Roosevelt and Louis McH. Howe.

Shipbuilding Labor Adjustment Board—V. E. Macy and A. J. Berres.

War Department—F. L. Hopkins and Major F. W. Tully.

APPENDIX NO. X

LABOR CLAUSES

The following clauses were adopted by the War Labor Policies Board for introduction into the contracts of—

1. War Department.
2. Navy Department.
3. Emergency Fleet Corporation.
4. U. S. Housing Corporation.

Clause on Laws and Restrictions Relating to Labor.

Adopted July 12, 1918.
Amended July 26, 1918.

All work required in carrying out this contract shall be performed in full compliance with the laws of the State, Territory, or District of Columbia where such labor is performed; provided, that the contractor shall not employ in the performance of this contract any minor under the age of fourteen years or permit any minor between the ages of fourteen and sixteen years to work more than eight hours in any one day, more than six days in any one week, or before 6 A. M. or after 7 P. M. Nor shall the contractor directly or indirectly employ any person undergoing sentence of imprisonment at hard labor which may have been imposed by any court of any State, Territory, or municipality having criminal jurisdiction. Provided, however, that the President of the United States may, by Executive Order, modify this provision with respect to the employment of convict labor and provide the terms and conditions upon which such labor may be employed. These provisions shall be of the essence of the contract.

Clause on Adjustment of Labor Disputes.[1]

Adopted July 19, 1918.

In the event that labor disputes shall arise directly affecting the performance of this contract and causing or likely to cause any delay in making the deliveries and the .... (head of department) shall have requested the contractor to submit such dispute for settlement, the contractor shall have the right to submit such dispute to the .... (head of department) for settlement. The .... (head of department) may thereupon settle or cause to be settled such disputes, and the parties hereto agree to accede to and to comply with all the terms of such settlement.

If the contractor is thereby required to pay labor costs higher than those prevailing in the performance of this contract immediately prior to such settlement, the .... (head of department) or his representative in making such settlement and as a part thereof may direct that a fair and just addition to the contract price shall be made therefor; provided, however, that the .... (head of department) or his representative shall

---

[1] The Labor Disputes Clause used by the Ordnance Department is similar to the above, although not identical with it. See A Report of the Activities of the War Department in the Field of Industrial Relations During the War, page 72.

certify that the contractor has in all respects lived up to the terms and conditions of the contract or shall waive in writing for this purpose only any breach that may have occurred.

If such settlement reduces such labor cost to the contractor, the .... (head of department) or his representative may direct that a fair and just deduction be made from the contract price.

No claim for addition shall be made unless the increase was ordered in writing by the .... (head of department) or his duly authorized representative, and such addition to the contract price was directed as part of the settlement.

Every decision or determination made under the article by the .... (head of department) or his duly authorized representative shall be final and binding upon the parties thereto.

Clause on Eight-Hour Basic Day, with Time and a Half for Overtime. Adopted June 28, 1918.

To be introduced into contracts which come under such a provision by reason of existing Federal laws:

Wages of laborers, operatives and mechanics doing any part of the work contemplated by this contract, in the employ of the contractor, shall be computed upon a basic day rate of eight-hours' work, with overtime rates to be paid for at not less than time and one-half for all hours in excess of eight hours. Compliance by the contractor with the provisions of this article shall be of the essence of the contract.

Title of Labor Adjusting Agency	How Created	Date	Connected with which Departments or Boards	Size of Labor Adjustment Board	Were Employers Represented?	Were Employees Represented?	Was Representation Equal?	Was Public Represented?	Employees' Representatives Selected by A. F. of L. or Affiliated Union?	Did Board Award Eight Hour Day?
Emergency Construction Wage Commission	Agreement Sec. of War with Pres. A. F. of L.	June 19, 1917	War and Navy	3	Yes (the Government)	Yes	Yes	Yes	Yes	Yes
Administrator Army Clothing	Order of Sec. of War	Jan. 18, 1918	War	1	No	No		Yes		Yes
Industrial Service Section—Ordnance Department	Order of Sec. of War	Jan, 1918	War	*	No	No		Yes		Usually
Industrial Relations Division Emergency Fleet Corporation	Order of Emergency Fleet Corporation	May, 1918	Shipping Board-Emergency Fleet Corporation	*	No	No		Yes		Usually
Industrial Service Section—Aircraft	Order of Sec. of War	Jan, 1918	War	*	No	No		Yes		Usually
Labor Bureau—Fuel Administration	Order of Fuel Administrator	July 23, 1918	Fuel Administration	2	Yes	Yes		Through final authority of administrator	Yes	Yes
Marine and Dock Industrial Relations Division	Order of Shipping Board	Sept. 19, 1918	Shipping Board	*	No	No		Yes	Yes	No
National War Labor Board	Proclamation Pres. of United States	April 9, 1918	No Special Department	12	Yes	Yes	Yes	Yes	Yes	Usually
National Adjustment Commission	Agreement Shipping Board, War and Labor Depts. with Employers, Longshoremen's Union and A. F. of L.	August, 1917	Shipping Board War	4	Yes	Yes	Yes	Yes	Yes	No
New York Harbor Wage Adjustment Board	Agreement Shipping Board with Employers and with Representatives Marine Workers in the Port of N. Y.	Oct. 20, 1917	Shipping Board War	(**) 7	Yes	Yes	Yes	Yes	Yes	No

Commission / Board	Created by	Date	Department or Board	No.						
National Harness and Saddlery Commission	Agreement War Dept. with Employers and Union	Sept. 26, 1917	War	3	Yes	Yes	Yes	Yes	Yes	Yes
Railroad Wage Commission	Gen. Order No. 5 Railroad Administration	Jan. 18, 1918	Railroad Administration	4	No	No	Yes	Through final authority of Administrator		Yes
Board Railroad Wages and Working Conditions	Gen. Order No. 27 Railroad Administration	May 25, 1918	Railroad Administration	6	Yes	Yes	Yes	Through final authority of Administrator	Yes	Yes
Railway Board of Adjustment No. 1	Gen. Order No. 13 Railroad Administration	March 22, 1918	Railroad Administration	8	Yes	Yes	Yes	Through final authority of Administrator	Yes	Yes
Railway Board of Adjustment No. 2	Gen. Order No. 29 Railroad Administration	May 31, 1918	Railroad Administration	12	Yes	Yes	Yes	Through final authority of Administrator	Yes	Yes
Railway Board of Adjustment No. 3	Gen. Order No. 53 Railroad Administration	Nov. 13, 1918	Railroad Administration	8	Yes	Yes	Yes	Through final authority of Administrator	Yes	Yes
President's Mediation Commission	President U. S.	Sept. 9, 1917	No Special Department or Board	5	Yes	Yes	Yes	Yes	Yes	Yes
Shipbuilding Labor Adjustment Board	Agreement Shipping Board, Emergency Fleet Corp., Navy Dept., Representatives Shipyard Unions	Aug. 25, 1917	Shipping Board Emergency Fleet Corporation	3	No, except through Shipping Board	Yes	Yes	Yes	Yes	Yes
Arsenals and Navy Yard Commission	Order of Secretary of War and of Navy	Aug. 15, 1917	War Navy	3	No	No		Yes	Yes	Yes

* Industrial Service Divisions consisted of a director and his assistants.

** Agreement first provided for board of three, one representative of Shipping Board, one of Department of Labor and one of Department of Commerce. This was later modified by adding to the board a representative of the private employers and one of the union and still later by adding a representative of the Railroads and a second representative of the workers.

INDEX

A.

Absenteeism, 185, 186, 205.

Adamson law, 83-85, 231, 252.

Administrator of Labor Standards in Army Clothing, 58, 161, 209.

Agreement, Atlantic, 34; creating Cantonment Adjustment Commission (Baker-Gompers), 15, 127, 190, 297; of Fuel Administration with miners, 102; Harness and Saddlery Adjustment Commission, 63; creating National Adjustment Commission, 39; Adjustment Commission of 1919, 42-43; Washington, 97; creating Shipbuilding Labor Adjustment Board, 22.

Air Craft, Industrial Service Section, 65, 72.

Allen, H. J., Governor, 145.

Alschuler, Judge Samuel, 55.

Amalgamated Association of Street Railway Employees, 116, 171.

Amalgamated Clothing Workers, 58, 60.

Amalgamated Textile Workers, note 1, 140.

American Federation of Labor, agreement creating Shipbuilding Labor Adjustment Board, 22; agreement creating National Adjustment Commission, 37; agreement with Secretary of War, 15; appeal to President, 53; company unions, note 2, 164; employers limit refusal to discriminate to affiliated unions, 57; failure to organize migratory workers, 258; influence on labor policy, 151; labor standards, 152; opposition to compulsory arbitration, 124; police unions, note 3, 142; to nominate members of Conference Board, 118; resolutions, 236.

American Telephone & Telegraph Co., 106.

American Woolen Co. strike, 138.

Anderson, Judge George W., opinion on enemy plots, note 1, 230.

Arbitration, causes of success of, in war, 276; difficulties of, in peace, 277; general discussion, 281.

Army Clothing, Administrator of Labor Standards in, see Administrator.

Atlantic Seamen strike, 35.

Attendance, irregularity of, see Absenteeism.

Award, anthracite miners, 98; Army Ordnance, Bridgeport, 77; Arsenal and Navy Yard Wage Commission, 63; bituminous miners, note 2, 100; Council of National Defense committee, 84; Harness and Saddlery, 63; National Adjustment Commission, 41-43; National War Labor Board, general, 122, Bridgeport (Eidlitz), 78, N. Y. Harbor (Macy), 51; New York Harbor Wage Adjustment, 46; N. Y. machinists, 67; first Pacific Coast shipyard, 23; railroad service, 93; railroad shopmen, 92; Railroad Wage Commission, 88; Shipbuilding Labor Adjustment, 22-31; Washington agreement, 97.

Awards, duration of, 194.

Rogers, Major Wm. C., 76-77.
Rome brass mills strike, 144.
Ryan, W. S., note 3, 109, 113.

S.

St. Paul and Minneapolis strikes, 112.
Sanitation, 4, 5, 20, 59, 259, note 1, 271.
Seamen's union, see International.
Seattle strike, 25-30, 283.
Secretary of Labor, 10; Arsenal and Navy Yard Wage Commission, 62; attempt to avert coal strike, 99; averted coal strike, 97; Chairman Mediation Commission, 54; New York longshoremen strike, 44; on change of standards, 170; on right to organize, 165; organization of labor administration, 118; organized conference committee, 129; proposed increase for miners, 100; statement on labor standards, 152; understanding with Fuel Administrator, 102.
Secretary of Navy, Arsenal and Navy Yard Wage Commission, 62.
Secretary of War, action in Smith & Wesson case, 7; demobilizes labor sections, 71; denies extension of closed shop, 170; establishes Arsenal and Navy Yard Wage Commission, 62; establishes Harness and Saddlery Commission, 63; signs agreement creating Cantonment Wage Adjustment Commission, 15.
Secret service agents, 167, 253.
Senatorial comment on Government labor policy, etc., see chapter XVIII.
Sherman, L. Y., Senator, 253.
Shipbuilding Labor Adjustment Board (Macy), cost of living, 193; creation, 20; extends collective bargaining, 161; overtime, 186; refers award to Conference Committee, 129; summary of agreement and per-

sonnel, 298; uniformity of rates, 198.
Shipping Board Industrial Relations Division, Atlantic agreement, 34; Emergency Fleet Corporation, 30; Marine and Dock, 33; National Adjustment Commission, 39; New York Harbor Adjustment Board, 46; hours, 180; see Shipbuilding Labor Adjustment Board.
Shoe workers' strike, 141-142.
Shop committees, see Collective Bargaining.
Slacking, 205, 231, 270.
Smith & Wesson, 70, 226, 252.
Springfield, Ill., general strike, note 1, 30.
Standardization, see Wages.
Standards, maintenance of, 175, 152, 170.
Steel strike, note 1, 173.
Street railways, 116, 117; note 2, 122; note 1, 192; 208.
Strikes, American Woolen Co., 138; Atlantic Seamen, 35; before Government controlled railroads, note 4, 86; Billings, note 1, 30; bituminous miners, 99-100; Boston police, 142; Bisbee, 264; Bridgeport, 67, 73, 226; canners, 104; clothing, 61; coastwise longshoremen, 44; concrete workers, note 1, 203; copper mines, 55; Dayton street railroad, note 1, 174; fishermen, 105; Fore River, Newark Bay, Baltimore, 24; for forty-four-hour week, 61, 181; General Electric, note 1, 158; Great Lake seamen ordered, 1917, 36; Great Lake seamen ordered, 1918, 37; in jurisdiction of Construction Wage Commission, 16; Indianapolis cantonment, 14; Jacksonville plasterers, note 2, 158; Kansas City, note 1, 30; Kansas Coal, 101, 145; Lawrence, 139; Lumber, 179, 260, 270; Lynn, 141; Newark, 68; New England Telephone, 112-114; New York, 67; New York Harbor threatened, 45; New York Harbor, 51; New

American Labor: From Conspiracy to Collective Bargaining

AN ARNO PRESS/NEW YORK TIMES COLLECTION

SERIES I

Abbott, Edith.
Women in Industry. 1913.

Aveling, Edward B. and Eleanor M. Aveling.
Working Class Movement in America. 1891.

Beard, Mary.
The American Labor Movement. 1939.

Blankenhorn, Heber.
The Strike for Union. 1924.

Blum, Solomon.
Labor Economics. 1925.

Brandeis, Louis D. and Josephine Goldmark.
Women in Industry. 1907. New introduction by Leon Stein and
   Philip Taft.

Brooks, John Graham.
American Syndicalism. 1913.

Butler, Elizabeth Beardsley.
Women and the Trades. 1909.

Byington, Margaret Frances.
Homestead: The Household of A Mill Town. 1910.

Carroll, Mollie Ray.
Labor and Politics. 1923.

Coleman, McAlister.
Men and Coal. 1943.

Coleman, J. Walter.
The Molly Maguire Riots: Industrial Conflict in the Pennsylvania
    Coal Region. 1936.

Commons, John R.
Industrial Goodwill. 1919.

Commons, John R.
Industrial Government. 1921.

Dacus, Joseph A.
Annals of the Great Strikes. 1877.

Dealtry, William.
The Laborer: A Remedy for his Wrongs. 1869.

Douglas, Paul H., Curtis N. Hitchcock and Willard E. Atkins, editors.
The Worker in Modern Economic Society. 1923.

Eastman, Crystal.
Work Accidents and the Law. 1910.

Ely, Richard T.
The Labor Movement in America. 1890. New Introduction by
    Leon Stein and Philip Taft.

Feldman, Herman.
Problems in Labor Relations. 1937.

Fitch, John Andrew.
The Steel Worker. 1910.

Furniss, Edgar S. and Laurence Guild.
Labor Problems. 1925.

Gladden, Washington.
Working People and Their Employers. 1885.

Gompers, Samuel.
Labor and the Common Welfare. 1919.

Hardman, J. B. S., editor.
American Labor Dynamics. 1928.

Higgins, George G.
Voluntarism in Organized Labor, 1930-40. 1944.

Hiller, Ernest T.
The Strike. 1928.

Hollander, Jacob S. and George E. Barnett.
Studies in American Trade Unionism. 1906. New Introduction by
   Leon Stein and Philip Taft.

Jelley, Symmes M.
The Voice of Labor. 1888.

Jones, Mary.
Autobiography of Mother Jones. 1925.

Kelley, Florence.
Some Ethical Gains Through Legislation. 1905.

LaFollette, Robert M., editor.
The Making of America: Labor. 1906.

Lane, Winthrop D.
Civil War in West Virginia. 1921.

Lauck, W. Jett and Edgar Sydenstricker.
Conditions of Labor in American Industries. 1917.

Leiserson, William M.
Adjusting Immigrant and Industry. 1924.

Lescohier, Don D.
Knights of St. Crispin. 1910.

Levinson, Edward.
I Break Strikes. The Technique of Pearl L. Bergoff. 1935.

Lloyd, Henry Demarest.
Men, The Workers. Compiled by Anne Whithington and
   Caroline Stallbohen. 1909. New Introduction by Leon Stein
   and Philip Taft.

Lorwin, Louis (Louis Levine).
The Women's Garment Workers. 1924.

Markham, Edwin, Ben B. Lindsay and George Creel.
Children in Bondage. 1914.

Marot, Helen.
American Labor Unions. 1914.

Mason, Alpheus T.
Organized Labor and the Law. 1925.

Newcomb, Simon.
A Plain Man's Talk on the Labor Question. 1886. New Introduction
   by Leon Stein and Philip Taft.

Price, George Moses.
The Modern Factory: Safety, Sanitation and Welfare. 1914.

Randall, John Herman Jr.
Problem of Group Responsibility to Society. 1922.

Rubinow, I. M.
Social Insurance. 1913.

Saposs, David, editor.
Readings in Trade Unionism. 1926.

Slichter, Sumner H.
Union Policies and Industrial Management. 1941.

Socialist Publishing Society.
The Accused and the Accusers. 1887.

Stein, Leon and Philip Taft, editors.
The Pullman Strike. 1894-1913. New Introduction by the editors.

Stein, Leon and Philip Taft, editors.
Religion, Reform, and Revolution: Labor Panaceas in the Nineteenth
   Century. 1969. New Introduction by the editors.

Stein, Leon and Philip Taft, editors.
Wages, Hours, and Strikes: Labor Panaceas in the Twentieth Century.
   1969. New introduction by the editors.

Swinton, John.
A Momentous Question: The Respective Attitudes of Labor and Capital. 1895. New Introduction by Leon Stein and Philip Taft.

Tannenbaum, Frank.
The Labor Movement. 1921.

Tead, Ordway.
Instincts in Industry. 1918.

Vorse, Mary Heaton.
Labor's New Millions. 1938.

Witte, Edwin Emil.
The Government in Labor Disputes. 1932.

Wright, Carroll D.
The Working Girls of Boston. 1889.

Wyckoff, Veitrees J.
Wage Policies of Labor Organizations in a Period of Industrial Depression. 1926.

Yellen, Samuel.
American Labor Struggles. 1936.

SERIES II

Allen, Henry J.
The Party of the Third Part: The Story of the Kansas Industrial Relations Court. 1921. *Including* **The Kansas Court of Industrial Relations Law** (1920) by Samuel Gompers.

Baker, Ray Stannard.
The New Industrial Unrest. 1920.

Barnett, George E. & David A. McCabe.
Mediation, Investigation and Arbitration in Industrial Disputes. 1916.

Barns, William E., editor.
The Labor Problem. 1886.

Bing, Alexander M.
War-Time Strikes and Their Adjustment. 1921.

Brooks, Robert R. R.
When Labor Organizes. 1937.

Calkins, Clinch.
Spy Overhead: The Story of Industrial Espionage. 1937.

Cooke, Morris Llewellyn & Philip Murray.
Organized Labor and Production. 1940.

Creamer, Daniel & Charles W. Coulter.
Labor and the Shut-Down of the Amoskeag Textile Mills. 1939.

Glocker, Theodore W.
The Government of American Trade Unions. 1913.

Gompers, Samuel.
Labor and the Employer. 1920.

Grant, Luke.
The National Erectors' Association and the International Association of Bridge and Structural Ironworkers. 1915.

Haber, William.
Industrial Relations in the Building Industry. 1930.

Henry, Alice.
Women and the Labor Movement. 1923.

Herbst, Alma.
The Negro in the Slaughtering and Meat-Packing Industry in Chicago. 1932.

[Hicks, Obediah.]
Life of Richard F. Trevellick. 1896.

Hillquit, Morris, Samuel Gompers & Max J. Hayes.
The Double Edge of Labor's Sword: Discussion and Testimony on Socialism and Trade-Unionism Before the Commission on Industrial Relations. 1914. New Introduction by Leon Stein and Philip Taft.

Jensen, Vernon H.
Lumber and Labor. 1945.

Kampelman, Max M.
The Communist Party vs. the C.I.O. 1957.

Kingsbury, Susan M., editor.
Labor Laws and Their Enforcement. By Charles E. Persons,
Mabel Parton, Mabelle Moses & Three "Fellows." 1911.

McCabe, David A.
The Standard Rate in American Trade Unions. 1912.

Mangold, George Benjamin.
Labor Argument in the American Protective Tariff Discussion.
1908.

Millis, Harry A., editor.
How Collective Bargaining Works. 1942.

Montgomery, Royal E.
Industrial Relations in the Chicago Building Trades. 1927.

Oneal, James.
The Workers in American History. 3rd edition, 1912.

Palmer, Gladys L.
Union Tactics and Economic Change: A Case Study of Three
Philadelphia Textile Unions. 1932.

Penny, Virginia.
How Women Can Make Money: Married or Single, In all Branches of
the Arts and Sciences, Professions, Trades, Agricultural and Mechanical Pursuits. 1870. New Introduction by Leon Stein and Philip Taft.

Penny, Virginia.
Think and Act: A Series of Articles Pertaining to Men and Women,
Work and Wages. 1869.

Pickering, John.
The Working Man's Political Economy. 1847.

Ryan, John A.
A Living Wage. 1906.

Savage, Marion Dutton.
Industrial Unionism in America. 1922.

Simkhovitch, Mary Kingsbury.
The City Worker's World in America. 1917.

Spero, Sterling Denhard.
The Labor Movement in a Government Industry: A Study of Employee Organization in the Postal Service. 1927.

Stein, Leon and Philip Taft, editors.
Labor Politics: Collected Pamphlets. 2 vols. 1836-1932. New Introduction by the editors.

Stein, Leon and Philip Taft, editors.
The Management of Workers: Selected Arguments. 1917-1956. New Introduction by the editors.

Stein, Leon and Philip Taft, editors.
Massacre at Ludlow: Four Reports. 1914-1915. New Introduction by the editors.

Stein, Leon and Philip Taft, editors.
Workers Speak: Self-Portraits. 1902-1906. New Introduction by the editors.

Stolberg, Benjamin.
The Story of the CIO. 1938.

Taylor, Paul S.
The Sailors' Union of the Pacific. 1923.

U.S. Commission on Industrial Relations.
Efficiency Systems and Labor. 1916. New Introduction by Leon Stein and Philip Taft.

Walker, Charles Rumford.
American City: A Rank-and-File History. 1937.

Walling, William English.
American Labor and American Democracy. 1926.

Williams, Whiting.
What's on the Worker's Mind: By One Who Put on Overalls to Find Out. 1920.

Wolman, Leo.
The Boycott in American Trade Unions. 1916.

Ziskind, David.
One Thousand Strikes of Government Employees. 1940.